COMMUNAL SOCIETIES IN AMERICA
AN AMS REPRINT SERIES

THE QUEST FOR PARADISE

*Europe and the
American Moral
Imagination*

AMS PRESS
NEW YORK

THE
QUEST
FOR
PARADISE

CHARLES L. SANFORD

*Europe and the
American Moral
Imagination*

Library of Congress Cataloging in Publication Data

Sanford, Charles L., 1920–
  The quest for paradise.

  (Communal Societies in America)
  Reprint of the 1961 ed. published by the University
of Illinois Press, Urbana.
  Includes bibliographical references.
  1. United States—Civilization. 2. United States—
History—Philosophy. 3. American literature—History
and criticism. I. Title. II. Series.
[E169.1.S245 1979]   973   76–42791
ISBN 0-404-60078-6

081045

First AMS edition published in 1979.

Reprinted from an original in the collections of the Ohio State University Library. [Trim size and text area of the original have been slightly altered in this edition. Original trim size: 15 × 22.7 cm; text area: 10.2 × 19.7 cm.]

MANUFACTURED
IN THE UNITED STATES OF AMERICA

Preface

The genesis of this book was a series of lectures in American literature at Middlebury College during the year 1950-1951. Because I did not then have the time or opportunity to incorporate them in a full-length book, in March, 1951, I summarized my findings in an essay called "The Garden of America," later published in the *Modern Review*. Since then, I have felt the need to penetrate more deeply into the origins and meaning of my subject and, above all, to show its broader application to such other aspects of our civilization as art, industry, politics, and foreign policy.

This representative cross section of American culture is treated in the following pages in a chronological order corresponding roughly to the period in which each area has had its greatest impact on American life and thought. The significance of each is then, insofar as possible, projected into the present. I have therefore attempted a broad survey without sacrifice of depth.

My work, as it has appeared chapter by chapter in published articles, has frequently been compared with that of Henry Nash Smith. His book, *Virgin Land* (1950), attempted to place Frederick Jackson Turner's frontier hypothesis within an intellectual tradition. I am concerned with something rather different, which is to define the intellectual tradition to which both the "philosophers of primitivism" and the "trailblazers of progress" have subscribed. The Edenic image, as I have defined it, is neither a static agrarian image of cultivated nature nor an opposing image of the wilderness, but an imaginative complex which, while including both images, places them in a dynamic relationship with other values. Like true myth or story, it functions on many levels simultaneously, dramatizing a people's collective experience within a framework of polar opposites. The Edenic myth, it seems to me, has been the most powerful and comprehensive organizing force in American culture.

Of necessity I have had to be selective, but always with an eye to what seemed to me the major configurations of American culture. This is true also of my analysis of such major figures as Thomas Jefferson and Henry James, where I am concerned primarily with the larger structure of thought and feeling rather than with textural detail. The result is not, I hope, caricature. At the same time, in dealing with the main tendencies of American culture, I have tried not to duplicate the investigations of other scholars who have published important works since the appearance of *Virgin Land.* I am thinking, for instance, of R. W. B. Lewis, whose book, *The American Adam* (1955), also looks for the images and "story" which animate the dominant ideas of a period. Professor Lewis attempts to capture the dramatic terms of the story through analysis of a "cultural dialogue" which has developed around the "hero" of the story, the American Adam. My own emphasis is more upon the story itself, its origins, growth, and extension to areas of American culture unexamined by either Lewis or Henry Nash Smith.

One always wonders, of course, to what extent significant omissions may weaken the thesis of an interpretative work such as this, which attempts to grasp the meaning of a whole culture through the study of key fragments. My own findings suggest that the Edenic theme may be central, though in subtly differing ways, to many Americans whose work would superficially seem to be an explicit denial of it. Charles Lane, a minor Transcendentalist, wrote in 1844, for instance:

The experiment of a true wilderness life by a white person must . . . be very rare. He is not born for it; he is not natured for it. He lacks the essential qualities as well as the physical substance for such a life, and the notion of entering on it must be considered merely an interesting dream. Some amalgamation may, however, be possible; and to unite the advantages of the two modes has doubtless been the aim of many. . . . To view all things as male and female is a favorite habit of many acute minds; and to such it may appear, that the forest and civilized lives are the male and female, from whose marriage an offspring shall result more conducive to human bliss. But it is difficult to conceive how corrupt parents shall have pure progeny, until their own corruption be annulled.[1]

Whether Charles Lane, in spite of his skepticism, nevertheless reflects in some important way what I have taken to be the dominant American mode of apprehending reality is a question left unexamined in this book.

Nor is there included a discussion of Edgar Allan Poe—surely a significant figure in our culture—who, as Perry Miller has written in *The Raven and the Whale*, extracted only evil from America, supposedly the land of nature and natural virtue. Also omitted are Parkman and Melville, for whom nature, whether in depths of forest or of ocean, often exhibited an inhuman cruelty. I have treated Poe separately in an article which, unfortunately, I do not have space to include as a chapter in this volume.[2] Those Americans who, like Parkman and Melville, have not always found nature beneficent have frequently felt in nature an indomitable grandeur which to attempt to reduce to merely human terms would be an act of colossal impiety and conceit. For them, too, nature has sometimes provided a chastening experience, a supreme test of character, similar in remedial function to Henry James' European "school of worldly experience."

I have endeavored to show that American critics of the sentimental primitivism surrounding the American Adam have an important place in my interpretation at the European pole of American experience. I have also tried to make clear the view that the paradisiac impulse and metaphor does not depend solely upon nature as its setting, but has been broadly associated with a rich abundance of inward and outward life in contrast to the fancied poverty of existing conditions. The metaphor of paradise,

---

[1] Charles Lane, "Life in the Woods," *The Dial*, April, 1844, reprinted in the Appendix to Henry David Thoreau, *Walden*, ed. Sherman Paul, Riverside Edition (Boston: Houghton Mifflin Co., 1957), pp. 236, 238.

[2] A recently published article on Poe which develops my point of view is Robert D. Jacobs, "Poe's Earthly Paradise," *American Quarterly*, XII (Fall, 1960), 404-413.

that is, must be understood not only to represent a hierarchy of desired goods, but to represent them in dynamic relationship to opposing subjective experiences of deprivation.

In America, for the most part, the concept of nature has flourished in the realm of ideality, as a standard by which to criticize different aspects of the developing civilization. In practice, Americans have consciously or unconsciously sought to establish a midpoint between savagery and civilization, to establish a national identity which was neither primitive in the frontier sense nor excessively civilized in the European sense. With respect to this midpoint, the American concept of nature has tended to be largely sylvan and rural. At the same time, it has not been limited to the agrarian elements of the population. One might argue that the dream of sylvan felicity has, in fact, dominated the imaginations of city dwellers even more than those of farmers. A recent public opinion poll shows, for instance, that to this day there exists considerably more criticism of urban life and urban dwellers by the farming population than criticism of rural life by city dwellers.[3]

Though the American dream of a plenitude of inward and outward life has characteristically been associated with such scenes of natural felicity as one finds in the rolling, stylized midwestern landscapes of Grant Wood, I have tried to indicate that such imagery has abounded in Europe as well as in America—with, of course, peculiar differences of emphases and detail traceable to time and place. What I have attempted to do, however, was to trace the transit of this imagery from Europe to America. This intention required that I abandon European parallels and background with the colonization of America. The development of urban-rural tensions in England which coincided with similar tensions in nineteenth-century America is therefore entirely neglected, though assumed. Similarly, a comparative study of the effects of science and industrialism upon agrarian preconceptions in both Europe and America is omitted as deserving special study in itself. Nevertheless, the main tenor of my work argues against the myth of American uniqueness and in favor of a national identity within the Atlantic community of nations. At the same time, I have

----

[3] Cf. Hadley Cantril, ed. *Public Opinion, 1935-1946* (Princeton: Princeton University Press, 1951), p. 497.

sought to connect Americans' ideas about themselves with something universal in human nature, remembering that although individuals may differ in their circumstances, as human beings they are generically more alike than different.

A number of chapters in this book have already been published, as I have indicated, but they were originally written as part of the larger plan so that I have been able to include them here with only slight revisions. Part of chapters 3 ("The Journey Pattern of Modern History") and 7 ("The Art of Virtue") was originally published as "An American Pilgrim's Progress," *American Quarterly*, VI (Winter, 1954), pages 297-310. Chapter 8 ("National Self-Consciousness and the Concept of the Sublime") is a revision of my article, "The Concept of the Sublime in the Works of Thomas Cole and William Cullen Bryant," *American Literature*, XXVIII (January, 1957), pages 434-448. Chapter 9 ("The Intellectual Origins and New-Worldliness of American Industry") appeared with the same title in *The Journal of Economic History*, XVIII (March, 1958), pages 1-16. Chapter 10 ("The Hope of Reform and the Promise of American Life") expands my article, "Classics of American Reform Literature," *American Quarterly*, X (Fall, 1958), pages 295-311. Parts of chapter 13 ("Conclusion") were drawn from my article, "Paradise and Hades: Aspects of American Nationality," published in the *Western Humanities Review*, XII (Winter, 1958), pages 11-27. I am greatly indebted to the editors and publishers of these journals for permission to use the above articles in this volume. A number of other chapters, particularly the early ones and the last few, appear for the first time in this book.

I am also indebted to numerous individuals for encouragement, help, and advice: to my old teacher Professor Reginald Cook of Middlebury College for enlisting me in the work; to my colleagues Professor William Pease and Mr. Richard Hathaway of Rensselaer Polytechnic Institute for reading and commenting upon a number of chapters; to Professors Edwin Rozwenc and George Rogers Taylor of Amherst College, upon whom I tried many of my ideas; to Mrs. Lisa Huse and Mrs. Nell Gadd for their patience in typing my manuscript; to Mrs. Sylvia Gerhart, who read proof with me; and to all the kindhearted people in the many libraries which I have haunted. I received a great deal of help in matters of tone and style from Professor Isadore

Traschen, who carefully read the entire manuscript. Finally, I am grateful to Rensselaer Polytechnic Institute for releasing me on part-time teaching and for the several generous grants which enabled me to complete the work. I myself am responsible, however, for its final form and for any faults which may be found in it.

Contents

1

The Quest
for Paradise:
Introductory

During some wryly amusing observations on the "messiness" of history, Kenneth Boulding, author of *The Image* and *The Organizational Revolution,* once told members of an American Studies Association that if he could "explain" President Eisenhower satisfactorily, he would hold the key to the meaning of human history. One sensed in his statement the unspoken assumption that, somehow, the entire history of mankind was summed up in the collective experience of the United States of America and projected through the public image of the President. However fanciful and exaggerated this suggestion may appear, it is worth entertaining, for throughout its short history the United States has notably been a land of quests, and philosophies of history have been largely the studies of quests: the quest for adventure, for riches, for salvation, for power, for survival.

In a very real sense President Eisenhower personifies an America which has turned its back upon the provincial isolationism which dominated its earlier history and has accepted global responsibilities in the world of nations. But the unaccustomed perplexities and frustrations attending this new outlook have made Americans impatient, baffled, confused; and in this time of grave international crisis they have tended to turn to Eisenhower as a kind of father image or savior who will somehow miraculously deliver them from the devil of Russian communism. This popular sentiment, which one finds everywhere, is summed up in a poem which calls Eisenhower "the man that God has sent." In this poem he is depicted as the greatest since the Christ Child's birth: "A greater General/Than Napoleon/More resourceful/Than Caesar . . .!/He stands/Where the Christ once stood."[1] Where one most needs a patient, mature, realistic approach to problems, one meets instead an irrational, immature demonology. This situation relates to the paradox that although Eisenhower is a representative of one of the most advanced, industrial nations on earth, his chief appeal seems to be a naïve simplicity which recalls America's preindustrial past. There is good reason to believe that if he had been running for election against Senator Kennedy in the campaign of 1960, he would have won.

The main source of his continuing appeal is underlined by contrast with his opponent, Adlai Stevenson. President Eisenhower has humble antecedents in the village life of the rural Midwest; he has fond memories of the pickle jar and cracker-barrel; he expresses an intuitive sense of right and wrong in a simple, forthright manner; reminiscent of the pioneer vigilante, he was a manly fighter for the right in Europe; he takes a smiling interest in the various "crusades" of his party; his first principle of public administration is integrity. Whereas Adlai Stevenson, representing what has historically been the less influential side of American character, has had to bear the onus of being regarded as an urban sophisticate with inherited wealth; an Ivy League education; a cool intellectual wit; a complex view of the subtle interplay between moral principle, human character, and events; and a divorced wife lingering in the background— in short, all the earmarks of a highly civilized, cosmopolitan person who is in public disesteem. Both public images sketched here are imbedded deeply in a historical past stretching from America to Europe, and possibly farther, and are related to images of value which have largely governed the movement of history.

It is presumptuous, perhaps, for me to pretend to more than an amateur's interest in the philosophy of history; it is infinitely

----

[1] Dennis Tenney, *The Song of Eisenhower* (New York: Whittier Books, Inc., 1956), pp. 4-5.

worse, however, both from the practical and scholarly points of view, to surrender in a time of historical relativism to history's terrors. Not without misgivings, therefore, I venture the view that human history, converging in the perspective of time on America, is best understood in relation to the pursuit of paradise —that is, as an imaginative undertaking. A tantalizingly brief hint of this view is contained in George Santayana's essay, "A Long Way Round to Nirvana," which in turn develops a suggestion found in Freud's *Beyond the Pleasure Principle*.[2] In this essay Santayana speculates upon a tendency in living organic matter to revert to an earlier, simpler condition of being which it has been forced to abandon by external disturbing forces and which each additional effort to regain by circuitous expedients puts farther beyond reach. This original condition is held to be a state of blissful quiescence so near to non-being that Freud can say—and Santayana agrees—"The goal of all life is death." The complex human organism evolved, paradoxically, not out of the *élan vital* of simpler organisms, but from the unconscious desire to return to the primordial unity. Such a theory, Santayana is pleased to note, requires a pluralistic metaphysics, "or at least duality, if you wish to get effectively into the bosom of the One. . . ." He concludes that this theory accords with what we know about nature—with its snares, but also its primroses.

Insofar as Santayana's metaphysics is concerned, a position of dualism would seem adequate to the dynamics of recorded history. The important thing to note about his essay at this point, however, is that the Nirvana of human striving which he depicts is perfectly expressed by the images of paradise found in the literature of all peoples. Santayana himself suggests this equivalence when he attributes the myths of the Original Sin and Fall to the continual chastisements, the deep anxieties, relentless pressures, pricks, noises, and pain with which life imposes upon us its tragic fatality. But Santayana's essay, taken alone, does not take one far toward a philosophy of history. It is speculative biology.

A number of recent studies, some of them documented and

---

[2] In George Santayana, *Some Turns of Thought in Modern Philosophy* (New York: Charles Scribner's Sons, 1934), pp. 87-101. The quotations from it are on pp. 91 and 89. In subsequent citations, single page numbers referring to direct quotes will be listed separately, in order of their appearance in my text.

historically oriented, support a more extended application of Santayana's point of view. The first of these is Maude Bodkin's *Archetypal Patterns in Poetry,* a perceptive, intuitive study of the most deeply felt emotional symbols in poetic classics of Western literature from Homer to T. S. Eliot.[3] In it she, influenced by Freud, finds a tensional equation between life-craving and the death wish, which begets (in the works she examines) a vision of paradise. The long, circuitous path which Santayana conceives to have been taken by life in its attempt to escape from environmental and inner pressures in order to return to origins is expressed in poetic symbols by an arduous night journey, a plunge into a sea of woes, or a descent into hell. At the extremity of endurance and struggle the afflicted soul sinks down into quiescence, bringing surrender, renewal, a new self-knowledge, and peace. If the night journey represents the search for origins, quiescence may signalize a return to life. Thus Dante passes through the horrors of the Inferno and an icy calm of near-death into the all-fulfilling light of heaven and a view of the celestial paradise. The "archetypal" symbol of life renewal, or rebirth, is the magical golden bough, branch, or sprig of lilac. The great poetry of Western literature rehearses symbolically the universal human impulse to return to origins. The image of paradise comprehends both the beginning and the end of striving.

The hardheaded historian will not be persuaded by Miss Bodkin's analysis. In the first place, her criterion of selection is frankly subjective: of the classics, she selects those which have "the deepest, most meaningful appeal" for her. In the second place, her method of imaginative sympathy—"to penetrate to forces within the experience of poet and reader alike"—requires introspection. In the third place, she would seem to be arguing from preconceived ideas not even acceptable to all schools of modern psychology. Finally, she is not primarily interested in historical relevance. Nevertheless, her work remains one of the modern landmarks in the study of aesthetic experience and contains many fertile insights which the historian might develop.

A related work more immediately useful to the historian is Mircea Eliade's *The Myth of the Eternal Return,* which, while

----

[3] Maude Bodkin, *Archetypal Patterns in Poetry: Psychological Studies of Imagination* (London: Oxford University Press, 1934).

heavily indebted to anthropological studies of myth and ritual, bears directly on the philosophy of history.[4] Interested in discovering the main source of that collective faith, belief, or tradition which enabled tens of millions of men and women "for century after century, to endure great historical pressures without despairing, without committing suicide or falling into that spiritual aridity that always brings with it a relativistic or nihilistic view of history," he investigates the myths of early Christian, non-Christian, and pre-Christian civilizations and finds that a common denominator of faith was something very akin to the ideas I have been discussing: the myth of eternal return. Everywhere—in ancient Mesopotamia and Syria, in India and Greece, among early Christians as well as among North American Indians—recur the myths of a lost paradise together with an eschatological view of history in which the end of time reactualizes the beginning of time. Everywhere he finds a periodic confession of sins, a tendency toward purification, which reveals the nostalgia of "fallen man" for the lost paradise of mythical memory.

Eliade does not show how these ideas enter into the stream of historical events or how they affect and are affected by the "influences"—social, economic, national, cultural—which modern historicism reads into history. Indeed, his bias is on the side of an ontological or theological history, which these ideas, in their appeal to a transcendent reality, would seem to him to support, and he chides Karl Mannheim for not daring to affirm an autonomy of the spirit as a way of avoiding historical relativism.[5] But it is to Karl Mannheim and the professional historians we must look if we are to discover the expression of the paradisiac impulse in history. The six modern works which seem to me epochal in their recognition of the importance of this impulse are Karl Mannheim, *Ideology and Utopia* (1936); Lewis Mumford, *The Conduct of Man* (1944); Ernest L. Tuveson, *Millennium and Utopia* (1949); R. W. B. Lewis, *The American Adam* (1955); Arthur K. Moore, *The Frontier Mind* (1957); and Norman Cohn, *The Pursuit of the Millenium* (1957). Three of these belong to the category of intellectual history. The one

---

[4] Mircea Eliade, *The Myth of the Eternal Return*, trans. Willard R. Trask (New York: Pantheon Books, Inc., 1954). The quotation comes from p. 152.
[5] *Ibid.*, p. 159n.

which is the richest in historical texture and detail and closest to the clash and jangle of recorded events, mass movements, and the activities of charismatic personalities is Cohn's *The Pursuit of the Millennium,* which focuses upon the rise of millennial movements in Europe during the late Middle Ages.

This last work clearly reveals to the thoughtful reader an affinity between the frenetic seekers of a messianic kingdom on earth and the believers in the myth of the eternal return, both of whom sought a restoration of an ideal past in the near future and read the signs of their coming bliss in the rapid deterioration of their present state. The revolutionary chiliasm which Cohn describes is an extreme manifestation of paradisiac longing transformed into impetuous social action. He finds that although millennial movements have occurred at many different times in history, in many different parts of the world, and in societies with very different technologies, institutions, values, and beliefs, certain recurring patterns are evident. These are related to a breakdown in the traditional fabric of society, whether from conquest and oppression, a series of natural calamities, or rapid social change: "The areas [of Europe] in which the age-old prophecies about the Last Days took on a new, revolutionary meaning and a new, explosive force were the areas of rapid social change—and not simply change but expansion: areas where trade and industry were developing and where the population was rapidly increasing. Life in such areas differed vastly from the agricultural life which was the norm throughout the thousand-year span of the Middle Ages. . . ." [6] Here, abject poverty was not by itself a decisive factor; revolutionary chiliasm did not run strongly among the peasantry under the manorial regime. It did run strongly among the displaced multitudes living on the margin of urban, industrial society and played upon by leaders with marked paranoiac tendencies. Such leaders surveyed with anxiety, envy, and hatred the sharp contrasts within this new world, where unparalleled opportunity, privilege, and prosperity flourished side by side "not only with great poverty but with great and unaccustomed insecurity." [7] The

---

[6] Norman Cohn, *The Pursuit of the Millennium* (Fair Lawn, New Jersey: Essential Books, Inc., 1957), p. 22. But see also pp. 24-32, *et passim.*
[7] *Ibid.,* p. 89.

grass seems greener on the other side of the fence, in other words, only if one can see through the fence.

The step from Millennium to Utopia and the ideas of linear progress which have found their richest material fulfillment in the United States has been marked by a similar contrast between newly acquired wants and aspirations and the inability to satisfy them under existing conditions. Thus, Lewis Mumford, the historian of utopias, writes: "The Utopia of Sir Thomas More, and those of later men of the Renascence, arose . . . from the contrast between the possibilities that lay open beyond the seas [since the discovery of America] and the dismal conditions that attended the breakdown of the town economy of the Middle Ages." [8] The line of historical development hinted at here, to be more fully examined later, indicates the main shortcoming of Cohn's otherwise magnificent study. For Cohn derives from his analysis of millennial movements something quite different: that is, an abnormal social psychology, a collective megalomania, which, according to him, is mirrored in the French Revolution and the totalitarian movements of our own day. He is, in an intellectual sense, out to "get" Hitler, and much of his documentation has to do with the persecution of Jews by fanatical chiliasts of the late Middle Ages. A broader view suggests that millennialism, stemming from the paradisiac longing, may have played an important part in producing the best as well as the more reprehensible features of civilization.

Historians have not, to date, carried their investigations of the paradise theme beyond the point outlined above, and not one, to my knowledge, has suggested it as the possible basis for a more comprehensive view of history. A major reason would seem to be a praiseworthy professional reluctance, fortified by a professional respect for "objective" documents, to venture into the shadowy area of social psychology. It is now necessary to push farther into this area, beginning with an attempt to ascertain in what sense the metaphor of paradise translates or expresses the commonly recognized goals of human endeavor.

The two main goals of human endeavor would seem to be, on the one hand, temporal satisfactions of wealth, power, adven-

---

[8] Lewis Mumford, *The Story of Utopias* (New York: Boni and Liverright, 1922), p. 114.

ture, and security, and, on the other, satisfactions dependent upon the salvation of the soul—a distinction which determined a basic difference of outlook between the early and late Middle Ages in Europe. The question to be asked first is whether other-worldly aspirations contain the idea of paradise. On this question Karl Mannheim states: "As long as the clerically and feudally organized medieval order was able to locate its paradise outside of society, in some otherworldly sphere which transcended history and dulled its revolutionary edge, the idea of paradise was still an integral part of medieval society. Not until certain social groups embodied these wish-images into their actual conduct, and tried to realize them, did these ideologies become utopian." [9] I shall leave until later the question of whether utopian, or secular, ideologies contain the idea of paradise. The peasantry of this early medieval period, relatively secure in their kinship ties and guaranteed in their conditions of tenancy by the feudal lord, compensated for whatever hardships they endured by locating their ambrosial meadows in heaven above.

To what extent was the orthodox Christian heaven, undoubtedly a solace for the millions during periods of social stagnation, conceived as a transcript of paradise? The orthodox view on this question during most of the Middle Ages followed Augustine. Augustine, in his commentary upon the Book of Genesis, held that the original terrestrial paradise, in all its original beauty and innocent delights, still existed, though now inaccessible to fallen man by virtue of its location on the summit of a gigantic mountain which reached into the third region of the air near the moon.[10] In *The City of God* he rejected the possibility of an earthly millennium and literal restoration to paradise. Nevertheless, the first condition of Adam and Eve was to be understood in a spiritual sense to contain "prophetic foreshadowings of things to come"—and not merely things to come under the dispensation of the New Testament wherein "Paradise is the Church; the four rivers of Paradise are the four gospels; the fruit-trees, the saints, and the fruit of their works; the tree of

---

[9] Karl Mannheim, *Ideology and Utopia: An Introduction to the Sociology of Knowledge*, trans. Louis Wirth and Edward Shils, Harvest Book (New York: Harcourt, Brace & Co., n.d.), p. 193.

[10] Cf. Washington Irving, *The Life and Voyages of Christopher Columbus* . . . , III (New York: G. P. Putnam's Sons, 1868), p. 518.

life is the holy of holies, Christ. . . ." [11] For he compared the final state of blessedness of the righteous on the Mountain of Holiness after the Day of Judgment to that of "our parents in Paradise," surpassing theirs only in its certainty of eternal felicity. Indeed, the terrestrial paradise could be made into "a perfect allegory of heaven," since evil did not reside in Nature, but in the human will.

Among the eternal blessings to be enjoyed by the resurrected body, St. Augustine numbered the loveliness of earth and sky and sea, the wondrous qualities of light in sun, moon, and stars, the shades of trees, the colors and perfume of flowers, the songs of multitudinous birds.[12] Leaving aside for the moment an apparent contradiction in metaphor between the future state conceived as a primitive paradise and the future state as a holy city, one may conclude that *The City of God*, under siege in contemporary Rome, transported the Garden of Eden from earth to heaven.

The spiritual aspirations of other, non-Christian peoples for rewards in an afterlife are commonly expressed by similar imagery, as in the Elysian fields of the Greeks, the Hindu Mount Meru, and the "happy hunting grounds" of the North American Indians. And Augustine's development finds many similar parallels in Christian tradition after him. One hardly need point out that Dante's master image for the heavenly city which translated the longing of the masses into high art at the end of the Middle Ages was, after all, *paradise*. Though the Protestant Reformation undoubtedly contributed its share to the later dismantling of the heavenly city in favor of an earthly one, many of its leaders and most devoted followers continued the tradition of Augustinian piety. Among these was Martin Luther, who in his break from Rome heralded the time "when the voice of the turtle is heard in the land, and flowers appear on the earth." In the Church's article of faith, as distinguished from mere outward obedience to Mosaic law, he found the true Christian liberty—but also an analogy with Adam and Eve before the Fall: "Such also are the works of a believer. Through his faith he has been restored to Paradise and created anew, has

---

[11] Augustine, *The Confessions; The City of God; On Christian Doctrine* (Chicago: Encyclopaedia Britannica, Inc., 1952), p. 371.

[12] *Ibid.*, pp. 322-329, 371-372, 385-386, 611.

no need of works that he may become or be righteous, but . . .
only to please God." The promised land of Canaan, which had
to be lost under the Old Testament's covenant of works, would
be recovered under the New Testament's covenant of faith when
man became a second Adam in Christ.[13] The Protestant Reformation, on its intellectual side, originated largely in the attempt
to put into actual practice what pious Catholics already believed. This spiritual mission, as will be seen, was carried into
the wilds of America, where the image of a heavenly paradise
or city rather quickly became subordinate to that of an earthly
paradise.

The imaginative way from the spiritual paradise to an earthly
one would seem to be opened whenever or wherever there exists
a marked emphasis upon moralism in religion.[14] Nowhere is
this development seen more clearly than in the Old Testament,
in which the moral content of paradise—the "paradise of righteousness"—is stressed and the rewards of this paradise are temporal: a land of milk and honey in Canaan, longevity, health,
great natural fertility, riches, peace. As Norman Cohn writes in
his study of the millennium, the chosen people of Israel believed that "there will arise a Palestine which will be nothing
less than a new Eden, Paradise regained." [15] Here one notes that
paradise is not quite identified with a state of primitive innocence, but rather with moral effort. "Everything we know about
the mythical memories of 'paradise' confronts us, on the contrary," Eliade writes, "with the image of an ideal humanity
enjoying a beatitude and spiritual plenitude forever unrealizable
in the present state of 'fallen man.' " [16] Purification rituals, jeremiads, and strict discipline would suggest a psychological motivation of nostalgia not for the lost paradise of animality, but for
the lost innocence which the adult abandons when he acquires
a mature sense of guilt.

Nevertheless, as the story of Job reveals, one finds in the

----

[13] Preserved Smith, *The Life and Letters of Martin Luther* (Boston: Houghton Mifflin Co., 1911), p. 229; *The Works of Martin Luther, with Intro-
ductions and Notes,* 6 vols. (Philadelphia: A. J. Holman Co., 1915), II, 330;
VI, 378.

[14] See, for instance, Joseph Haroutunian, *Piety versus Moralism: The Passing
of the New England Theology* (New York: Henry Holt & Co., Inc., 1932).

[15] Cohn, *op. cit.,* p. 2.

[16] Eliade, *op. cit.,* p. 91.

orthodox Mosaic view of the connection between moral behavior and future rewards not only elements of bribery and hypocrisy, but an emphasis on temporal conditions which points in the direction of a materialistic hedonism. Increasingly in Western civilization during modern times the lost state of innocence to be regained is associated with or interpreted as a paradise of material bliss. This association rests upon a primitivistic assumption somewhat similar to what is discovered in Augustine—that things in their natural abundance as originally created by God retain the innocence of God. This assumption underlies the modern vogue of Utopia which, beginning in the Renaissance, has encouraged the enjoyment of creature comforts on a large scale without awakening a correspondingly uncomfortable sense of guilt. This egalitarian state of nature is foreshadowed, for instance, by Sir Thomas More, who defines virtue as a life lived according to nature and commends to Europeans as ordained by God the kind of Epicurean communism supposedly practiced by the Indians of North America.[17] The stream of utopian thought has made it possible for modern man to retain his vision of the primitive moral paradise while living in the midst of smoking factories, grinding gears, and honking motorcars. He has identified moral and spiritual "advance" with material progress.

It is only too easy to show the many ways in which the image of paradise corresponds to and expresses the temporal goals of rich material abundance, sexual fulfillment, ease, power, security—and even adventure. In times of great economic scarcity accompanied by social stagnation, narrow horizons, and a pessimistic outlook, however, such images are assigned to an irrecoverable past. The Golden Age visualized by the early Church fathers and especially by the classic writers of Greece and Rome is thus assigned to the past. Lucian, living in the second century, addresses the imagined god who reigned in that longlost time:

Now I hear poets tell that in the old days, when you were king, things were otherwise in this world; earth bearing its fruits for men without being sown or ploughed—for each man a meal all prepared, and more than enough of it; rivers flowing with wine, and others with

---

[17] Thomas More, *Utopia*, ed. with Introduction and Notes by J. Churton Collins (Oxford: The Clarendon Press, 1904), pp. 7, 41-43, 76-77, 84-85. But God follows nature in things reasonable, and not foolish, as in the pursuit of false pleasures.

milk, and others again with honey. And most important of all, they say that at that time people themselves were of gold; poverty never approached them. Whereas we are hardly even men of lead, but rather of some still meaner metal; most of us eating our crust of bread in the sweat of our brow; forever saddled with poverty and want and helplessness, crying out "Alas!" And "Oh, what a fate!"— that is how we poor men live. And believe me, all this would be less galling to us if only we did not see the rich enjoying such a good time . . . and not deigning even to cast a glance at us, the many, let alone share anything with us.[18]

In times of expanding horizons, such as the early Renaissance, images of a material paradise mark a similar contrast between present conditions and an ideal state, but project that ideal state into a realizable future. I have chosen to quote Lucian, however, as one example from among hundreds illustrative of the material paradise, whether past or future, because he combines, not without an edge of satire, this image with an image of power. Note the class consciousness which he affects, the mock self-pity, the envy, the desire to vault into the throne of gold in the place of the mighty.

Paradise as an image of power is frequently encountered in world literature. Jean de Meun's *Romance of the Rose,* one of the earliest renderings of the egalitarian state of nature since antiquity after the long lapse of the Middle Ages, coupled paradisiac images of power with sexual eroticism. One meets this association so often that one is tempted to conclude that the drive for power and the erotic impulse are related and that all self-assertion in relation to any of the fancied goods of life may be a manifestation of this dual impulse. Thus, the Jewish vision of a promised land in Canaan helped the Jews to assert themselves against the threat or reality of oppression by the Egyptians, and their military leaders in the conquest of Canaan —Samson, Joshua, David—displayed strong sexual appetites. Most images of paradise would seem in some sense to express an assertion of individual or group freedom and self-government as against the constraints of parental or societal authority. *The Romance of the Rose* delineated an ideal past state—as contrasted with the ideal future state conceived by Sir Thomas More some two centuries later—in which there was once plenty to eat and drink; perfect equality and harmony without kings,

---

[18] "Letter I," quoted in Cohn, *op. cit.,* pp. 196-197.

princes, or laws; and finally, free love on beds of flowers cur-
tained by tree leaves—in as much as "love and authority never
yet dwelt companionably together." [19] The rule of love was
preferable to the rule of princes.

Power-craving, with de Meun, comes to be one with the satisfaction of sexual desire. Similarly, Hawthorne and Dostoyevsky
frequently depict in their works supposedly public-spirited reforms advocated by professed "lovers of mankind" which, by
much the same process of displacement, become the guises for
power-seeking. The triumphant do-gooder of Dostoyevsky's
Notes from Underground even becomes involved in a "naughty"
scene in the bushes. "Dostoyevsky," Professor Traschen writes,
"identifies idealism and power, and both with the erotic impulse; put in harsher terms, public idealism and private depravity are all of a piece." [20] One need not, however, impute a
depravity of motive to all such behavior. The instances where
sexual satisfaction finds a truly ideal embodiment and fulfillment in a divinely sanctioned paradise—and, conversely, the
religious sublimation of sexual feeling directed toward God—
are almost as numerous as evocations of the more mundane material paradise described by Lucian. Indeed, thoughtful students
have found a source of all religion in ancient fertility rites which
celebrated the fertility of the womb in conjunction with the
fecundity of nature. For the moment, however, I am only concerned with showing instances where the felt correspondence of
sexual desire and the paradise image is made explicit.

Certain passionate temperaments during the Middle Ages
took advantage of the assumed innocence of God's creation to
form a cult of Adam and periodically stripped themselves naked
in public to dramatize their emancipation from sin. They likened
themselves to "the First Parents in Paradice before the Fall."
In 1330, Suso, a Catholic mystic sympathetic with such notions,
wrote, "I belong to the Liberty of Nature, and all that my nature desires I satisfy. . . . I am a natural man." A member of the
Homines Intelligentiae called the sex act itself "the delight of
Paradise." [21] About this time Boccaccio was slyly writing a story

---

[19] *Ibid.*, pp. 205-208.
[20] Isadore Traschen, "Dostoyevsky's 'Notes from Underground,'" *Accent*,
XVI (Autumn, 1956), 262.
[21] Cohn, *op. cit.*, pp. 187, 189-190.

about a priest who, by distracting a man with a series of arduous rituals for finding the way to the heavenly beatitude, was able to seduce the man's wife. The moral of this story was that "there are many persons who, what while they study to enter Paradise, unwittingly send others thither." [22] One is reminded, also, of the many cults of free love which flourished in the nineteenth century in such religious communities as that of John Humphrey Noyes and of the less innocent sexual orgies which took place under the banner of frontier revivalism. But lest we suppose such parallels to be found only in exceptional instances, we might examine briefly the more common varieties of secular love and religious aspiration. Throughout the New Testament and in the many theological commentaries thereupon the union of the faithful with Christ in the heavenly paradise is depicted by the imagery of marriage. In 1660, Thomas Shepard, the venerable New England theologian, even derived from Matthew's "Parable of the Ten Virgins" news of Christ's Second Coming to inaugurate in New England the new heaven and the new earth.[23] And John Donne, in his most famous holy sonnet, yearned so passionately for the expected consummation that he could not wait for the wedding!

The many testaments to secular love are also clear-cut in their affirmation of paradisiac longing. Indeed, the object of one's desire often becomes, as with Dante's Beatrice, a god-bearing image. The classical setting for the consummation of secular love in prose and verse is a delightful garden, meadow, or forest. The artificiality of the indoor bedroom is commonly, if not always, reserved for illicit love, as in the tales of Boccaccio and Chaucer. Even the most saintly of secular lovers often find their highest bliss in an exotic earthly paradise. The English poet, Edmund Spenser, for instance, writes of his betrothed in the "Amoretti":

> Hart need not wish none other happinesse
> But here on earth to have such hevens blisse.

In "Epithalamion" he likens his lot to "Jove's sweet paradice, of Day and Night," and speaks of Venus' "paradice of joys" in the springtime of love.

---

[22] Giovanni Boccaccio, *The Decameron*, trans. John Payne (New York: Blue Ribbon Books, 1931), pp. 144, 147, 204.

[23] Thomas Shepard, *Works*, 3 vols. (Boston: Doctrinal Tract and Book Society, 1853), II, 370-634.

The favorite season for lovers is spring, the season not only of the birth of gods, but of the flowering of nature. The loved one is described in the sexually seductive language of nature in the full flower of springtime or summer. We do not need to go to Shakespeare's *Venus and Adonis* for passion's adornment of the female body. Almost any uninhibited account will do—and even some of the inhibited accounts, as Hawthorne's sultry treatment of Zenobia with the exotic blossom in her dark tresses who, in his novel, *The Blithedale Romance*, reminded him of the original Eve. But here is Ariosto describing the fair Angelica, bound naked to a rock, statue-like:[24]

> But that he saw distinct a tear which streamed
> Amid fresh-opening rose and lily fair,
> Stand on her budding paps beneath in dew,
> And that her golden hair dishevelled flew.

Or the equally fair Olympia:

> . . . above were seen
> Two rounding paps, like new-pressed milk in show
> Fresh-taken from its crate of rushes green:
> The space betwixt was like the valley low,
> Which oftentimes we see small hills between,
> Sweet in its season. . . .

This poet was somewhat more reticent than Shakespeare in adorning other parts of the female body with nature's garlands, but the point is clear.

The various images of paradise examined above—the images of power, ease, sexuality, and worldly riches—are those in the name of which it is assumed, without for the moment investigating, that human beings act to better their lives. All suggest self-assertion against some cramping restraint or restriction within the social environments out of which these images arise. The freedom that is desired is the fancied freedom to be enjoyed in a luxuriant state of nature, as opposed to the censorship, the rules and regulations, the economic deprivations, the class distinctions, the forms and ceremonies, the logic-chopping, the emotional repression, the tyranny of rulers, the burden of taxes, the responsibilities of adulthood, the boredom of routine—the very complexities of social relationships experienced in advanced stages of ancient or modern civilization.

But the impulse of self-assertion may be triggered by the

---

[24] Ludovico Ariosto, *The Orlando Furioso*, trans. William Stewart Rose, 2 vols. (London: George Bell and Sons, 1907-1910), Canto X, st. xcvi; Canto XI, st. lxviii.

opposing impulse which craves a Nirvana of peaceful acquies-
cence. The repeated frustrations of life in whatever new situations people find themselves, according to this theory, force them
continually to assert themselves in order that they may, in effect,
annihilate themselves. Yet these two opposing impulses, paradoxically, can be reconciled in the single image of paradise,
which is at once an image of desire and an image for the release of desire, an image for the realization and fulfillment of
self and an image for the surrender of self. Let me examine
this paradox briefly, looking first into the subjective experience
of sexual assertion, then of power-craving, and finally of the
spirit of adventure in relation to the opposing desire for security.

In the literature of sexual self-assertion, where the paradise
image is either explicit or implicit, one encounters also an extreme ecstasy involving both the complete domination of, and
utter surrender to, one being by another being. The surrender
of oneself to another in sexual self-annihilation has much in
common, indeed, with the loss and the expansion of the individual ego in that perfect union which lies at the heart of the
most profoundly felt religious experience. It is not surprising,
therefore, that Lady Chatterly's lover in D. H. Lawrence's novel
of that title experiences an almost religious self-transcendence
or expresses the desire to die at the moment of sexual orgasm.
Similarly, John Donne writes in his sonnet, "Batter My Heart,
Three-Personed God":

> That I may rise and stand, o'erthrow me and bend
> Your force to break, blow, burn and make me new.

In order to conjoin one's individual identity with a larger whole,
one begs to be utterly ravished. The successful total merger in a
larger self brings with it, in effect, "the peace which passeth
all understanding."

Sexual domination is one of the many forms which the power-
craving impulse takes. But searching analyses of human motive
such as Tolstoi's *The Death of Iván Ilých*, suggest that power-
craving may also express the desire for status, prestige, and ultimately, by a roundabout route, the desire for security. That is,
one desires to manipulate people and things in such a way as
to erect around oneself all kinds of safeguards for one's security
—fawning courtiers, adoring fans, subservient officials, approv-
ing supervisors, cringing populations—until one hopes to feel,

but seldom does feel, "as happy as a clam." Complete satisfaction of power-craving in these respects would require in theory a final satiation of desire and so quiescence, just as Madame Bovary's urgent sexual demands led progressively to satiety and death. No longer did she and her lover experience "in their mutual possession, that wonder that multiplies the joy a hundredfold. She was as surfeited with him as he was tired of her. Adultery, Emma, was discovering, could be as banal as marriage." [25] A power-hungry political leader like Hitler finds no final resting point in life because the world will not allow him to impose his will upon it.

The desire for security, which has obviously motivated millions of people, would seem to lie at the opposite pole from power-craving and the spirit of adventure. Yet the spirit of adventure is essentially a desire for new experience based upon a dissatisfaction with old routines and conventions. It, too, seeks a greater bliss in paths of glory leading to new levels of satiation and quiescence, and so, perhaps, to renewed activity. Sometimes the greater bliss, as with Walt Whitman, lies in the process itself or in erotic submission to the process. The dedication of many Americans to the Open Road has, indeed, been a dedication to endless process itself rather than to any easily definable end point. Nevertheless, as Jack Kerouac's *On the Road* testifies, one wants to wrest from swift-passing experience some holy eternal moment, some indefinable essence, unnameable Word, ineffable grace; and one becomes utterly ravished and exhausted and must withdraw, like Achilles sulking in his tent, to restore himself for the next and the next assault upon experience.

Of the last impulse, the desire for new experience, one observes finally and tentatively that it becomes historically operative on a large scale only when expanding social horizons afford new possibilities for its fulfillment. This happened during the Renaissance, when a significant social transformation in Europe coincided with the opening of new lands beyond the seas. But the new experience which the seafaring adventurers sought had a great deal to do also with the myth of El Dorado, believed to exist in the interior of the newly discovered Eden. And mixed

---

[25] Gustave Flaubert, *Madame Bovary*, trans. Francis Steegmuller (New York: Modern Library, Inc., 1957), p. 330.

with the lure of the El Dorado, as the letters of "stout Cortez" plainly show, was the power-craving impulse to worldly glory, an interest in the sexual paradise of Indian maidenhood, the desire to found a religious paradise among the natives for the Dominican fathers and the pope, and a preference for the simple, rugged life of Central American jungles over the effete and ostentatious civilization of Spain.

The image of paradise, in conclusion, helps to order on the physical plane of existence a desire for material ease without labor or hardship as opposed to the grinding poverty of previous existence; on the psychic plane, an infantile regression from the cares of adult life to the warm Nirvana of the womb or mother breast; on the sexual plane, a yearning for the frank, free affectional life prescribed by one's inner nature as opposed to the emotional starvation often felt in an overrationalized civilization; on the moral plane, a wish to recapture the lost state of innocence which the adult abandons when he acquires a sense of guilt or shame; on the religious and aesthetic plane, a wish to transcend all that is merely human and temporal; on the political plane, an assertion of individual freedom and self-government against the constraints of parental and societal authority; on the plane of individual rhythms in temperament, a rebellion against established routine in behalf of new experience—in short, assertion in behalf of all the fancied goods of life in a world which must remain forever restrictive and imperfect, therefore evil. The quest for paradise necessarily takes the "long way round to Nirvana." There would seem to be no final resting point.

2

The Poles
of History

The analysis in the preceding chapter suggests that the image of paradise is born of a tension between two impulses: the impulse to self-assertion, and the impulse of submission. Psychological motivation would seem to involve movement between these poles; historical change would follow. Santayana is doubtless right in saying that the monolithic idea gets us nowhere. In any event, the interpretation put forth here requires a dualism, a psychological dualism and a metaphysical dualism. The inner dualism reflects a felt distinction between subjective experience and objective fact; the metaphysical dualism reflects what we presently know about the workings of nature, including human nature.

The science of physics has advanced our understanding of the structural contrasts in nature: "Cause and effect became effective tools for studying nature, as did stability and change, rest and motion. As quantum mechanics has replaced the classical atomic view of matter, nature has been most fruitfully studied by calculating structures of fields of force which persist intact but yet which emit determinable quantities of force. Atoms remain themselves, yet continuously change by radiation into others beside themselves. With the abandonment of static substances physics has resorted to terms which calculate dynamics and relativities that are meaningful just as they combine contrary, e.g. particle and wave-like, properties." [1] Alfred North Whitehead,

[1] Louis William Norris, *Polarity: A Philosophy of Tensions Among Values* (Chicago: Henry Regnery Co., 1956), p. 2.

in his *Science and the Modern World*, would extend the relational poles of physics to chemistry and biology. He sees the sum total of what we call "reality" as a vast complex of interrelated events structured within polarized electromagnetic fields.

Man has also found himself to be, in some sense, an expression of polar opposites. This discovery is not remarkable once we concede his rightful place within the natural scheme of things. Human beings are amphibians, C. S. Lewis has his Screwtape say: their minds can be directed to an eternal object, but their bodies, passions, and imaginations continually change. "Their nearest approach to constancy, therefore, is undulation—the repeated return to a level from which they repeatedly fall back, a series of troughs and peaks . . . periods of emotional and bodily richness and liveliness . . . alternate with periods of numbness and poverty." [2]

During the peaks of vitality individuals are more self-assertive and therefore interested in exploring the *differences* in the texture of experience which make for individualism, competition, novelty, adventure, chaos. They are governed, in the terminology of Thomas and Znaniecki, by the wish for new experience and the wish for social recognition.[3] During troughs, however, they become more quiescent and take comfort in the *likenesses* within the texture of experience which make for routine, tradition, uniformity, authority, cosmos. At such times, Thomas and Znaniecki say, they are dominated by the wish for security and the wish for social response. When the assertive individual ventures too far from the tribal ways and received truths in the direction of discrete, novel experience, his curiosity may give way to fear, his self-confidence to anxiety, his amoral egoism to guilt—and he scuttles back into the fold. If the extreme menace at the pole of assertiveness is a self-annihilation of insanity, the danger at the other extreme of submission is the living death of automatism such as one frequently finds in primitive forms of life. Truly autonomous individuals seek a delicate balance, or tension, between the two poles.

Because of the extreme fragmentation and dislocation of values in modern life, many of our best creative minds have been forced

----

[2] C. S. Lewis, *The Screwtape Letters* (New York: The Macmillan Co., 1954), pp. 44-45.

[3] Cf. William I. Thomas and Florian Znaniecki, *The Polish Peasant in America and Europe*, III (Boston: The Gorham Press, 1919), pp. 5-88.

to confront the spectacle of chaos. Out of this confrontation has come, for instance, T. S. Eliot's remarkable poem, "The Waste Land," which places isolated fragments of sordid contemporary experience in ironic juxtaposition to both the romantic images of an earlier age and the symbols of a restorative tradition found in primitive myth and ritual. The presence in the poem of irony, holding mutually exclusive points of view together in tension, suggests the kind of psychological equilibrium which is proof against mental breakdown. Nevertheless, one already finds T. S. Eliot inclining in this poem in the direction of tradition. Later, of course, he embraced the Anglican faith. Henry Adams also recoiled from multiplicity to seek in medieval history the unity of the Church. On the other hand, Ezra Pound, whose *Cantos* influenced Eliot's techniques, suffered a mental derangement.

On the level of personal psychology, it would seem that Eliot derived a new vitality from his return to tradition; within its framework he has explored and developed new themes and modern techniques for verse drama. But his great experimental period came earlier. Fortunate are those individuals, like William James or Ralph Waldo Emerson, who are able continually to feel at home in a pluralistic universe. Yet even James drew close to the One when he proposed a theory of "pansychism" and recommended for religion a pluralistic pantheism. Emerson's transcendentalist group constitutes a special case where vitality would apparently lead to cosmos rather than chaos. But this anomaly is only apparent. The position represented in Emerson's mature essays is actually a fine equipoise which holds the One and the Many within a single instantaneous vision. His doctrine of Correspondence intuits a cosmos *in* chaos. Whatever private troughs underlay his cheering public affirmations can only be surmised through study of his journals and letters.

The investigation of chaos for signs of order is the search for *likenesses* amidst a sensory welter of *differences*. The principle of likeness-and-difference, or parallelism-and-contrast, corresponds roughly to the organizing poles of submission and assertion, which give rise to the image of paradise. That this is so can be demonstrated, at least theoretically, by examining the analytical and imaginative faculties of intelligence, the one giving a conceptual order to the external world and the other a more subjective metaphorical order.

There is not nearly as sharp a distinction between the two

functions as many logicians would like us to believe. As Morris Cohen says, mere intellect cannot supply the motive power which sets inquiry going. He considers imagination "the fundamental basis of our whole mental outlook."[4] It furnishes the motives for inquiry, the fundamental assumptions, hypotheses, and criteria for selection which go into the making of so-called "objective" knowledge. Both functions of intelligence, moreover, depend fundamentally upon the principle of likeness-and-difference. Let me briefly note first how the principle of likeness-and-difference is involved in logical processes. In scientific inquiry the main concern is to discover, in any particular problematical situation, the relationship of concrete data to abstract formulation, the particular to the general, the many to the one, individual instances to uniform law. This relationship is clearly one of likeness-and-difference, or parallelism-and-contrast. The motives for inquiry assume a restless curiosity, or *assertiveness*, as the "disturbed" mind, confronted with an intellectual problem, seeks a satisfying resting point. The research scientist has his intellectual paradise and passes through an intellectual hell.

In the analytical process of abstracting, one discovers what things are *like* in order to place them in a general category such as "cat" or "liquid" only by seeing how they *differ* from such other things as dogs or solids and by *comparing* them with many particular cats and liquids. This act of discrimination lies at the base of all induction and deduction in scientific inquiry. Michelson's famous experiment with the interferometer would effectively demonstrate this point. A less dramatic, but equally good, example of the scientific mind at work is Schneirla's and Piel's published study of the army ant, which has the advantage of being extremely lucid scientific reporting.[5] It also presents some reliable

---

[4] Morris Cohen, *A Preface to Logic* (New York: Meridian Books, 1956), p. 195; *Reason and Nature* (New York: Harcourt, Brace & Co., 1931), p. 57. The principle of similarity-and-difference as a basic, common structural principle in both imaginative and conceptual reconstructions of our experience has been developed by Professor Sterling P. Olmsted in an informal paper presented at a Rensselaer faculty colloquium. For an extended treatment of that principle as it applies to imaginative literature, see Wentworth K. Brown and Sterling P. Olmsted, *Three Uses of Language* (Ann Arbor: Edwards Brothers, Inc., 1960), pp. 78-106, 202-207.

[5] Theodore Christian Schneirla and Gerard Piel, "The Army Ant," *Scientific American*, CLXXVIII (June, 1948), 16-23; reprinted in *Scientific American Reader* (New York: Simon and Schuster, 1953), pp. 411-422.

data by which to check Santayana's disturbance theory of biological evolution and the tendency of living organisms to revert
to origins.

Schneirla's investigations, as reported in collaboration with
Gerard Piel, began with the problem of how such essentially
primitive creatures managed such a highly organized and complex social existence. As an example of scientific inquiry, the
investigation thus began with the experience of *difference*, contrasting ant simplicity with a paradoxical complexity of behavior,
measuring the degree of simplicity and complexity by *comparison*
with other social creatures, including man. I shall leave until
later the consideration of how the results of this inquiry bear
upon Santayana's speculation.

The motive for the investigation was partly the scientist's
motive of curiosity, to impose order upon discrete new experience
(likeness and difference), and partly, as Piel admits, the more
passionately human interest to throw some light on rather similar
human problems of the relationship of the individual to society
(parallelism, analogy). From these motives might also be in-
ferred an element of self-concern involving not only the assertive
ego of the discoverer, but also his remembered experiences of
discomfort (his hell) as an individual having to adjust to society.
Some sense of the latter must be present to his imagination if
he is to perceive the problem of adjustment as parallel in human
and ant societies. Finally, the very word "society" when applied
to ants by Piel is a metaphorical analogy.

Having recognized a problem, Schneirla's "disturbed" mind
sought a satisfactory explanation and temporary resting point—
his intellectual paradise. First, he examined several widely held
theories, or hypotheses, for their correspondence to known fact,
rejecting them on the ground of anthropomorphism (faulty
analogy, observed differences). In the process of testing these
hypotheses he logged a dozen ant armies through one or more
complete life cycles (repetition), looking for hitherto unrecorded
uniformities and correlations in their behavior (likenesses). He
discovered that their migratory cycle coincided precisely with
their reproductive cycle (parallelism, suggesting a repeating
interaction). This observation required a new hypothesis capable
of being tested, which Schneirla derived from the already established concept of "trophallaxis." Ant armies, that is, alternated

between periods of fixed bivouac and nomadic wandering neither
for reason of food supply nor to protect the vulnerable queen
and her helpless young, but because of the role of active larvae
in stimulating callow workers by means of an interchange of
coenzymes.

The testing of a hypothesis is preceded by inferential reasoning based on the syllogism. The pattern of likeness-and-difference
during the deductive phase of this successful empirical study
is obvious in the symbolic equivalent for Schneirla's unspoken
syllogism:

$$\text{M.P.} \quad A \subset B$$
$$\text{m.p.} \quad C \subset A$$
$$\text{C.} \quad C \subset B$$

Using control groups, Schneirla found that, as predicted by his
syllogism, tampering with the trophallactic relationship indeed
disrupted the behavior cycle.

Schneirla's findings have some bearing on Santayana's speculative biology. In the first place, ant life oscillates rhythmically
between periods of intense activity and periods of quiescence
preparatory to new life. The period of activity is brought on
by a chemical disturbance. In the second place, during periods of
activity, characterized by large-scale foraging expeditions, only
the unevenness of the terrain as the ants follow paths of least
resistance counteracts their natural propensity to destroy themselves in suicide mills. In the third place, the whole complex
process grows out of fortunately unsuccessful attempts to per-
petuate or return to a profoundly simple, stereotyped nature.

So much for the orderly thought processes of scientific inquiry. The main distinction between rational and imaginative
thought processes would seem to be one of conscious intent and
degree of abstraction. Both functions are polarized by impulses
of assertion and submission; both make use of the principle of
likeness-and-difference; both abstract from experience in conformity to this principle. The difference seems to be that evocative structures are infinitely more concrete in reference and
texture, relating more immediately to the emotive-sensory content of experience. People like to recreate in imagination as
nearly as possible the lives that they have lived or would like
to have lived. Actual experience always comes originally not in
the abstract, but in a panoply of particular colors, sounds, smells,

tastes. These are simultaneously referred to, and filtered through, emotional likes and dislikes. Much of the richness and subtlety is necessarily lost in the process, but much also remains. What remains transforms spontaneous, day-to-day life metaphorically into a kind of drama of good and evil played by saints and sinners. "We are condemned to live dramatically in a world that is not dramatic," Santayana once wrote, attributing the disappointments of life not so much to hostility and contrary purposes, as people are wont to do, but to contrary facts.[6] This brief review of physics, biology, and human thought processes—both imaginative and analytical—suggests that the human impulses of assertion and submission with their image of paradise have considerably wider ramifications than can be studied in this book.

Giving facts a human significance is a function of "myth." Malinowski claims that myth is an indispensable ingredient of all culture. "Myth is a constant by-product of living faith, which is in need of miracles; of sociological status, which demands precedent; of moral rule, which requires sanction." [7] To the true believer, myth is not a fiction, but "a retrospective, ever-present, live actuality" which puts humankind in touch with some transcendent destiny. It helps to make life meaningful, coherent, and ordered, however miserable the present. Myth functions especially "where there is a sociological strain, such as in matters of great difference in rank and power, matters of precedence and subordination, and unquestionably where profound historical changes have taken place."[8] But myth also contributes to historical change, for people try to behave in conformity to myth pictures which portray, as Ernst Cassirer says, a dramatic world —"the world of actions, of forces, of conflicting powers."[9] History moves, if it moves at all, in the mass, and mass psychology is peculiarly dependent on myth.

The image of paradise belongs in the context of what is perhaps mankind's most compelling myth: the myth to which Judeo-

---

[6] George Santayana, *Realms of Being* (New York: Charles Scribner's Sons, 1942), pp. 463, 478.

[7] Bronislaw Malinowski, *Myth in Primitive Psychology* (New York: W. W. Norton & Co., Inc., 1926), p. 92.

[8] *Ibid.*, pp. 58-59.

[9] Ernst Cassirer, *Essay on Man* (New York: Doubleday & Co., Inc., 1953), p. 102.

Christian lore has given the name of the Garden of Eden. This myth is organized by an evocative structure of parallelism-and-contrast. It presents a narrative of actions, forces, and conflicting powers. There is a god and there is a devil contending for the soul of man. The ways of the devil embody the theme of appearance and reality in a story of temptation, deceit, and seduction. The good things of life are paralleled by the image of paradise. The contrastingly evil things of life are paralleled by man's estate after the Fall, which is also the syndrome of hell. The over-all rhythm of action is a tragic one containing the burden of suffering. The hope for a final triumph of spirit is symbolized by the rivers and tree of life and by God's covenant with the chosen seed of Adam, renewed through Noah, Abraham, Isaac, the children of Israel, and Christ.

According to students of myth, the images of God and Satan would express psychologically the child's divided feelings for the authoritarian parent. By projection, Satan would personify all the harrassments of life which press in on the ego. Similarly, Eve as temptress and Eve as madonna would split off from the mother image, releasing a repressed eroticism, but linking man's apprehension of ideal beauty to love throughout nature. Adam is the wish-embodiment of god-man, poised between divinity and devilishness and associating man's hope for a rebirth out of sin or guilt with a return to nature. All these images, Miss Bodkin believes, express conflicting factors of self-assertion and surrender.[10] All express, in some sense, divided feelings toward authority. Although the particulars and the names in this story may change from culture to culture, its large outlines have been everywhere much the same. Every people has apparently envisaged in its past or future a sinless paradise, frostless gardens, purifying streams, a tree of knowledge, and a tree of life.[11]

---

[10] Cf. Maude Bodkin, *Archetypal Patterns in Poetry: Psychological Studies of Imagination* (London: Oxford University Press, 1934), Ch. IV ("The Image of Woman") and Ch. V ("The Images of the Devil, of the Hero, and of God"). Also see Northrop Frye, *Anatomy of Criticism* (Princeton: Princeton University Press, 1957), pp. 139-239.

[11] William F. Warren, *Paradise Found* (Boston: Houghton Mifflin Co., 1885), pp. 3-32, 117-190, *et passim.* Also pertinent is Arthur K. Moore, *The Frontier Mind: A Cultural Analysis of the Kentucky Frontiersman* (Lexington: University of Kentucky Press, 1957), pp. 30-37. The latter work came to my attention too late to make full use of it in my own investigations.

As a framework for interpreting historical events, the myth of the Garden of Eden helps to rescue man from the terrors of his swift-passing and often painful existence on earth by reconciling the transitory and the eternal. It becomes a powerful fulcrum for historical change, however, when a "chosen people" convert it into a rationale for temporal status, independence, power. The chosen people try to make historical events conform to their image of a temporal future which holds for them an earthly paradise. They tend to regard this earthly paradise as a type of the original Eden. They locate their second Eden in such places as Palestine, the Garden of the Hesperides, the Fortunate Islands, or, as shall be seen, America. Urgency is given to heroic, assertive action in regaining Eden by the need to combat the devil and forward God's divine plan on earth. Human enemies become instruments of the devil to sabotage this plan. Heroes who come forward to help the chosen people whenever the outlook is especially bleak are looked upon as saviors sent by God. It would be difficult to exaggerate the extent to which such mythology has contributed to the dynamism of history.

The demonic view of history is, to be sure, extremely immature, not to say irrational; but history, we are told, is seldom made by logic. Cohn's study of millennial movements shows that "there are always very large numbers of people who are prone to see life in black and white, who feel a deep need for perfect saviors to adore and wicked enemies to hate. . . ."[12] The more mature tragic sense of life is held by relatively few people. It probably contributes little in the short run to the making of history, because, keyed to the understanding of human limitations rather than human potentiality, it is not aggressive. It transcends a simplistic moralism by seeing elements of good and evil intermixed in human character and events. The tragic hero cannot play the role of god or savior. He has already won to and passed over the heights of exaltation in a private, inward victory over passion. This story is contained in the part of the myth of the Garden of Eden which has to do with the Fall.

At this point one should distinguish between secular tragedy and its religious counterpart. The Christian story of man's Fall has a "happy ending," and for that reason has sometimes been

---

[12] Norman Cohn, *The Pursuit of the Millennium* (Fair Lawn, New Jersey: Essential Books, Inc., 1957), p. 312.

called "divine comedy." The Christian paradox of the fortunate
fall is that although the Fall cannot be sufficiently condemned
and lamented, it is nonetheless, in the words of Arthur Lovejoy,
the condition "both of a greater manifestation of the glory of
God and of immeasurably greater benefits for man than could
conceivably have been otherwise obtained." [13] The greater rewards of sinful experience over callow inexperience and untested
innocence tend to encourage an activistic acceptance of the Fall.
In secular tragedy, by contrast, there is no redress, no reprieve,
no "second chance." The tragic hero's acceptance of the Fall,
therefore, represents his restoration to a common humanity which
will never know the joys of heaven or enter into an earthly
promised land. His only salvation is to rescue from crushing
defeat a measure of fortitude and dignity. When Lear remarks
with simple dignity, "Pray you, undo this button," he has discovered a compassionate fellow-feeling before the mysterious,
terrifying forces of the universe.

The myth of the Garden of Eden expresses the relationship of
the individual or the group to authority. When this myth becomes an important factor in history, it is apt to be the rationale
of an underprivileged group of social upstarts in conflict with
an entrenched authoritarian class or old established civilization.
"Civilization shouts, gives orders, writes rules, puts man in institutions, and intimidates him with a thousand irritating directives." [14] All these authoritarian features are rendered, as in
Dante's *Inferno*, by the image of hell. The chosen people assert
themselves against authority in behalf of a restoration to a paradisiac state of nature which, in imagination at least, hurls no
directives. The impulses of assertion and submission expressed
in the myth of Eden thus tend to polarize history in the most
general terms of civilization and nature.

The polarity of nature and civilization generated the dynamism
of Hebrew history. Originally, the concept of a chosen people
in covenant with God and the vision of a new promised land
were devices by which the Jews consoled, fortified, and asserted
themselves against oppression in Egypt, where a simple agrarian

---

[13] Arthur O. Lovejoy, "Milton and the Paradox of the Fortunate Fall,"
Essays in the History of Ideas (Baltimore: The Johns Hopkins Press, 1948),
pp. 278-279.
[14] Walter Prescott Webb, *The Great Frontier* (Boston: Houghton Mifflin
Co., 1952), p. 32.

folk came into conflict with a highly organized urban culture. The basically agrarian orientation of the Jews is revealed not only in the general character of Biblical imagery, but also in the characteristic indictment of urban civilization. In the mouths of the Old Testament prophets—Amos, Hosea, Jeremiah, Nehemiah, and others—city cultures become synonymous with sinful backsliding, the main symbol of which is sexual lust as personified by painted Jezebels and mincing harlots. The prophecies of doom which will overtake a sinful people invariably envision the destruction of a city. Nehemiah preached the destruction of even his own capital city, Jerusalem. But, in the main, the chief places of sin in the Old Testament are the cities of the authoritarian oppressors: Nineveh, Sodom, Gomorrah, Babylon, and the cities of Egypt. The chief villains are those in authority—as cultured as they are tyrannical, as powerful as they are wealthy, subtle in deceit, and perfect instruments of the devil.

The same bias is present in the New Testament, which holds in special veneration shepherds, fishermen, small children, lambs, a manger in the rural village of Bethlehem, and such quiet retreats from urban cares as the garden of Gethsemane. The most famous of Psalms reads: "He maketh me to lie down in green pastures: he leadeth me beside the still waters." The primitive regression to nature is also apparent in the Jewish attitude toward intellectual sophistication. The Jews distrusted learning as the cause of Adam's downfall and intellect as a source of deception. The serpent deceived Eve through a stratagem of cold, reasoning intellect, just as Delilah consciously, deliberately, used her sex to deceive Sampson and Jezebel deceived Naboth. The preacher in Ecclesiastes expressed a popular sentiment when he wrote that knowledge increased one's sorrow. Hebrew writers did not like to express themselves analytically, but wrote poetically in symbols, epigrams, and parables. The prophets in particular aspired to truth through the outpouring of the unreasoning heart. Among the animals which one so often meets in the imagery of the New Testament, as Erasmus noted, the ones which pleased Christ most were those with a reputation for least slyness. He chose to ride upon a donkey, though it was believed that He could make a lion lie down with a lamb and could therefore ride a lion safely if He had chosen. The Holy Spirit descended in the likeness of a dove rather than an eagle

or hawk; and hares, fawns, and other guileless creatures are frequently mentioned. These animals had not eaten of the tree of
knowledge! The only beings who could do so safely were God
and the saints in heaven. Knowledge, with the other marks of
cultural sophistication, was otherwise the special sanctuary of
Satan.

Hebraic providential history demanded action. Hebrew history
is one long tale of conquest and bloodshed. But the Jews could
not hope to contend successfully with powerful empires like
Assyria. When they could not move mountains, therefore, they
produced a Lamb, and were disappointed that Christ was not a
temporal savior like Moses or David. Yet, ironically, their most
characteristic imagery, revealing their deepest emotional attach-
ments, shows that they asserted themselves to achieve ultimately
in Palestine through their worldly saviors the very state of paradisiac bliss for which Christ stood in a spiritual or psychological
sense. Even their worldly saviors and anointed leaders were conceived as simple men. Moses was so diffident in speech that he
needed Aaron and Miriam to speak for him. "O my Lord," he
said, endearing himself to his people, "I am not eloquent . . .
but I am slow of speech, and of a slow tongue." Isaac favored
the rough hunter, Esau, over the smooth-spoken, tent-dwelling
Jacob although Jacob later became the eponymous hero of the
tribe. The "city slicker," Joseph, did not receive grace until he
had outgrown his worldly vanity, symbolized by the coat of
many colors. Samson was a rural strong man. When Saul went
the way of oriental luxury and despotism, he was replaced by
David, a youthful shepherd. All these heroes were followers of
the Mosaic code whose lack of sophistication and refinement of
manner, in the main, guaranteed their moral rectitude. They
succumbed to sinful temptation, as with Saul and David, in
proportion as they became powerful and worldly. In Hebraic
history the main poles of good and evil, for the most part, correspond to the opposition of nature and civilization. This dichotomy governed the contrast of country and city and opposed
freedom to tyranny, modest prosperity to corrupt materialism,
simplicity of manner to sophistication, moral rectitude to carnal
lust, heart to intellect, truth to falsehood. The devil of Hebraic
imagination tended to be a powerful, sophisticated city-dweller.

The city of Hebraic thought is the archetypal home of conspiracy, envy, and division. The murderer Cain built a city; Abel did not, because he was a "sojourner" who belonged to God. The tower of Babel symbolized the dissension which the Jews found in urban civilization: Babylon means "the city of confusion." The engineer Nimrod, who was believed to have built Babylon, is depicted as a rebel against God. Nevertheless, attitudes toward urban culture were not simple, but compounded servility and rebellion, admiration and loathing, pride and inferiority. Psychological movement between the poles of assertion and submission requires just such a love-hate relationship to authority. There was, after all, a holy city—Rome. The image of the city in human thought splits off into dual components comparable to the ambivalent god-man, god-devil, and madonna-temptress. Let us briefly see what the image of the city, on its positive side, stands for. As men congregated together, they located at the center of the mythical paradise a temple, palace, or royal residence which they imagined to be constructed of gold, richly studded with jewels and other splendors. Out of this developed the idea of a holy, or sacred, city. Because the center of creation was believed to exist at the summit of a sacred mountain where heaven and earth met, every sacred city of actual history became by extension, as Eliade says, a "Sacred Mountain." [15] Thus, when the American colonists said that they were going to establish in the New World "A City on a Hill," they meant to found a sacred city and a new paradise.

Babylon was originally so settled. An ancient map shows it at the center of a vast circular countryside bordered by a river, "precisely as the Sumerians envisioned Paradise." [16] Indeed, the sacred city takes on the character of the country surrounding it. Hebrew and Christian writers frequently used the terms "Jerusalem" and "Paradise" interchangeably. Thus, Baruch, in the Syriac Apocalypse, has God complain of worldly Jerusalem, "This building now built in your midst is not that which is revealed with Me, that which was prepared beforehand here from the time I took counsel to make Paradise, and showed it to Adam before he sinned. . . ." [17] Augustine similarly located his holy city

---

[15] Mircea Eliade, *The Myth of the Eternal Return,* trans. Willard R. Trask (New York: Pantheon Books, Inc., 1954), pp. 11-12, 16-17.

[16] *Ibid.*, p. 10.

[17] *Ibid.*, p. 8.

in paradise. A monk during the Crusades called Jerusalem "the navel of the world, the land fruitful above all others, like another paradise of delights." [18] The pilgrimages of the Middle Ages were duplicated by thousands of American pioneers belonging to evangelical religious sects, who pushed westward into the wilderness to set up the New Jerusalem and await the Second Coming of Christ. But insofar as the image of a holy city conflicts with that of a primitive paradise, it is a symbol of civilized progress. The sacred city therefore expresses the buoyant hope of a glorious future paradise rather than a nostalgia for the lost paradise of the past. As the Spanish philosopher Unamuno says, however, "Everyone who fights for any ideal whatever, although his ideal may seem to lie in the past, is driving the world on to the future." [19] Conversely, the forward-aching impulse may act unconsciously in the name of its opposite.

Since the earthly, temporal city is always corrupt, progress is thought of in terms of an ideal city. But the ideal city lies at the center of creation. Therefore, the idea of progress partakes of a spiritual, sociological, or geographical search for the "center." The many journey patterns of antiquity and modern times represent, according to this view, a search for the center, or paradise, which is in part regressive. But the vision of paradise is determined and preceded by a state of intense suffering symbolized by the passage through hell, a night journey, or descent into the sea. Every historical period of great persecution and suffering by the Jews and other peoples is accompanied by such images, illustrative of psychological motion between poles of assertiveness and submissiveness. Classical examples abound in the Old Testament.

The sad experience in Egypt produced the journeys of Joseph, the wilderness trials in the deserts of the Sinai Peninsula, and the passage across the Red Sea, whose waters opened a gateway to the promised land. The Babylonian exile produced the jeremiads of the prophets and their promise of a messiah; it also produced Daniel's descent into the lion's den and his eschatological vision of the Last Days; its memory produced, above all, the lamentations of Job, whose imagery is full of the dark night of the

---

[18] Cohn, op. cit., p. 44.
[19] Miguel de Unamuno, The Tragic Sense of Life (New York: Dover Publications, Inc., 1954), p. 321.

Hebrew soul. "He is thrust from light into darkness, and driven out of the world. . . . Job spake, and said, Let the day perish wherein I was born. . . . Let that day be darkness. Lo, let that night be solitary, let no joyful voice come therein. . . . Why is light given to a man whose way is hid, and whom God hath hedged in?" Job passed from spiritual arrogance in contending with the Lord, through pain, to acceptance and submission, for which he was rewarded with "twice as much as he had before." The tragic rhythm was completed in his final surrender and self-abnegation.

The passion play was a product of Roman domination heaped upon a heritage of oppression. The passage of Jesus through the streets of the city carrying the burden of the cross to Cavalry symbolically re-enacts the suffering of His people, His resurrection, their hope of deliverance. But this is also the story of Jonah, who fled from the sins of the city of Nineveh and whose passage took the form of a sea journey and resurrection from the depths of despair:

The waters compassed me about, even to the soul: the depth closed me round about, the weeds were wrapped about my head.

I went down to the bottoms of the mountains: the earth with her bars was about me for ever: yet hast thou brought up my life from corruption, O Lord my God.

His initially rebellious spirit, chastened by fear and guilt, was replaced by a submissive attitude, and he returned to Nineveh, where God caused a shade plant to grow, signifying the quality of life-renewing forgiveness. The narrow legalism and exclusiveness of Mosaic teaching was transcended on a higher plane. In Christ, the earlier geographical searches for the center had become a spiritual quest—and so remained for some thousand years afterward.

During this long period, which witnessed the contraction of the Roman Empire and the corresponding expansion of Christianity, the peoples of Europe were, for the most part, reconciled to their temporal conditions. Growth and change, of course, continued, but proceeded quietly beneath the surface, to erupt more violently in the late Middle Ages. Life was by no means easy, for extreme poverty, oppression, and severe plagues were the rule. Nevertheless, people did not revolt against these fatalities. They had no blueprint for utopia, according to historians, and no new frontiers presented themselves for development. Indeed, they tended to locate their earthly paradise in a distant past, listening to the sorrows of Cyprian or Augustine. When the search for the center was once again renewed on the geographical and sociological level, it was preceded by the awakening of millennial fervor and the displacement of the earthly paradise with its holy city from the past to the future. When this happened, a contrast of present and future rose to parallel the dynamic polarities of town and country, prosperity and poverty, liberty and authority, morals and manners, heart and head. Also, the geography of Europe became polarized around Rome and the outposts, just as the Near East had been polarized in ancient Biblical times around Jerusalem and Babylon. The renewal of the search for the center on a geographical and sociological plane is the subject of the next chapter.

Before this is taken up, however, one other question needs brief attention. That is the question whether the myth of Eden, as it is examined here, promises a comprehensive theory by which all history is both caused and explained. Certainly it is reasonable to assume an interplay between myth as interpretation and myth as one cause among many. It should be the duty of the historian wherever possible to point out and demonstrate this connection without losing sight of obvious discrepancies between myth and historical fact. Kenneth Boulding, in his book, *The Image*, has argued plausibly that people try to behave according to their myth pictures of the world.[20] They do not always succeed because their pictures may be faulty, and external circumstances may be beyond their control. In that case they may modify their pictures. Boulding would distinguish between those processes in history which are relatively independent of the images held and those processes which are sharply dependent on the image. He calls the former processes "latent" and the latter "manifest."

The myth of Eden has not only shown itself capable of assimilating all the broad areas of human experience to which historians have commonly attributed causation, but it also expresses and organizes some of mankind's most imperative emotional needs. The main poles of modern history, it is tentatively pro-

---

[20] Kenneth Boulding, *The Image* (Ann Arbor: University of Michigan Press, 1956).

posed, correspond to the poles of self-assertion and submission, which structure the myth of the Garden of Eden. Viewed psychologically, history would then be the movement between these poles projected upon events, but also affected by events. Such a view treats myth both as manifest cause and as effect of latent causes, depending upon the particular historical situation. It is by no means a total explanation of history.

On the other hand, some biological speculation already introduced, when taken with other scientific theories and the kind of analysis attempted here, would tend to support something like a total explanation of history. This explanation would argue that the evolutionary energies of organic life show the same basic rhythmic patterns which shape human history and the myths of human history. All history would then be regarded as a constant active effort by living matter to overcome obstacles in order to sink back toward origins. Written history would be a fantastic chronicle of fact straining to become myth. While this theory will be kept before the reader as an intellectually intriguing, even ironically amusing possibility, it is not offered as demonstrable truth.

3

The Journey
Pattern of
Modern History

The journey pattern of modern Western history would seem to begin with the imaginative transfer of the second paradise from a heavenly future to an earthly future. Norman Cohn contends that dreams of a future earthly paradise were kept alive among the populace of the Middle Ages by the millennial tradition. That is not quite true, for Augustine held that the earthly paradise was forever inaccessible to fallen man and that Christian peoples were already living in the millennium of the Church prior to the Last Days. Only a small minority of the Church fathers had held out with Lactantius for "a thousand years of carnal bliss."

More important were early pagan ideas of geography and the influence of medieval exploration. What evidence we have suggests that a few intrepid adventurers such as Marco Polo and the not very trustworthy Sir John de Mandeville did more than anyone else to help earthbound imaginations, where they existed, to reach out from the tiny island of the known world toward the great, nebulous, fabulous unknown. Through such men, medieval fable with its strange wonders and miraculous beings located the kingdom of earthly desire vaguely and variously in romantic places like Abyssinia, in Cathay or Ophir somewhere in the Far East, or in unknown lands beyond the Western seas. The name

"Ophir" comes, of course, from Old Testament accounts of King Solomon's mines. But these men owed as much to pagan legend as to the Bible for their ideas: the pagans held that men had even visited these places!

When the way West replaced the trade routes to the East in the imaginations of the explorers, the ancients of Greece and Rome helped to instruct them: Aristotle, Plato, Seneca, Strabo, Pliny.[1] Thus, writing in the fifth century before Christ, Aristotle was describing incredibly fertile, sweet-scented islands which Carthaginian merchants had discovered after several days sail "beyond the Pillars of Hercules." In his *Timaeus* and *Critias* Plato told of an invasion of Europe from Atlantis, an idyllic island in the western ocean which an earthquake had since sent sliding into the sea. The famous geographer Strabo later envisaged a continent existing beyond the Atlantic, while the elder Pliny claimed that the whole western and northern oceans had been largely explored under the auspices of the Emperor Augustus.[2] And, of course, medieval explorers believed with Ptolemy that the earth was round. Many of these ideas appeared in the cartography of medieval map makers and geographers even before Ptolemy's geography was rediscovered to the Western world. The two most immediate sources of Columbus' ideas, Pierre d'Ailly's *Imago Mundi* and the globe of Martin Behaim, mixed Christian cosmography with known fact, interpolations of medieval travel accounts, and pagan legend.

Plato's Atlantis appeared on the Pizigani map of 1367. Behaim's globe showed the large islands of Antilia and St. Brendan appearing between the mainland of Europe and the islands of Asia. That these legendary islands were associated with paradise and influenced maritime expectations is illustrated by the popular, long-lived myth of Brendan. He was a monk living in the sixth century A.D. who founded a monastery in Ireland and learned

---

[1] Cf. William H. Babcock, *Legendary Islands of the Atlantic, A Study in Medieval Geography* (New York: American Geographical Society, 1922), Ch. I and pp. 2-5.

[2] Cf. Peter Albinus, *A Treatise on Foreign Languages and Unknown Islands*, trans. Edmund Goldsmid (Edinburgh: privately printed, 1884), pp. 40-49. This historiographer of Saxony, who died in 1598, was more impressed by the possible influence of these ideas upon Columbus than is Samuel Eliot Morison in his definitive biography of Columbus. In any event, during the Middle Ages their influence would have been indirect, since many of the original writings had not yet been recovered.

to be something of a navigator. Legend had him disappearing into the Western seas. According to the medieval *Book of Lismore,* he heard an angel say to him one night, "Arise, O Brenainn, for God hath given thee what thou soughtest, even the Land of Promise." Another version found him hiding away from sinful mankind on an island "just under Mount Atlas," which was "the first home of Adam and Eve." [3] Already, long before Columbus, the transfer of Eden and the sacred mountain from Mesopotamia to America was underway; already the Renaissance utopia loomed in the imagination. The myth of Brendan stimulated hundreds of excited eyewitness reports of mysterious, disappearing islands, and the Canaries were constantly being discovered and rediscovered. With the discovery of America, Edenic expectations entered the main stream of history, assured of a prophetic fulfillment in the West. Without this westward-looking promise, the masses of Europe might never have stirred, the industrial revolution never begun, the social revolutions never launched.[4]

We see the process of fermentation in Dante, who works out his spiritual allegory with the sharp imagery of rich sensory life. Anticipating the future march of history, he has Ulysses, another archetypal hero of the journey pattern, sailing through the Straits of Gilbraltar to reach the West, seeking "the new experience/ Of the uninhabited world behind the sun." [5] Shouldering the dawn, Ulysses comes upon Mount Purgatory, where one begins the ascent to the Celestial City. Dante's sacred mountain is none other than Brendan's Mount Atlas, though at this time the lure of the East and the kingdom of Prester John spoke more authoritatively in Europe than did the Atlas of the West.[6] On the other hand, Columbus' saturation with European medieval legend partook of both poles East and West. He clung to the belief that

----

[3] Babcock, *op. cit.,* pp. 34-35.

[4] This is the thesis of Walter Prescott Webb, *The Great Frontier* (Boston: Houghton Mifflin Co., 1952). Webb is not concerned with the Edenic myth.

[5] Dante, *The Divine Comedy: I, Hell,* trans. Dorothy L. Sayers (Baltimore: Penguin Books, Inc., 1951), p. 236.

[6] Professor Edward Cheyney's two books on the Renaissance period, *European Background of American History, 1300-1600* and *The Dawn of a New Era, 1250-1453,* both stress "The Revelation of the East." My stress is rather "The Revelation of the West." But these two views need not be incompatible.

the Garden of Eden existed at "the end of the East," as described in Genesis. But one sailed West to get to the East, just as one seeks one's beginning in one's end, and the end of time recovers the beginning of time.

Much has been made of Columbus' ruling motive to open trade with the Orient by sailing West. One cannot deny this since Samuel Eliot Morison so ably refuted the theories of Henry Vignaud. Nevertheless, Professor Morison does not take Columbus' cosmographical ideas and paradisiacal conceits with sufficient seriousness. Columbus was not only saturated with medieval legends about the location of the earthly paradise, but was also greatly influenced by millennial movements of the late Middle Ages whose rise coincided with the earliest stirrings of geographical excitement. Moreover, the economic objectives of spices, incense, jewels, and gold is perfectly comprehended by the image of the material paradise.

Columbus was secondarily interested in the paradise of innocence and beatitude. He wished to open the world to the Gospel in fulfillment of Biblical prophecy of the Second Coming. When on his third voyage he realized that he had discovered a new continent—which he named Ophir because he still believed himself to be in the Far East—he was convinced, as he reported, that literally "there is the terrestrial paradise." [7] He explained his reasoning: calculations of latitude seemed to indicate that the earth was not quite round, as he had assumed, but pear-shaped, and that his ships skirted a kind of "cosmic breast" rather similar to Dante's Mount Purgatory, at the top of which must exist the Garden of Eden. He believed that the strong, fresh-water currents found far out in the Gulf of Paria had their source in the four rivers which watered the Biblical garden. Moreover, all the evidence of his senses—the delightful climate, the luxuriant vegetation, the perfume of a thousand tropical flowers—seemed to confirm speculations of the mind. It is no

----

[7] For information about Columbus' cosmographical ideas see Samuel Eliot Morison, *Admiral of the Ocean Seas,* 2 vols. (Boston: Little, Brown & Co., 1942), II, 283-284; Washington Irving, *The Life and Voyages of Christopher Columbus,* III (New York: G. P. Putnam's Sons, 1868), Appendixes no. 13, 19, 23-26, 35; Le Roy Edwin Froom, *The Prophetic Faith of Our Fathers,* II (Washington, D.C.: Review & Herald Publishing Assoc., 1948), 159-175; *Select Documents Illustrating the Four Voyages of Columbus* (London: Hakluyt Society, 1933), pp. 42, 30-50, *et passim.* Columbus' pear-shaped theory has recently been reaffirmed.

wonder that at first, before disillusionment set in, he attributed to the Caribbean Indians the innocent qualities of Adam and Eve. The earliest delineation of the so-called "noble savage," which was to dominate seventeenth- and eighteenth-century imaginations, was created by Columbus.

Columbus' vision of paradise was determined by the afflictions of old age, by a succession of disappointments, and by his troubles at the Spanish court. He had not mentioned paradise in his first voyages and had been explicit only in his belief that he had been divinely inspired to discover new lands. But everywhere in his writing one finds a compulsive conviction that the prophecy about proclamation of the gospel to the ends of the earth must be fulfilled before the approaching end of the world. That Columbus assumed the Second Coming of Christ to restore the earthly paradise to the faithful on this grand occasion is indicated by *The Book of the Prophecies* which he wrote shortly before his last voyage to America and after he was released from chains in Seville. It amplified a statement which he had made to the former nurse of Prince John: "God made me the messenger of the new heaven and the new earth, of which He spoke in the Apocalypse by St. John, after having spoken of it by the mouth of Isaiah; and He showed me the spot where to find it." [8] In his book he wrote that the blessed event was to be preceded by the opening up of the New World, the conversion of the heathen, and the destruction of Antichrist, or Satan. In it he cited the famous medieval millennialist, Joachim of Floris, who seems to have indicated long before that Spain was to play an important role in this glorious enterprise. The Spanish, in other words, were to be the chosen people, successors of the children of Israel.

The noted nineteenth-century geographer, von Humboldt, says that these ideas of Columbus had little success in Spain or Italy, where, already by this time, "le scepticisme en matières religieuses commençait à germer." [9] But a literal acceptance of these ideas was not necessary to impart a dynamism to history if they flourished in a richly metaphorical sense, as they did. Thus,

----

[8] Froom, *op. cit.*, II, 170.

[9] Friedrich Alexander von Humboldt, *Examen Critique de l'Histoire de la Geographie du Nouveau Continent,* 5 vols. (Paris: Gide Press, 1836-1839), III, 117.

even the sophisticated Vespucci felt the lure of paradise in the trade winds off South America.[10] Columbus' tales, taken metaphorically as richly descriptive of a bonanza land called El Dorado, helped the Spanish conquistadors, few of whom did not feel divinely appointed, to fill Spanish galleons with Aztec gold. The influx of gold, in turn, contributed to the social transformation of Europe. Contrary to the assertion of George Sarton and George Sellery that the Renaissance humanists either ignored or failed to appreciate the supreme importance of the new geographical discoveries, that release of energies known as the Renaissance was largely stimulated by geographical excitement as interpreted by the myth of Eden. History began to move again toward the pole of self-assertion, because the revelations of new earthly possibilities encouraged a radical departure from old traditions, beliefs, and social institutions. The jealous individualism of the Spanish explorers was one with the cult of personality of Renaissance Italy. The humanists showed their awareness of the importance of geographical discovery directly by attempts to interpret its meaning and indirectly by their use of figures of speech, modes of expression, and New World themes.

As early as 1498, one Annius attempted to identify the American Indians with the ten lost tribes of Israel, an undertaking which later supported the belief of American colonists that the New Jerusalem would be founded in America.[11] The wider meaning of the New World was at once interpreted by the great humanist Poliziano, who, from Florence, complimented the King of Portugal upon "opening up new lands, new seas, new worlds, even new constellations."[12] The New World metaphor betokened a voyage of imagination which swept up Ariosto, Machiavelli, Castiglione, Erasmus, Sir Thomas More, Dürer, Raphael, Michelangelo, Copernicus, Galileo, Donne, and others. The great influence over scientific investigation is suggested by the words of the famous Italian doctor Fracastoro, who once entertained Sebastian Cabot in his home as well as noted mathematicians, philosophers, and astronomers. He declared at the end of the

[10] Morison, *op. cit.* II, 285; *The Letters of Amerigo Vespucci,* ed. Clements R. Markham (London: Hakluyt Society, 1894), p. 48.

[11] Don Cameron Allen, *The Legend of Noah* (Urbana: University of Illinois Press, 1949), pp. 119-120.

[12] Cited in Lewis Mumford, *The Condition of Man* (New York: Harcourt, Brace & Co., 1944), p. 234.

fifteenth century, "We have attained a whole world different from ours both in its peoples and even in its heavens where shine new stars." [13] Renaissance letters became filled, as never before, with allusions to an earthly paradise and a golden age. In 1495, Charles VIII of France found a seventh heaven of delight in Naples. He wrote characteristically, "You cannot believe what beautiful gardens I have seen in this city. Upon my faith, I think that only Adam and Eve are wanting to make them the earthly paradise. . . ." In the next year Cardinal Briçonnet was describing Florence as the earthly paradise.[14] The Renaissance vogue of Arcadia blended accounts of the New World with Biblical reminiscences of Eden, medieval stories of the earthly paradise, and classical fables of a golden age. The "Columbus of this visionary hemisphere," as Symonds called him, was Jacopo Sannazzaro, whose *Arcadia*, significantly, was not published until 1504.

That representative man of the Renaissance, Erasmus, wrote in 1517 that he anticipated "the approach of a golden age." [15] This pronouncement, so frequently repeated in the period following Columbus' discovery, meant, if it meant anything, that the golden age was no longer considered something long past and forever lost. But Erasmus' indebtedness to geographical discovery had been revealed earlier and more directly by his *Praise of Folly*, published in 1509. The birthplace of Folly was "the Fortunate Isles, where there is no labor and where all things thrive naturally." [16] The book's main theme was a satirical contrast of nature and civilization associated indirectly with the contrast between civilized Europe and Vespucci's account of the New World. One of its models, Sebastian Brant's *The Ship of Fools*, published in 1494, also reflected the influence of the geographical journey. At the time Erasmus wrote, he was visiting

[13] Quoted in Myron P. Gilmore, *The World of Humanism, 1453-1517* (New York: Harper & Bros., 1952), p. 267.

[14] Quotation is from F. Funck-Brentano, *The Renaissance* (New York: The Macmillan Co., 1936), p. 160. Briçonnet on p. 163.

[15] Desiderius Erasmus, *The Epistles of Erasmus, from His Earliest Letters to His Fifty-first Year*, ed. and trans. Francis Morgan Nichols, 3 vols. (New York: Longmans, Green & Co., 1901), II, 506. Similar allusions recur throughout these letters.

[16] Desiderius Erasmus, *The Praise of Folly*, trans. Leonard F. Dean (Chicago: Packard & Co., 1946), p. 28.

his friend, Sir Thomas More, in England. The distance from Erasmus' *Praise of Folly* to More's *Utopia* in 1517 is as short as a straight line can be. *Utopia* is pre-eminently a New World symbol and equally a symbol of all the multifarious stirrings of the Renaissance period. The book exhorted Europeans, particularly the princes of Europe, to follow the noble example of laws and institutions in "those newe founde lands." [17] Of course, the mass movement of people to realize a better life as furnished by this ideal standard and as stimulated by the westward-looking promise of the future was slow in coming to fruition, as any great movement must be, but its roots lay here.

The Abbé Raynal, writing at the end of the eighteenth century, attributed the modern fanatical spirit of discovery to the bold attempts of Columbus and Vasco da Gama. Summarizing the content of the revolutionary myth of our own time, Lewis Mumford says: "We shall find that it rested on a devout faith in the 'New World' of science, capitalism, mechanization, and colonial expansion. So that it was not by accident that Thomas Paine spent his spare time inventing an iron bridge; that the Saint-Simonians projected the Suez and Panama canals; and that the greatest triumph of the French revolution was the extension of its benefits, as succinctly incorporated in a legal code, to the peoples subdued by the last of the great conquistadors, Napoleon I." [18] But we must not linger here, for we have hardly hinted at the extent to which the men of the Renaissance responded imaginatively to the geographical voyage. About the time More's *Utopia* appeared, there also appeared Ariosto's *Orlando Furioso*, which Galileo thought "divine," and which the literary historian John Addington Symonds has considered the supreme point of the fifteenth century. Though it recaptures a romantic, chivalric past in order to glorify the Italian house of Estes, it presents in its thirty-fourth and thirty-fifth cantos an image of the earthly paradise as an excuse for satirizing the foibles of civilized Europe. The knight Astolpho is sent on a journey to the moon to procure the herb which will cure Orlando's madness, occasioned by his fall from the sexual paradise with the loss of his beloved Angelica. On his way to the moon,

----

[17] Thomas More, *Utopia*, ed. J. Churton Collins (Oxford: The Clarendon Press, 1904), p. 7.

[18] Mumford, *op. cit.*, p. 322.

Astolpho visits the sources of the Nile; looks in on Prester John,
who mistakes him for the coming Messiah; enters hell, like
Dante, to see the tortures of the damned; leaves hell afflicted,
again like Dante, with paradisiac longing; and climbs the sacred
mountain, which takes him near the third circle of the moon,
as described earlier by Augustine.

But this is no heavenly paradise at the summit, even though
the grass is so green, the birds so melodious, the region with its
gleaming palace so lovely that the earth below seems foul and
more like hell than earth. For John the Evangelist, who greets
him there, sets before him and his horse a meal so bountiful as
to make the sin of Adam forgivable. Moreover, in sharp conflict
with Augustine's spiritualized paradise, the saints assembled
there by Ariosto expect to hear angelic trumpets proclaim
Christ's Second Advent on earth. That earth sorely needs it is
indicated by the heaped up excrescences from Renaissance Italy
which Astolpho finds on the moon: the sycophantic offerings of
courtiers to "greedy prince and patron," jewels symbolizing the
oppressive authority of great lords, the ruined castles of conspiracy, the broken bottles of servitude, and a bunch of stinking
flowers—"The gift (if it may lawfully be said)/Which Constantine to good Sylvester made." [19] Here we find in Ariosto, as in
Erasmus and Boccaccio, the savage indictment of the papacy
which anticipated the Reformation. Here, too, we find the contempt for authority, both secular and ecclesiastical, which not
only characterized Renaissance letters but also the individualism
at the core of the social movements which followed. Renaissance
artists, as a class, belonged to a social élite far removed from the
ignorant peasants, mechanics, artisans, and journeymen, who
increasingly thronged into the urban centers; but under cover of
servile flattery for their patrons and disguised by satire, their
works spread heretical ideas far and wide.

Satire is the gift of those not yet ready or audacious enough
to break openly with solidly constituted authority. The fate of
Lollardy, of John Huss, of the Waldenses, and Savonarola
showed what could happen to innovators who were dangerous
to the social order at a time when that order was still strong
enough to defend itself. Social evolution had to precede revolu-

---

[19] Ludovico Ariosto, *The Orlando Furioso*, trans. William Stewart Rose, 2
vols. (London: George Bell and Sons, 1907-1910), Canto XXXIV, st. lxxvi.

tion. As the sixteenth century progressed, social criticism became bolder, more direct. In a public lecture at the University of Salamanca in 1532, Francisci de Victoria, the famous Spanish theologian and political theorist, dared openly to challenge Spain's divine right to conquer the New World by force. Before a royal council of Emperor Charles V, Bishop Bartholomew de Las Casas attacked Spanish brutality in the New World. Martin Luther had recently posted his defiance of the Pope. These people were listened to all over Europe and had to be countenanced by those in authority. At the climactic moment of Luther's career, for instance, when his very life should have been at stake under the old dispensation, Pope Clement VII was disposed to sit down to talk things over. The Pope was not only faced with social and political unrest all over Europe, but forced to accede to the sack of Rome itself. But the important thing to note is that New World idealism, releasing long pent-up energies of self-assertive individualism, was chiefly responsible for the new intransigence toward authority. As Luther said, "We are living in a New World today, and things are being done differently." [20]

The high point of the Renaissance in France was reached by Rabelais' *Gargantua*, which appeared in 1534. It was the broadest burlesque of French life yet written. It, too, received its life from the news from abroad, and its ideals, if not its humors, derived from the impact of the New World upon European imaginations. The sensual giant is represented as a "masterpiece of nature," a world-wide traveler, and a taster of "the joys of paradise." He marries Badebec, daughter of the king of the Amaurots in Utopia, who becomes the mother of Pantagruel. The chief occupation of Gargantua, aside from eating, drinking, and fornicating, is to expose the senselessness of European warfare, the vanity of courtiers, the pomposity of princes, and above all, the hypocritical worldliness of the Church. Rabelais sets up a utopia of his own in a monastery converted into a sexual paradise. The friar who builds it is an individualist. He wants it fashioned after his own "minde and fancie," and he wants to "institute his religious order contrary to all others." [21] It is a monastery

---

[20] Quoted in Mumford, *op. cit.*, p. 235.

[21] François Rabelais, *The Lives, Heroic Deeds and Sayings of Gargantua and His Son Pantagruel*, trans., Sir Thomas Urquhart and Peter le Motteux (London: Chatto & Windus, n.d.), pp. 161, 160-180 *passim*.

without walls, without regulations, without vows of chastity, poverty, or obedience. Its only inhabitants are young men "comely, personable and well-conditioned" and maidens "faire, well-featured, and of a sweet disposition" who have free access to one another in orchards, parks, gardens, swimming pools, archery ranges, and riding stables. The only law governing their behavior is the motto: "DO WHAT THOU WILT." An inscription on the gate of this abbey expressly bars from "our earthly paradise" peddlers of deceit, lawyers, clerks, scribes, commissaries, judges, etc. The book ends with a prophetic riddle of a new world coming.

The Renaissance period impresses us with its diversity, but underlying this splendid diversity, as water to waves, one finds also a great cultural uniformity. Everywhere one turns, from Boccaccio to Rabelais, from Sannazzaro to Tasso, from More to Spenser and Shakespeare, from Savonarola to Luther, one finds variations on a single theme and a common source of inspiration in paradisiac yearning. The garden isle of Tasso's *Aminta*, published in 1573, for instance, was suggested by the myth of Brendan. The theme hinged upon the contrast, sometimes tragic, more often merely sentimental, between the known world of strife, treachery, and sordid ambition and an ideal world of peace, loyalty, pleasure, and tranquil leisure. The characters are divided between a state of nature and civil society, the laws of honor and the obligations of love, the easy morals of paradise and the stiff manners of Italy. If we substitute lush Egypt for paradise, these are also the poles of Shakespeare's *Antony and Cleopatra;* if we substitute the island of Prospero for Tasso's gardens, we almost get *The Tempest.* But these contrasts—and most of the main contrasts and tension of Renaissance literature—were organized by the poles of nature and civilization. These poles, in turn, were related to actual life by the encroachment of European town life upon the country consequent to the opening up of possibilities beyond the seas. They also reflected the resulting polarization of Europe between Rome as the established center of authority and the dispersed civilization at the western and northern peripheries of the old empire which were profiting most from the revenue from abroad.

The oscillation between these poles which sent Europe on its long historical journey is marked by the rise of mixed attitudes of rebellion and submission, awe and jealousy, self-pride and inferiority in discontented peoples on the one hand and on the other by patronizing, superior attitudes of individuals in power toward their supposed inferiors. The humanists in Rome, for instance, tended to regard the people living in the hinterlands of Europe, in whom feelings of national pride were beginning to awaken, as "barbarians." The so-called barbarians, on the other hand, were alternately repelled and attracted by Rome —attracted by virtue of Rome's reputation as the traditional center of learning, religion, and empire; repelled by uncomfortable feelings of dependency, especially cultural, and by their "frontier" sense of Italy's urban depravity. This discomfort was augmented by criticism. Thus, when Benvenuto Cellini traveled in France, he complained that the French were less civilized than the Italians. Machiavelli once appealed to Lorenzo de Medici as a savior to rid Italy of the Swiss, Spanish, and French. "This rule of the barbarians," he said, "stinks in the nostrils of us all."[22] Indicative of the antagonism aroused on this score is the fact that otherwise excellent French and German copyists of ancient manuscripts became sulky and perfunctory when they had to do this work in Rome.

Savonarola, who came from a mountain village in the north of Italy, suffered a great deal from a sense of cultural inferiority. He was considered a foreigner in Florence, alien in eloquence, manners, and dress. Once informed of the poor grace of his delivery in comparison with that of Florence's own elegant Mariano, he said, "Elegance of language must give way to the simplicity of the preaching of sound doctrine." [23] Even the great Erasmus, as an outlander from the low countries, experienced a similar polar tension. When he was in England, he yearned toward Rome; when he was in Rome, he longed for England. Speaking of a mutual friend, he once wrote to Reuchlin, "Perhaps he is thirsting for Italy, but in these times England has an Italy to offer, and unless I am much mistaken, something better than Italy." After he had remained in England for a while,

----

[22] Quoted in John Addington Symonds, *Renaissance in Italy*, 7 vols. (London: John Murray, 1930), I, 288.

[23] Cited by Piero Misciattelli, *Savonarola*, trans., M. Peters-Roberts (New York: D. Appleton & Co., 1930), pp. 46-47. Burckhart is my authority for the behavior of French and German copyists in Italy.

he wrote: "I dreamed of a golden age and the Fortunate Islands, and then, as Aristophanes says, I awoke." To Robert Fisher, an Englishman in Italy, he wrote, "You are in a country where the walls are more learned and more eloquent than our men; so that what we here think eloquent and beautiful cannot but seem poor and rude and tasteless there." [24] All his life, Erasmus alternately wooed and debunked authority.

Ariosto of Ferrara was also attracted to Rome, as much as he knew and ridiculed its corruption under Leo X. His sixth canto of *Orlando* expressed a longing to be conducted by accomplished poets through the city of ruins, to seek learned counsel there, to see the treasures of the Vatican library. In Spain, Peter Martyr, who was sending his Decades of the New World to such patrons as Count Sforza, Pope Leo X, and Cardinal Ludovico d'Aragon, once delivering them through Castiglione, frequently apologized to the purists of Rome for his ignorance and corrupt Latin. The Spanish Bishop Bartholomew de Las Casas defended the reputation of Columbus against the usurpation of Amerigo Vespucci, claiming that Vespucci had the unfair advantage of being "a Latinist, and eloquent." [25] In England, Roger Ascham ascribed to Italy the "enchantments of Circe." He thanked God that he himself had remained in Rome but nine days. "And yet," he said, "I saw in that little time, in one city, more liberty to sin than ever I heard tell of in our noble city of London in nine years." [26] As sensitive pride moved farther toward the pole of unequivocal self-assertion, the psychology of a chosen people arose throughout northern and western Europe, sometimes as an expression of class feeling, more often as incipient nationalism. The old international society of the Middle Ages was breaking down. The geographical journey was being transformed by imagination into a sociological and political journey toward the "Center."

The strong religious sentiment rising against Rome, even among the staunchest Catholics who remained faithful to the Church throughout the Reformation, can hardly be understood

---

[24] Erasmus, *Epistles,* II, 192, 375; I, 225.

[25] Vespucci, *op. cit.,* p. 69.

[26] From Roger Ascham, *The Schoolmaster,* Book I, in *The Renaissance,* ed. Robert Whitney Bolwell (New York: Charles Scribner's Sons, 1929), pp. 63, 72.

apart from national, political, economic, and sociological considerations. Those considerations became part of an Edenic mission. One finds, for instance, an alliance between national sentiment, religion, and empire in Las Casas' statement: "God has made choice of *Spain* to carry his blessed Gospel into the *Indies*, and to bring many populous Nations to the knowledge of himself." [27] Cortez and the other conquistadors, almost without exception, considered themselves divinely appointed to gain glory for Spain in the New World. Wherever this concept of a chosen people appears, indeed, the affairs of this world are interpreted in an eschatological framework which locates in history the objective of regaining Eden.

This is particularly true of Luther and the German Reformation. Luther's pilgrimage began in a love-hate relationship to Rome and a sense of cultural inferiority. For several years after issuing the ninety-five theses he tried to placate the Pope. He wrote, for instance, "I come unwillingly before the precarious and divided judgment of the public, I who am untaught, stupid and destitute of learning, before an age so fertile in literary genius that it would force into a corner even Cicero. . . ." [28] For many years Luther tried to educate the young of Germany and cultivate a pride in the German language so that other lands would see "that we, too, are human beings, able to learn useful things . . . we have too long been German beasts." Luther followed the lead of other western nations who had passed laws against economic vassalage to Rome in recommending the same to the German nobility: "How comes it that we Germans must put up with such robbery and such extortion of our property, at the hands of the pope. If the Kingdom of France has prevented it, why do we Germans let them make such fools and apes of us?" [29]

Luther was explicit in his view that the Germans were a chosen people. "Did [God] not hear the children of Israel, crying to Him, and release them out of the hand of Pharoah, and

[27] Bartholomew de Las Casas, *An Account of the First Voyages and Discoveries Made by the Spaniards in America* . . . (London, 1599), 133.

[28] Preserved Smith, *The Life and Letters of Martin Luther* (Boston), Houghton Mifflin Co., 1911), p. 45.

[29] *The Works of Martin Luther with Introduction and Notes,* 6 vols. (Philadelphia: A. J. Holman Co., 1915), II, 82-83; IV, 125.

can He not today deliver His own?" All Christians, but especially the Germans, were the true Israelites in spiritual descent from Adam. Before the Peasants' Revolt, Luther's sympathies reflected the nature of his following. He favored the lower classes in their opposition to any authoritarian principle: "this poor populace has alone remained in the land and in the right estate, while the better people and the leaders were carried off to the devil with tonsure and cowl to Babylon." [30] Increasingly, he identified the Pope with the devil, or Antichrist—as had the millennialists before him—Rome with Babylon, and the condition of his people with the Egyptian bondage. In 1545, he changed his mind about the Revelation of John, which he had previously rejected, and embraced the apocalyptic doctrine of a new heaven and a new earth. The pattern of the myth of the Garden of Eden was now complete in his thinking.

If one wishes to account for the Protestant Reformation, one must examine the relationship of large groups and classes to authority: authority secular, religious, political, and otherwise. Luther was supported by the nobles who wished to extend their authority over Germany at the expense of the old Roman Empire and Emperors, by all patriotic Germans who wanted a stronger country freed of the foreign yoke, and by the lower classes who looked toward a millennium of equality, prosperity, and freedom. The peasants, for the most part, remained Catholic only because their aspirations had been so sternly suppressed by the nobles and they felt that Luther had betrayed them. All over Europe, a similar pattern is found.

Country people who had remained untouched by economic oppression were unmoved by the Reformation. Sometimes, as in the Swiss mountain cantons, rural folk stayed Catholic chiefly out of resentment toward urban centers which went Protestant. The rising, aggressive middle classes everywhere provided the richest soil for Protestant doctrine because they were trying to

---

[30] *Ibid.* IV, 120-121, 211; VI, 441-442. A follower of Luther who later became a disciple of Thomas Müntzer claimed that Adam and all his descendants spoke German up until the tower of Babel came into existence. See also Norman Cohn, *The Pursuit of the Millennium* (Fair Lawn, New Jersey: Essential Books, Inc., 1957), p. 119; and Ernest L. Tuveson, *Millennium and Utopia* (Berkeley: University of California Press, 1950), pp. 24-29.

make their way against the established authority of priests, kings, and noblemen. In France, as Funck-Brentano points out, "Neither Protestantism, nor Jansenism, nor the Civil Constitution would have roused such bitter strife if there had been in France a national instead of a Roman Church." [31] On the other hand, it was largely due to French Gallicanism, which shut out the sale of indulgences, special Church benefices, and inquisitions, that France was able to pass through the strife of the Reformation without leaving Rome. The Reformation touched only lightly in countries which had been converted to Catholicism by persuasion, deeply where Catholicism had been imposed by a conqueror's force of arms.

That the new social unrest and aspirations were originally released by the possibilities across the seas is suggested also by a rhetoric of spirit which fused the way West with the sociological and political movements of chosen peoples toward a place in the sun. In the journey patterns of Scripture as well as in the language of medieval Church symbolism the spiritual quest had traditionally been known as a "journey toward light." [32] According to this view, if the bower of light was paradise, or the celestial city, the original source of the bright beam was God, symbolized by the life-giving sun. The sun in medieval popular thought represented God's truth and righteousness, illuminating the dark corners of sin with His saving radiance in its solar cycle from east to west.

In his *Commentary on the Four Gospels*, published in 1521, Lefèvre d'Etables, a noted humanist, philosopher, theologian, and friend of Erasmus, compared the rising ascendancy of the light of the gospel with the contemporary discovery of the physical world. But God's divine light did not shine everywhere with equal brilliance. "Wheresoever the children of Israel dwelt," Genesis maintained, "*there* was light." In other words, His brightest beams were reserved for God's elect, the chosen people. Gradually, following Luther, the Reformed Churches of Europe and England revived the Hebraic conception of a chosen

---

[31] Funck-Brentano, *op. cit.*, p. 273.

[32] This is expounded in Helen F. Dunbar, *Symbolism in Medieval Thought and Its Consummation in the Divine Comedy* (New Haven: Yale University Press, 1929), *passim*; and in Dorothy Donnelly, *The Golden Well: An Anatomy of Symbols* (London: Sheed & Ward, Ltd., 1950), pp. 115-153.

people and claimed that the light of the true gospel dwelt in their house. It became almost commonplace for the favored ones to suppose, since the Reformation spread westward from Germany to France, the Netherlands, and England, that succession to the spiritual, cultural, and political leadership of the world followed the solar cycle of the sun from east to west.

Settlement of the New World by militant Protestants completed the identification of geographical westering with moral and spiritual progress and, with the secularization of millennial hopes, contributed to the eighteenth- and nineteenth-century ideas of progress. Before and during the settlement of America, the English considered themselves a chosen people. Shakespeare's England was not only "this blessed plot, this earth, this realm"; it was also a bower of light, "this other Eden, demi-paradise, this fortress built by Nature" for the heirs of the apostolic succession. On the eve of settlement, as Louis B. Wright has pointed out, Protestant theologians were frantically transferring the Ark of the Covenant from Abraham to the English.[33] There were undoubtedly many laymen who in their hearts cried with the Baptist Henry Nicholas, "We have it, we are the Congregation of Christ, we are Israel, lo here it is!" Or with the Anglican William Crashaw, "The God of Israel is . . . the God of England." [34] But there were also many Englishmen who were not loath to see the succession pass westward to America, so long as it enhanced the power and glory of England. Indeed, the English were divinely appointed to establish themselves in the promised lands of the New World! Thus, Richard Hakluyt included in his *Discourse of Western Planting* the argument that the Western discoveries had provided England a heaven-sent opportunity for the spread of the gospel, "whereunto the Princes of the refourmed Relligion are chefely bounde." [35] John White of Dorchester, author of *The Planters Plea*, considered England to be singled out for that work, "being of all the States that

----

[33] Louis B. Wright, *Religion and Empire* (Chapel Hill: University of North Carolina Press, 1943), p. 91ff.

[34] See especially the promotional tracts and sermons calendared in Alexander Brown, *The Genesis of the United States*, 2 vols. (Boston, 1890) and many similar rhetorical pronouncements quoted in William Haller, *The Rise of Puritanism* (New York: Columbia University Press, 1938).

[35] Quoted in Wright, *op. cit.*, p. 45.

enjoy the libertie of the Religion Reformed" the most orthodox and sincere.[36]

As early as 1583, Sir Humphrey Gilbert thought England's "full possession of those so ample and pleasant countreys . . . very probable by the revolution and course of Gods word and religion, which from the beginning hath moved from the East, towards, and at last unto the West, where it is like to end. . . ."[37] The belief that the bounties of God followed the course of the sun westward brought numerous prophecies of a bright future for America and contributed, in part, to their fulfillment.[38] Sir William Alexander, who was to become proprietor of Nova Scotia, wrote in 1616:

> America to Europe may succeed;
> God may stones raise up to Abram's seed.

The poet John Donne predicted in 1622 that the Virginia Company would make England a bridge between the Old World and the New "to join all to that world that shall never grow old, the kingdom of Heaven." A few years later another Anglican poet, George Herbert, noted in his *Church Militant* that

> Religion stands tip-toe in our land
> Ready to pass to the American strand.

Whereupon, Dr. Twiss, "considering our English Plantations of late, and the opinion of many grave divines concerning the Gospel's fleeing westward," asked his fellow clergyman, Joseph Mede: "Why may not that be the place of the New Jerusalem?" His question was later echoed by American colonists who founded cities in the wilderness. Influential Colonial leaders such as Samuel Sewall and Increase and Cotton Mather took explicit notice of Dr. Twiss' question and answered it in the affirmative.

The image of a New Jerusalem in the Western world accompanied dreams of empire and higher civilization. Among the blessings which God had bestowed upon fallen reason, and

[36] Peter Force, compiler, *Tracts and Other Papers Relating Principally to the Origin, Settlement, and Progress of the Colonies in North America*, 4 vols. (Washington, D.C., 1836-46), II, 3, p. 12.

[37] *Early English and French Voyages*, ed. Henry S. Burrage, Original Narrative Series (New York: Charles Scribner's Sons, 1906), p. 183.

[38] The prophecies quoted below come from Edward D. Neill, *The English Colonization of America* (London, 1871), pp. 177-178n.

whose great revival, according to seventeenth-century chiliasts, was to usher in the last stage before the millennium, was culture and learning. "Learning, like the sun," the English theologian Thomas Burnet wrote in his *Archaelogiae* in 1692, "began to take its Course from the *East*, then turned *Westward*, where we have long rejoiced in its Light. Who knows whether, leaving these Seats, it may not yet take a further Progress? Or whether it will not be universally diffused, and enlighten all the World with its Rays?"[39] Already the secular idea of progress was emerging from the millennial stages of Christian eschatology. The English Puritan divine John Edwards, who was writing at about the same time, also traced the advance of culture and religion as a westward movement. In 1725, Jeremy Dummer, Massachusetts' agent in London, hoped, apropos of his collection of books for the new Yale library, that religion and polite learning would not rest in their westward progress until they took up their chief residence in America.[40] Two years later, Dummer's kindly friend and patron Bishop Berkeley summed up for posterity ideas which had been in circulation for more than a century. His famous poem beginning, "Westward the course of empire takes it way," restated the familiar solar analogy to conform to the imperial vision of eighteenth-century Englishmen.

Although Englishmen transplanted to America shared this dream of imperial grandeur, they quickly assumed a role for themselves which in their imagination eclipsed that of the mother country and unconsciously hastened the separation of the colonies. They believed, on the whole, that they were the chosen instruments to set up in the New World a "city on the hill" as an example of the true Reformation to Europe and the rest of the world. In this mission they regarded themselves as the heirs of all history, curiously unappreciated by Englishmen at home, for whose salvation they prayed. Their pre-eminence on the stage of history seemed guaranteed not only by the westward progress of religion and culture, but also by God's providence in concealing America from European eyes until the time

---

[39] Quoted by Tuveson, *op. cit.*, p. 166.
[40] In his letter to Timothy Woodbridge, *Transactions of the Colonial Society of Massachusetts* (Boston, 1895-present), VI, 201-202.

of the Reformation.[41] There was little doubt in their minds that the final drama of moral regeneration and universal salvation was to begin here, with them. They continued to express their sense of mission through the conventional solar analogy as they followed the sun toward sunlit gardens in the West. But their sun-worship dedicated them to the standard of nature as much as to concepts of Christian progress, for this was the selfsame sun which once shown over Eden. The Renaissance standard of nature had merely been absorbed by Christian tradition.

---

[41] This idea recurs frequently in American Colonial writing, but see especially Cotton Mather, *Magnalia Christi Americana,* 2 vols. (Hartford, 1820), I, 40-41; Jonathan Edwards, *Works,* 4 vols. (Boston, 1843), III, 314-315.

4

The Renaissance Standard of Nature

The journey pattern of modern history combines elements of progress with impulses of infantile regression. One sought a paradisiac fulfillment now in primitivism, now in the march of civilization. But even the town life of Utopia, as contrasted with the existing city cultures of Europe, rested upon a rural foundation. The vision of paradise in connection with discoveries in the New World was chiefly responsible for the great emphasis during the Renaissance upon nature as a norm for aesthetic standards, for ethical and moral standards, for behavior, for social and political organization.

The contextual meaning of paradise, finally, made it possible for Renaissance culture to reconcile Christian belief with the pagan conceptions of nature rediscovered in the literature of antiquity. Thus, the young humanist, Ulrich Hugwald, prophesied that mankind would return "to Christ, to Nature, to Paradise." [1] He saw no contradiction in these terms. On the ground that a peasant's life was nearest to that which God had granted Adam and Eve, he became a peasant. His behavior in this respect was somewhat extreme and unusual, but nonetheless indicative of the inner logic of the Renaissance position.

That Italian writers were among the earliest to discover the world of man in nature was not only owing to a historical sympathy with classical civilization as a symbol of past greatness,

---

[1] Cited in Norman Cohn, *The Pursuit of the Millennium* (Fair Lawn, New Jersey: Essential Books, Inc., 1957), p. 258.

but also—and more importantly—to the fact that Italy was the first home of geographical literature, which up through the sixteenth century was published and distributed throughout Europe in Latin. A sentimental vogue of Arcadian primitivism, to be sure, was already being realized through acquaintance with the writings of Horace, Virgil, Ovid, Lucian, and other classical writers; but it needed to be put into touch with a living reality to rescue it from artificiality and nostalgia for the past, project it into the future, and make it a vital directing force in men's lives.

The letters which gave the New World its name of America contributed largely to this end. Though Vespucci's letters described cannibals and bestial giants, nature was depicted for the most part as devoid of the taint of sin and of the demoniacal powers with which the medieval imagination liked to invest it. During his third voyage he claimed to discover a gentle, naked, well-built people: "They have no cloth, either of wool, flax, or cotton, because they have no need of it; nor have they any private property, everything being in common. They live amongst themselves without a king or ruler, each man being his own master, and having as many wives as they please. . . . They have no temples and no laws, nor are they idolaters. What more can I say! They live according to nature, and are more inclined to be Epicurean than Stoic."[2] He also noted that the women were libidinous, but comely; that the people lived sometimes for 150 years; that the land was immensely fertile. One finds here already the egalitarian state of nature in the name of which future revolutions would be fomented, the psychic paradise of youth and longevity which would start Ponce de León on his search for the fountain of youth and medical doctors on the study of regenerative tissue, the libertarian paradise which would topple established authority in every field of endeavor, and the sexual paradise which, though largely unappreciated by the Protestant reformers, would eventually enable millions, without becoming libertines, to live more comfortably with their consciences.

Peter Martyr had little to add to this picture, except confirmation in detail. He did serve an important function, however, in discrediting the golden age of antiquity and replacing it with conceptions of a present and future golden age: "Every day the

---

[2] *The Letters of Amerigo Vespucci*, ed. Clements R. Markham (London: Hakluyt Society, 1894), pp. 46-47.

harvest increases, and overtops that of the last. The exploits of Saturn and Hercules and other heroes, glorified by antiquity, are reduced to nothing." Or, speaking of the Indians' faith in the powers of the Virgin Mary: "O what purity of soul and blessed simplicity, worthy of the golden age."[3] He also contributed to a growing cult of simplicity which was to be turned against any superrefinement of thought, manner, dress, speech, and social custom which one encountered wherever the seats of authority coincided with the great centers of urban civilization and learning. Such writing was largely responsible for the reasoned anti-intellectualism of Renaissance and Reformation intellectuals. Finally, he spread far and wide the legend of a "spring whose waters restore youth to old men."[4] He began to think that nothing was impossible for creative nature, where once he believed that such power was the prerogative of God alone. In Peter, as in Vespucci, romantic naturalism and cultural primitivism are far advanced.

Bartholomew de Las Casas was even more struck than Peter Martyr with the primitive innocence of the Indians and went far to exonerate them from the conquistadors' charges of cannibalism and idolatry. His accounts follow thematically the Biblical story of the Fall in that they chronicle the story of a virgin world despoiled and ruined. The main poles of his thought are nature and civilization as associated with America and the wicked Old World. "The Spaniards," he wrote, almost as if he himself belonged to an alien culture, "might have built great and flourishing Cities in so pleasant and commodious a Country, where they might have liv'd in the midst of Pleasure and Plenty, as it were in another Earthly Paradise: but their Stupidity, their Avarice, and the enormous Crimes they committed in America have render'd 'em unworthy of these Advantages."[5] He charged them with infringing the "Laws of Nature."

It is significant that the first extensive modern development of natural law theory comes in connection with the discoveries of the New World. This was Francisci de Victoria's *De Indis et*

---

[3] *De Orbe Novo: The Eight Decades of Peter Martyr d'Anghera,* trans. Francis Augustus MacNutt, 2 vols. (New York: G. P. Putnam's Sons, 1912), I, 334, 244.

[4] *Ibid.,* I, 274.

[5] Bartholomew de Las Casas, *An Account of the First Voyages and Discoveries Made by the Spaniards in America* (London, 1599), p. 53.

De Jure Belli Hispanorum in Barbaros, published in 1523. Before teaching theology and law at Salamanca, Victoria had studied at the Sorbonne, where he became intimate with Renaissance humanists. But we have the authority of Ernest Nys that he did not derive his ideas from Paris. Rabelais' contempt for the faculty at Paris would seem to confirm this view. Victoria first began to formulate his ideas as he lectured on the rights of the American Indians in relation to the rights of the Spanish sovereign. He put it this way: "The question . . . arises, what rights does the sovereign possess? The author has learned from a reliable source [probably Las Casas] that the aborigines of the countries just discovered by Christopher Columbus are men endowed with reason —mild, pacific, and capable of rising to the level of our religion. They have no private property, but cultivate certain lands in common. They are addicted to polygamy, which results in the disorganization of their families. Are they free? Yes, for God has given liberty to all men. . . ." [6] He approached the issue from the point of view of divine law, rather than human law, but tended to identify the laws of God with the laws of nature and right reason. The mere fact that many of the Indians refused to accept Christianity, he argued, gave the Spaniards no right to make war upon them and despoil their property. Their right of dominion over temporal goods, even if they did not exercise property rights, was as natural as the rising of the sun and the falling of the rain. Had not God granted a similar dominion to Adam and Eve "over the fish of the sea, and over the fowl of the air, and over every living thing that moveth upon the earth," as well as "every herb bearing seed?" [7]

Francisci de Victoria's work became an important source for Hugo Grotius, who, writing a century later, is usually credited with being the prime mover. Grotius and John Locke were the foremost authorites for natural law cited by American revolutionary leaders. Like Victoria, John Locke and Grotius supplemented their readings in classics and scripture with the more "scientific" evidence of travelers in the New World. Locke's second "Treatise of Government," which sanctioned the parlia-

----

[6] Francisci de Victoria, *De Indis et De Ivre Belli Relectiones,* ed. Ernest Nys (Washington, D.C.: Carnegie Institute of Washington, 1917), pp. 83-84.

[7] *Ibid.,* pp. 125-126.

mentarian revolution of 1688, discovered the hypothetical enactment of his natural law in the wilds of America and used as a working model of primitive society the Biblical example of Adam and Eve in Paradise. Reports about the Canadian and Carib Indians suggested to Jean Jacques Rousseau, a major spokesman for the French Revolution, an ideal state of innocence as a standard by which to measure European civilization. The archetypal Adam living in a state of nature was thus endowed by his creators, who included Thomas Jefferson, with inalienable rights to life, liberty, property, and the pursuit of happiness. The revolutionary doctrines which grew out of the discoveries of the New World were first developed by European savants only to be borrowed by American colonists and turned against Europe.

The reign of natural law theory historically preceded the more sentimental cult of the noble savage. But this later development was also foreshadowed by Renaissance writers and took its rise primarily from the fusion of humanistic thought and Christian messianism converging upon the New World. Nowhere is this development more clearly adumbrated than in the first drama said to be written specifically about America, Lope de Vega's *The Discovery of the New World by Christopher Columbus* (1614), which again locates in nature the seeds of perfectionism. The messianic impulse is revealed by Pinzon's exhortation to a mutinous crew: "God would show him the new land as he did to Moses and Aaron after so long a struggle. For that was God's promise." [8] In the light of what follows, Pinzon's statement generates a fine irony. Under the pretext of religion the crew seeks only the hidden treasures of the country. This gives Vega the opportunity to lecture his fellow Spaniards on their excessive greed and cruelty. They are told, in effect, not to found their happiness on avarice and gold, but to follow the example of the noble Indian. Thus, the Chieftain Dulcan declares, "Nature and fortune have joined forces to give me happiness. Nature has given me body, intelligence, strength," as well as rich bounty in land. America is then called "the Promised Land," where Columbus, with the help of the noble savage, is

---

[8] Lope de Vega, *The Discovery of the New World by Christopher Columbus,* trans. Frieda Fligelman (Berkeley: The Gillick Press, 1950), p. 23.

"to begin to achieve the redemption of the whole human race." [9]
Columbus is regarded as a type of Christ, "the light of the
New World," and Pinzon finally expects God himself to descend
from Heaven and inaugurate the millennium. The polarity of
nature and civilization is obvious; only the pantheism of a later
period is lacking, the deification of nature which makes moral
and spiritual regeneration a process of nature itself.

The standard of nature has, of course, as Professor Lovejoy
has demonstrated, meant different things to different people.
This was true of the men of the Renaissance. To Machiavelli,
who does not reveal the direct influence of geographical discovery, the standard of nature meant truth-telling, a hatred of
sham and hypocrisy, but also an acceptance of the necessity to
achieve ends by something less than ideal means. Ariosto, too,
was struck by a duality in nature. Although, for the most part,
his pages are filled with the plastic beauty of lovely maidens,
idyllic gardens, and landscapes, he could observe of the intransigency of human nature:

> . . . the heart that is of churlish vein,
> Wher'er it be, its evil kind will shew.
> Nature inclines to ill, through all her range,
> And use is second nature, hard to change.[10]

The passionate temperament of Ariosto's contemporary Pietro
Aretino, on the other hand, would admit no taint of sin in nature. He once wrote a series of sonnets for pornographic illus-
trations of "twenty-six Modes of Copulation," which, like the
writings of Machiavelli, were too primitive ethically for even
the Renaissance sensibility. Like Machiavelli, he thought of himself as a truth-teller. But Aretino was also supremely an artist
and enunciated what was everywhere the aesthetic ideal of the
Renaissance:

Go to Nature and study her habits. . . . Look at a nurse suckling a
child, see how she slips her nipple into its mouth, how she moves
its feet and teaches it to walk, how she lends her smile to its eyes, her
words to its lips, and her gestures to its motions until, as the days
pass, Nature develops its own aptitudes. This is how a student should
study the poets and, taking only the breath of their spirit, develop
the music of his own organs. I tell you again, poesy is nothing but

[9] *Ibid.*, pp. 26, 32, 40.
[10] Ludovico Ariosto, *The Orlando Furioso*, trans. William Stewart Rose, 2
vols. (London: George Bell and Sons, 1907-1910), Canto XXXVI, st. ii.

a delightful lunacy of Nature. . . . The man who writes without being born to write is a cold pumpkin. . . . Learn from the painter who, when he was asked whom he imitated, pointed to a group of men, meaning that he drew his models from life and truth. . . . Nature, of whose simplicity I am the secretary, dictates what I compose, and my native speech unties my tongue when it twists itself up in superstitious knots and foreign jargons. . . .[11]

Aretino's recommendation of the natural passions and instincts as the source of truth and art was a kind of psychic primitivism which caused Renaissance writers to value fools over wise men, youth over age, feeling over reason, and simplicity over sophistication. As Leonard Dean has pointed out, Erasmus was scornful of most of the scholars of his day. His, and other humanists', fondness for the literature of antiquity was in large part a fondness for a supposedly primitive simplicity of style and thought as opposed to the learned pretensions of a more complex civilization. He liked the English humanist, John Colet, because Colet was so different from the "sophistical and supercilious divines" who had no respect for the new literature. He was attracted especially to the sweet simplicity of Sir Thomas More's nature and applauded in young neophytes such as Antony Lutzenburg a "simple and natural style." When, in his *Praise of Folly*, he took to truth-telling himself, he chose for his spokesman a fool, a fool conceived in passion and born out of wedlock, whose parents were Youth and Plutus, king of intoxication, and whose birthplace was the Fortunate Isles.[12]

In *The Praise of Folly* he half-playfully, half-seriously argued the thesis that just as fools alone were candid and truthful, being closest to the unstudied paradise of childhood, so they were also the happiest. He wrote:"The people of the golden age lived without the advantages of learning, being guided by instinct and nature alone. . . . Isn't it true that the happiest creatures are those which are least artificial and most natural?"[13] He praised the lot of birds and flies, who lived "for the moment and by the light

---

[11] Quoted in Ralph Roeder, *The Man of the Renaissance. Four Lawgivers: Savonarola, Machiavelli, Castiglione, Aretino* (New York: The Viking Press, Inc., 1933), p. 514.

[12] Desiderius Erasmus, *The Epistles of Erasmus, from His Earliest Letters to His Fifty-first Year*, ed. and trans. Francis Morgan Nichols, 3 vols. (New York: Longmans, Green & Co., 1901), I, 141, 149, 220-221, 226, 315; III, 390. Desiderius Erasmus, *The Praise of Folly*, trans. Leonard F. Dean (Chicago: Packard & Co., 1946), pp. 16, 28, 75.

[13] *Ibid.*, pp. 71-72.

of nature," at the same time upbraiding "stupid intellectuals." The very reverse of this simple wisdom of the creation was followed, he thought, in the urban centers of authority by merchants who were honored for lying, stealing, and cheating, by philosophers who claimed to be possessed of the inmost secrets of nature, by conceited theologians who dealt in supersubtleties, by monks who tyrannized people with ridiculous ceremonies and noisy pedantries, by affected courtiers, power-lusting kings and nobles, and warrior popes who imitated a courtly way of life under pretense of imitating Christ. All this was, of course, a product of folly also, representing our dual human nature, but folly warped and twisted out of its natural growth by civilized institutions. Erasmus favored above all that divine madness which transformed nature's fool into a Christian fool. In the concept of the Christian fool were reconciled the opposing tendencies of the Renaissance—the impulses of assertion and submission, the lure of culture and the love of simplicity, the pagan cult of nature and Christian tradition, but not Christianity as Erasmus knew it to exist.

The Christianity which he valued was the Christianity of Biblical times, which venerated little children, women, fishermen, and sheep;[14] so that even in Erasmus' religion the standard of nature was controlling. In *Utopia*, Sir Thomas More, with a few sideward glances at religion, applied the standard of nature chiefly to economics. It was impossible to govern well, he thought, in the states of Europe where possessions were private and "where moneye beareth all the stroke." The natives of America, without money and without possessions, knew no such strife, no anxiety, no envy. As contrasted with the complex rules, restrictions, amplifications, duties, decrees, and ramifying legalities of Europe, which still did not prevent strife, the American natives lived at ease with a few simple laws dictated by nature. One of these laws was a patent taken out in Eden, the law of work. The one main "science" of the inhabitants of Utopia was, accordingly, husbandry. Nature supplied all the *necessary* things—as contrasted with Europe's superfluities—so abundantly, however, that nobody had to work longer than six hours a day.

The rule of nature was also the rule of love and pleasure, there
_____
[14] This characterization of primitive Christianity is Erasmus' own. *Ibid.*, pp. 124-125.

being no contradiction between nature's command to love one's fellowman and the command to enjoy oneself because God so ordained the course of Nature that, in desiring and refusing things, one was ruled by reason. In spite of this qualification, however, More had no more use for reason than Erasmus. It was the rule of love, not reason, which erased the boundaries between peoples of Utopia. "The felowshyppe of nature," he wrote, "is a stronge league." Valuing the heart over head, the inhabitants of Utopia "sette great store by fooles." [15] Their laws were so simple as to be understandable by common farmers. They banished lawyers and all other peddlers of deceit who used intelligence to manipulate people for selfish ends. It is true that one found philosophers in Utopia, but these surpassed European philosophers chiefly by virtue of their want of "subtle intentions." The Utopians carried natural simplicity and honesty so far, indeed, that men and women were required to see each other stripped naked before they married! The utmost concession which More would make to an age of reason was the hope that truth would finally prevail if error were permitted to exist in the market place of ideas. Therefore, More permitted religious tolerance in Utopia. In actual life he died a martyr to prevent the extension of Protestantism in England.

One cannot very well say that Sir Thomas More charted the course of our modern Western civilization, but he succeeded admirably in compressing into a single image all the explosive forces of the future. The great irony is that the great material expansion of our time has taken place under the banner of a return to nature, tracing "the long way round to Nirvana." Dissatisfaction with the old civilization produced not a state of nature, or even a modest agricultural civilization, but a more intricate, inconceivably artificial industrial order which, in turn, is breeding new unrest and dissatisfaction, together with renewed yearnings for new lands, new frontiers, new planets. Sir Thomas More himself was not naïve in his hopes for the future. His narrator and fugitive from European civilization, Raphael Hythlodaye, discounted the good news from Utopia, saying, ". . . it is not possible for all thynges to be well, onles all men

---

[15] Thomas More, *Utopia*, ed. J. Churton Collins (Oxford: The Clarendon Press, 1904), pp. 104-105, 108-109.

were good: which I thynke will not be yet thys good many yeares." [16]

In *The Tempest*, Shakespeare also questioned whether human nature was capable of achieving a "brave new world." In the end of that play, however, the regenerative powers of nature produce a masterful triumph for the forces of good over cold, calculating, civilized evil. The reconciliation of all the characters to one another under the rule of love is celebrated by vegetation rites presided over by Ariel, a fertility god, and Ceres, goddess of harvest. Prospero must relinquish his Faustian power over nature; in return, his enemies acknowledge his right to govern Milan—more humanely, we suppose—and the brutish Caliban, who, after all, has been unfairly put upon, is given his freedom. It is not certain that Shakespeare had read *Utopia*, but we do know that he was influenced by voyagers' tales. He undoubtedly relied upon Montaigne's essay *Of Cannibals* for the character of Caliban, and he had at least read Raleigh's *The Discoverie of the Large, Rich, and Bewtiful Empyre of Guiana*, an exciting account of the explorations of 1595.[17]

It is a mistake to think that Shakespeare's extravagant imagination would touch only once, and in a single play, a vision which had awakened all Europe—as if the whale, having spouted once, no longer communicated with the medium which sustained him. Shakespeare's villains—Claudius, Antonio, Edmund, Iago, the Caesar of *Antony and Cleopatra*—are usually rationalists whose main weapon, like the devil's, is deception. Many of them have some contact with Hades through residing or holding office in Italy. One learns to distrust in Shakespeare's plays any "supersubtle Venetian." His heroes, on the other hand, try like Hamlet, not always successfully, to be true to themselves and nature. When they are most themselves, their language strains against reason to express deep emotional reserves and intuitive wisdom.

In Shakespeare, the professional fool is a wise man, while the

---

[16] *Ibid.*, p. 41.

[17] For Raleigh, see Jarvis M. Morse, *American Beginnings: Highlights and Sidelights of the Birth of the New World* (Washington, D.C.: Public Affairs Press, 1952), p. 23; for Montaigne, John M. Robertson, *Montaigne and Shakespeare* (London: Adam and Charles Black, 1909), chs. II, III, VII, and pp. 228-231.

supposed masters are most fool-prone. Viola thus says of the
Clown in *Twelfth Night,*

> This fellow is wise enough to play the fool;
>
> For folly that he wisely shows, is fit;
> But wise men, folly-fall'n, quite taint their wit.[18]

As truth sayer, the Clown is the first to draw attention to the
quality of self-indulgence in Olivia's romantic fixation, the first
to make Malvolio show that he is "sick of self-love," the first to
hint at the coming marriage of Maria and Toby. It is the other
clown, Fabian, who first confesses and repents of the cruel joke
against Malvolio, understanding that excessive fun-making at
the expense of others can be as destructive of human relationships as excessive virtue or excessive self-love. It is the Clown,
finally, who holds up the mirror of nature to the madness which
hides us from ourselves.

The people in this play who would appear to be what they
are not, for the most part, are misled by the affectations of a
superior civilization. Olivia must publicize her virtuous mourn-
ing for her dead brother and the Duke his infatuation. Ague-
cheek affects French and long, learned syllables of which he does
not know the meaning. Viola alone is without affectation, but at
one point in the play, Olivia and Viola, who masquerades as a
youth, lisp to each other in couplets, according to courtly conventions of love, so that the contrast of appearance and reality
comes to be the difference between worldly affectation and the
sincerity of nature. This contrast is further underlined by the
division of scenes organized around Olivia's orchard on the one
hand and on the other the Duke's palace or Olivia's house. Folly
is hatched under supposedly civilized roofs; it is exposed out
of doors. The various miscarriages of sentimental love, in particular, are keyed with fine irony to idyllic outdoor settings.

The comic spirit and the tragic spirit are one in their exposure
of human folly. In *Hamlet* the standard of nature is plain. Critics
tell us that we are not to take seriously the high-sounding plati-
tudes of the deferential, maundering Polonius. That is, of course,
true. But aren't he and his son Laertes judged precisely by their
failure to live up to the more general code which he preaches?
And isn't that code precisely the Renaissance code of truth:

---

[18] *Twelfth Night,* Act III, sc. i, lines 67-75.

> This above all—to thine own self be true,
> And it must follow, as the night the day,
> Thou canst not then be false to any man.[19]

The main tragedy in *Hamlet* comes from the failure of each character, including Hamlet, to observe this rule of nature.

Hamlet holds up the mirror of nature to each, one by one. The true colors of Claudius, who appears to be wholly the magnanimous, kindly prince and stepfather, are mirrored in the players' re-enactment of the murder, imitating nature. Hamlet's mirror shows Ophelia with the painted face, ambling gait, and lisping manner of a wanton woman. His mother also presents to him an image of carnal wantonness masquerading as virtue. For an image of true virtue he makes her look upon a portrait of his dead father in contrast to a portrait of Claudius. Similarly, Hamlet tests Polonius, Rosencrantz, Guildenstern, and Osric. The obsequious affectation of these courtiers displays itself in their nervous haste to mold themselves in outward compliance with his every whimsy: yes, the wind is cold; the wind is sultry; he needs a hat; he does not need a hat. Whereupon Hamlet observes of Osric, "He did comply with his dug before he suck'd it. Thus has he, and many more of the same bevy that I know the drossy age dotes on, only got the tune of the time and outward habit of encounter. . . ." [20] Laertes, too, has been infected with the falsity of Claudius' court. At the beginning of the duel he pretends to the same scrupulous honor as Hamlet, swearing not to wrong the love which Hamlet offers him. Yet we have seen him outdo Claudius in ruthless cunning, and we know that he intends to betray his word. The contrast between human pretension and the true condition of man is summed up with ironic finality in the graveyard scene.

Hamlet is more in sympathy with the humble grave diggers than with the mighty of the earth. They uphold Adam's profession and, like the Clown in *Twelfth Night,* are Shakespeare's inspired mirrors of truth. But the graveyard scene is revealing in other ways. Hamlet's descent into the grave climaxes his hellish nightmare of spirit. The scene also extends the analogy between the spreading corruption in Claudius' court and the progressive stages of a disease in nature. As Hamlet has said earlier, " 'Tis

---

[19] *Hamlet,* Act I, sc. iii, lines 78-80.
[20] *Ibid.,* Act V, sc. ii, lines 194-197.

an unweeded garden/ That grows to seed; things rank and gross in nature/ Possess it merely." [21] Bearing out the theme of bodily dissolution to symbolize moral decay, Hamlet has sent Polonius, hiding behind the arras, to supper—"not where he eats, but where he is eaten." But disease is not a natural state of nature; it is unnatural, hence the revulsion it evokes. It is the sins of an artificial, ambition-ridden civilization headed by Claudius which has made nature diseased.

In his deepest consciousness Hamlet shows that he is aware of this. Then why doesn't he take forthright action to set nature right? The conventional answer is that he is inhibited by divided loyalties. Christian scruple cannot countenance the courtly code of revenge. But his soliloquies do not fully bear this interpretation out, any more than they fully confirm Ernest Jones' theory of the Oedipus complex. They do show an outraged moral sense, an exaggerated self-guilt, dominated by a simple angel-fiend, god-devil antithesis. The youthful Hamlet has indeed been too long in Wittenberg, not so much because scholarly study has impaired his capacity for action, but because he has acquired an oversimple moral outlook based on the Paradise-Hades archetype which did not prepare him for the complicated situation in Denmark. When his father ruled, as Hamlet would have it, before his mother took off "the rose/From the fair forehead of an innocent love" and Ophelia was still the "rose of May," Denmark was an Edenic garden. But the ghost revealed a serpent in the garden, "the serpent that did sting thy father's life." Hamlet has lost Eden and also lost a throne.

Hamlet reacted to the traumatic experience of his homecoming by converting all Denmark into an image of Hades, finding the work of Satan everywhere in this fallen garden. The supposed treachery of Gertrude and Ophelia, more than that of Claudius, echoes within him. The bewildered sense of treachery within as well as without, as Maude Bodkin suggests, makes strong self-assertion impossible, and he moves toward his goal obliquely, intriguing against Claudius, Rosencrantz, and Guildenstern in much the same way they have intrigued against him. Hamlet's view of the world has become a conspiratorial one. The strong sexual yearning at the base of his personality has been thwarted

----

[21] *Ibid.*, Act I, sc. ii, lines 135-137.

and crippled so that the sympathies of nature can only seem carnal. That is the tragedy of Hamlet.

The main sin in *King Lear* is also a falsity to nature. The fool in this play is again the truth sayer, holding up the mirror of nature to Lear's unreality. The villains of the piece—Edmund, Regan, and Goneril—are rationalists representing a diseased nature who most frequently speak in a businesslike prose, while the noble Lear, Gloucester, and Kent—men of sentiment—deliver themselves in poetry. Lear is initiated into the magnetic chain of humanity with his full realization of the false, foolish pride of one who has been too long accustomed to authority. He expresses this awareness by divesting himself of the same symbols of affectation and authority which have marked the court of Claudius.

His conversion and rebirth of spirit is preceded by a dark storm of suffering and self-torment which is reflected outwardly in the warring of the elements themselves. This storm in nature accompanies an interesting dialectical development of the issue whether nature is to be considered fundamentally just or essentially amoral. Speaking for the latter viewpoint, Edmund, the archvillain and illegitimate son of Gloucester, says early in the play: "Thou, Nature, art my goddess; to thy law/ My services are bound." [22] Albany puts the issue clearly:

> If that the heavens do not their visible spirits
> Send quickly down to tame these vile offences,
> It will come,
> Humanity must perforce prey upon itself,
> Like monsters of the deep.[23]

The play *King Lear*, like the others, finally upholds the standard of nature—and in a way of argumentation which is more convincing than that of *The Tempest*. The heavens do tame "these vile offences"; they do inculcate a respect for the "natural, unaccommodated man." That Lear suffers more then he would seem to deserve is evidence only that Shakespeare's feeling for nature is not sentimental.

In *Antony and Cleopatra*, the hero and heroine are somewhat overripened children of nature. The aging Cleopatra, by her artifice, is said to excel the portrait of Venus, "where we see/

---

[22] *King Lear*, Act I, sc. ii, lines 1-2.
[23] *Ibid.*, Act IV, sc. ii, lines 47-51.

The fancy outwork nature," [24] while Antony, also past his prime, is likened to a great towering pine. The poles of nature and civilization which generate the action are represented by the conflict between Antony's love for Cleopatra and his duty to the state; the contrast between the lush permissiveness of Egypt with its fertile, flower-scented Nile Valley and the cold, circumscribed practicality of Rome; the impulsive openness of Antony's character as compared with the calculated cunning of Caesar; the wantonly loyal Cleopatra as opposed to Antony's self-contained wife in Rome, whose sisterly regard for Caesar outweighs her wifely feeling for Antony; the soft, yielding armor of love's flesh and the cruel, unyielding armor of the battlefield; Antony's preference for manly combat on land and Caesar's crafty maneuvers at sea; Antony's easy reign over his men and Caesar's anxious, domineering habit of authority. The scenes alternate between Rome and Alexandria, but the visions of Cleopatra and a paradisiac bliss become most vivid for Antony in Rome, where Cleopatra's absence leaves "a gap in nature."

The paradise evoked in *Antony and Cleopatra* is largely a sexual one. Some critics see in it elements of decadence. In any event, the two lovers, having found an eternity in lips and eyes, bear the stroke of death "as a lover's pinch." They translate their earthly paradise to heaven, "where souls do couch on flowers." The play's sexual imagery consists of two main types: the images of carnality by which the priggish Caesar and his friends interpret the relationship of Antony and Cleopatra, and the images of desire and frank sexuality by which Antony and Cleopatra express themselves. Shakespeare's own point of view would seem to be that pagan sexuality can be a wholesome, creative, integrating experience. The vilest things, as he puts it, become transformed by Cleopatra, so that "the holy priests/ Bless her when she is riggish." [25] Whether this is decadence or not, the tragedy of Hamlet lies primarily in his inability to respond in a similar way. Shakespeare's most consistently held belief, if we read between the lines of his plays, appears to be that the evil which men do in the service of lust, ambition, power-craving is caused by the displacement of sexual sympathies which lie at the heart of nature.

---

[24] *Antony and Cleopatra*, Act II, sc. ii, lines 193-200.
[25] *Ibid.*, Act II, sc. iii, lines 237-239.

In Montaigne, whose writing brought to a close the Renaissance in France, we find a similar stress: to know oneself was to study nature. This was the single theme underlying the many points of view of his *Essays*, lending them whatever coherence they have. He studied nature close about him within his own experience; he studied the classics, whose epigrams interlace his work; but he also studied the news from abroad which he received from a man who had participated in the disastrous French attempt to colonize the coast of Brazil during 1556 to 1559. "This discovery of so vast a country," he wrote in his essay *Of Cannibals*, "seems to be of very great consideration." [26] After deciding that ancient accounts of the lost Atlantis did not agree with descriptions of the new lands, he concluded that his informant deserved better to be heard on the wonders of nature than Plato or Aristotle, especially since he was "a plain ignorant fellow, and thereby the more likely to tell truth." [27] He then evoked a vision similar to Vespucci's of a golden age which lay still ahead, not in the past.

The poles of nature and civilization which he outlines here formed the basic terms for all his *Essays*. Self-realization, he argued in essay after essay, consisted in establishing an inner harmony with outer nature. This was a harmony of contrarieties— "of diverse tones, sweet and harsh, sharp and flat, sprightly and solemn." A certain amount of pain was inevitable; it made pleasure the sweeter, and it taught moderation. We should learn to find our enjoyment within these limits, accepting nature's gifts, living in the present, not worrying about the need to repent, which represents a foolish attempt to contradict our natures, and learn to be good healthy animals. The only laws which deserved to be respected were these—"the most rare, the most simple and general." In his essay *Of Experience* he wrote, "Nature always gives [laws] better and happier than those we make ourselves; witness the picture of the Golden Age of the Poets, and the state wherein we see nations live, who have no other. . . ."[28] His respect for the simplicity of nature made his whole outlook

----

[26] *The Essays of Michel Eyquem de Montaigne*, trans. Charles Cotton (Chicago: Encyclopaedia Britannica, Inc., 1952), pp. 91-92.
[27] *Ibid.*, p. 93.
[28] *Ibid.*, pp. 517, 529.

toward civilized society sceptical, antiauthoritarian, and individualistic.

A nobleman by birth and education and a good Catholic, he was nevertheless distrustful of priests and kings and other wielders of authority. He placed greater faith in simple folk, in peasants, ignorant seamen, and youth. He once wrote, "I have an inclination toward the meaner sort of people." [29] He was especially interested in the education of children. The ideal program of education which he sketched out, while in some respects tailored to the Renaissance courtier, and in his own day requiring an outlay of time and money which only members of a leisure class could afford, nevertheless anticipated the more democratic ideas of a later period. At least one could say with confidence that its over-all emphasis was antiauthoritarian. The first object of study, according to Montaigne, should be nature, not books; practice, not learning by rote. One should question the supposed authority of pedants, and, at the same time, not cultivate the class-conscious habit of authority himself. Let the student "avoid these vain and uncivil images of authority, this childish ambition of coveting to appear better bred and more accomplished, than he really will, by such carriage, discover himself to be." [30] For nature teaches, as he puts it elsewhere, that both "kings and philosophers go to stool, and ladies too." [31]

Among the uncivil images of authority he included philosophy's "thorny subtleties of dialectics." "Take the plain philosophical discourses," he advised.[32] Nature inculcated truth and virtue by ways simple, direct, sincere, cheerful, and not after the fashion of Catholic Rome. The most manifest sign of wisdom was a continual cheerfulness which had nothing to do with the querulousness of philosophy or the morose ill nature of pedagogues. Imperious authority of any kind made the school a house of correction for imprisoned youth, when learning should be as pleasant as tennis, running, swimming, riding, dancing, and other recreations. The rationalistic, authoritarian tutor, not knowing how to allure the natural appetites and affections, used "rods

---

[29] *Ibid.*, p. 534.
[30] *Ibid.*, p. 67.
[31] *Ibid.*, p. 526.
[32] *Ibid.*, p. 72.

and ferules, horror and cruelty." "Away with this violence! away
with this compulsion! than which . . . nothing more dulls and
degenerates a well-descended nature." Montaigne rendered the
alternative in attractive Edenic imagery: "How much more decent would it be to see their classes strewed with green leaves
and fine flowers, than with the bloody stumps of birch and wil-
low?" [33] His schoolhouse would have been a libertarian paradise
not greatly different in theory from that of our modern, progressive education.

The main poles of Montaigne's thinking correspond to those
of Shakespeare's *Antony and Cleopatra*. His hell would be the
quarrelsome state of man in civilized Europe. His paradise would
be a state of nature influenced by imagined conditions of the
New World. His Satan would be a confidence man masquerading
now as king, now as bishop, now as merchant prince, now as
pedant and philosopher. His Adam would not quite be Shakespeare's or Erasmus' fool, but would describe children, seamen,
farmers, peasants, and the ideal Renaissance man. Eve is conspicuous by her absence, though Montaigne pretended to have the
healthy sexual appetites of an animal. His is not a sexual, but
a moral and libertarian, paradise. Yet in the over-all image of
paradise we find, as Montaigne said, "that men by various ways
arrive at the same end." [34]

After the deaths of Shakespeare and Montaigne, a chosen people of England, composed mainly of the middle classes whose
ascendancy had attracted them to the rising sun of Protestantism, where antiauthoritarianism in religion complemented and
abetted the challenge to secular authority, decided to locate
their earthly paradise in the New World. Their geographical
migration was speeded by a revival of millennialism, providing
a perfect sanction and parallel for their earthly hopes. The new
eschatology differed from medieval millennialism primarily in
being more attuned to history. Its assignation of the main events
of the Apocalypse to current history not only contributed to the
settlement of America, but also aggravated the European struggle for empire in the New World. How this came about is the
subject of the next chapter.

[33] *Ibid.*, pp. 73-74.
[34] *Ibid.*, p. 3.

5

The Protestant

Millennium

and the Struggle

for Empire

More than almost any other modern nation the United States was a product of the Protestant Reformation, seeking an earthly paradise in which to perfect a reformation of the Church. But the Protestant Reformation upheld the standard of nature quite as much as did the Renaissance. This is evident in the works of Savonarola, who stood as a colossus between the two movements, marking the continuation of the one into the other as well as new departures. Though he eventually disavowed the writings of the humanists as the work of the devil, he clung to their aesthetic ideals in his own writing and sermons.

His main articles of faith, moreover, expressed much the same quality of psychological primitivism found in Erasmus, More, and other Renaissance writers. He organized 5,000 children, for instance, to lead the attack upon the orgiastic carnival festivals preceding Palm Sunday because the youth had not yet been contaminated by a corrupt civilization. What he has to say about them reveals, also, his distrust of intellect: "O Lord, from the mouths of these children will come your true praise. The philosophers praise by natural enlightenment, these by supernatural; the philosophers with the tongue, these with deeds." Early in his career he had said in a similar vein, "There is no longer one man, no, not one who desires the good. . . . We must learn from women and children, for they are the only ones who still preserve some shade of innocence." [1] His primitivism was also expressed in imagery from the Old Testament. He likened himself to Moses leading a chosen people to God: "The good are oppressed, and the Italian people has become like the Egyptian which held the people of God in bondage. . . . Open, open, O Lord, the waters of the Red Sea and submerge the impious in the waves of Your Wrath." [2]

This imagery was not merely fanciful. He longed for a literal restoration in the present of a past glory, the glory of the primitive Church before its degeneration under the leadership of Rome. In treatise after treatise he reiterated the view that "were there no bad priests and friars Florence would return to the simplicity of life of the early Christians, and would be a model of religion to the whole world." [3] Protestantism at large is to be understood similarly, as will be seen, in the light of a restoration of a past state, not as a movement to extend the present establishment. The war cry of Protestantism, like that of Savonarola, was: "The Church will be first scourged and then regenerated."

But any active attempt to restore primitive Christianity, if one were to hasten the coming kingdom, necessitated determined self-assertion against entrenched authority. Thus, the reformers, like the humanists, were staunch individualists and the favorite target of each was *authority*. Like the humanists, Savonarola traced the organizing seats of all authority to Rome and the great urban centers of Europe and Italy. He early identified the Pope with Antichrist and called the palaces and courts of the worldly Italian princes "Babylon." He said, "It is the city that God will destroy." He continually prophesied the coming of great floods in which "Everybody is drowned and the city of Babylon is destroyed." [4] A paradisiac rebirth could come only

---

[1] Ralph Roeder, *The Man of the Renaissance. Four Lawgivers: Savonarola, Machiavelli, Castiglione, Aretino* (New York: The Viking Press, Inc. 1933), pp. 7, 72.

[2] *Ibid.*, p. 7.

[3] Piero Misciattelli, *Savonarola*, trans. M. Peters-Roberts (New York: D. Appleton & Co., 1930), pp. 171, 191.

[4] *Ibid.*, pp. 81-82; Ernest L. Tuveson, *Millennium and Utopia* (Berkeley: University of California Press, 1950), p. 22.

out of death and utter destruction of existing structures. Thus, the main poles of Savonarola's thinking were, essentially, nature and civilization.

Perhaps because Savonarola was more emotional than reformers like Luther and Calvin, periodically exhausting his nervous vitality, his psychological rhythms are more easily observable. According to his biographer, he was influenced by two wholly diverse impulses: he had the mystic's yearning for solitude and communion with God; yet he had to lead an active, public life. He took it upon himself to lead a chosen people against the Pope and Emperor at great personal risk; yet he dreamed "of creating a tranquil refuge to which he could resort, far away from the bustle and strife of the city." [5] These contrary impulses of submission and self-assertion discharged into one another. Savonarola *had* to assert himself against authority if he were to restore the bliss of the primitive Church. Prolonged periods of exertion, however, brought frequent collapses during which he was filled with self-doubts, questioned the validity of his prophetic inward voices, and temporarily tried to make peace with authority. These periods were rendered in the imagery of the night journey, the ocean voyage, the descent beneath the waters. But out of his suffering came quiescence and renewed vitality to do battle; out of his suffering also came millennial visions of Christ's Second Coming.

After he was first censored by the Pope, for instance, he said, "[T]he Lord placed me in a vessel and carried me out to the open sea. . . . I cannot see the shore. *Undique sunt angustiae* [Sufferings are on every side of me]. . . . Oh Lord, oh Lord, where hast thou led me?" Later, under interdiction, he said, "I have embarked on a stormy sea, I am assailed on all sides by contrary winds. . . . Arise, oh Lord, and help me, since Thou wouldest have me pass through this deep sea, and let Thy Will be done." For a short while, he was all supplication and abasement before the Pope and gave up his preaching, as directed. Gradually, his strength and courage returned, and he returned to the pulpit without authorization. His next action, the burning of the vanities, led to his excommunication and loss of his large following among the Florentines. Once more he collapsed. "If

---

[5] Misciatelli, *op. cit.*, p. 63.

I am deceived," he cried out in his distress: "Thou, Oh Christ, hast deceived me. Holy Trinity, if I am deceived, Thou hast deceived me. . . . I saw from the start that I was about to embark upon a rough sea, but it was said to me: 'Have no fear; this sea will soon be crossed.' Had I foreseen everything from the beginning I might have fled, as Jonah did. Everybody mocks at me. . . . I am called a fool. I am said to be mad." [6] He did not regain courage in time to go through the trial of fire demanded by sceptics and by his worldly enemies, but he stood up nobly to weeks of torture and, finally, burning at the stake.

It is said that as his strength waned under torture, he would confess his errors and later recant, but the only evidence comes from his persecutors, who would not have continued to torture him if he had not resisted heroically. They finally forged a false confession in which the meaning of his actual words was twisted by the significant omission of such "redundant" words as *the glory of God*" so as to suggest a carnal lust for power: "I reply that it was glory and to have reputation and credit; and for this purpose I sought to maintain myself in good esteem in the city of Florence, which seemed to me an apt instrument to increase this glory and gain credit abroad as well, particularly when I saw that I was believed." [7] Whether or not Savonarola's religious fervor can be explained as a form of power-craving, it is perhaps fortunate that he did not succeed in gathering the faithful aboard his Ark. As intolerant as were Luther and Calvin in dividing mankind into sheep and goats, they were not nearly as fanatical as this simple backwoods preacher and holy mariner.

The Reformation's main point of difference from the Renaissance stream of thought and feeling is symbolized by Savonarola's famous "Burning of Vanities" on the Piazza della Signoria of Florence in 1497, the year before Columbus claimed to have discovered the "terrestrial paradise." Savonarola not only caused to be burned such tokens of worldliness as jewelry, powder, rouge, perfume, carnival masks, tambourines, mandolins, and viols, but also Renaissance paintings of nude women and the poems of Pulci, Petrarch, and Boccaccio. The Reformation, insofar as it bypassed modern history, was a continuation of the

---

[6] The quotations from this paragraph come from Roeder, *op. cit.*, p. 4; Misciattelli, *op. cit.*, pp. 120, 114, 193-194.

[7] Roeder, *op. cit.*, p. 124.

ascetic, pietistic strain of medieval Catholicism. But its other-worldliness was greatly modified by Renaissance worldliness and stirrings across the seas. The Protestant doctrine of the millennium contributed considerably to the dismantling of the celestial city in favor of an earthly one by merging earth and heaven in one historical continuum, and it promoted energetic action to realize temporal goals by dramatizing the events of history in the light of a cosmic struggle on earth between the forces of the Lord and the powers of Antichrist.

Protestants were assuredly not people to whom things happened, but people who made things happen, and they tried to make them happen according to a divine plan operative in history. For most, the climactic feature of this plan was the Second Coming of Christ to His chosen people either before the millennium or after the millennium preparatory to the Last Day—the Day of Judgment. Savonarola, the great forerunner of the Reformation, was obsessed with this idea and was intent on making the city of Florence the setting for the final scene of human history. "You, my people," he promised Florentines in 1495, "will begin the reform of all Italy and spread your wings in the world, to bring the reform to all peoples. Remember that the Lord has given evident signs that He means to renew all things, and that you are the people chosen to commence this great enterprise." [8] But Savonarola was not really attuned to history. His was a mystical, therefore an *a*historical, mind, and he made little attempt to identify the symbolical events of the Apocalypse with historical periods of the Christian era in which he lived, beyond singling out Rome as the seat of the Beast.

In his second commentary on the Revelation of John, Luther went far, much farther, to fix Protestant eschatology in history. He was not explicit about the millennium, but he perceived five distinct stages in the fulfillment of prophecy which he assigned to five corresponding historical periods. The revival of knowledge during the Renaissance, the reformation and spread of the gospel, his certainty that the papacy was the Antichrist of prophecy—these things told him that Protestants were living in the fourth stage of history, which began with the thousand-year binding of Satan. The fifth and last stage, according to Luther, would see Satan loose again in the world for a very short time until he was

---

[8] *Ibid.*, p. 63.

finally destroyed in the Saints' cataclysmic battle with Gog and Magog, whom Luther identified with the Turks. That battle would be followed by the second advent of Christ and the Last Judgment.[9] Luther's interpretation of the five stages of history anticipated ideas of linear temporal progress toward a paradisiac state on earth.

Luther's interpretation was epochal in its repudiation of the Augustinian Catholic calculation, which computed the thousand-year binding of Satan from Christ's first advent, or from Constantine's time, and which, in Luther's day, made the millennium a thing of the past. Luther's interpretation, partaking of the optimistic futurism of New World idealism, became extremely influential among Protestant reformers. It is true that Calvin, the other great reformer, did not elaborate upon Luther's ideas on this particular point, but he contributed to their later development with his emphasis upon an elect Church and a national covenant. Only an elect people, it is remembered, was held to benefit by the millennium and Second Coming of Christ. The Protestant Reformation was fought against the Antichrist of Rome and his minions in behalf of the restoration of Christ's elect to a paradisiac state of blessedness which would have temporal and social manifestations. The new Protestant concept of the millennium signalized a marked change in emphasis from the otherworldliness of the Middle Ages to a fresh interest in the physical world as the stage, and possibly even the prize, of the spiritual drama. For the New World, the net effect of the Protestant Reformation was accordingly to adjust collective dreams to the realm of the practical and to produce a group of people sufficiently dedicated to endure the first hardships of colonization.

Increasingly it became clear in the writings of such reformers as Heinrich Bullinger, John Bale, Thomas Brightman, Thomas Rogers, Charles Dumoulin, and others that the Reformation represented not merely an attempt to reform religion, but basically and more importantly a hastening of the great day of paradisiac bliss. The Reformation timetable allocated five, more frequently seven, periods to the temporal journey, somewhat as

---

[9] *The Works of Martin Luther, with Introduction and Notes,* 6 vols. (Philadelphia: A. J. Holman Co., 1915), VI, 480-486; IV, 114, 146-147.

follows: [10] the first period was the uprising of the Waldenses, the Lollards, and the Hussites against the Antichrist at Rome; the second saw the opening of the whole world to the gospel with the discovery of America; the third began with the purification and spread of the gospel by Luther and his reformers; the fourth, already launched, would witness the destruction of Antichrist in a series of conflicts of which the Thirty Years War was but one; the fifth would complete the universal enlightenment of mankind which began with the Renaissance; the sixth would be the conversion of the Israelites, as reformers called the Jews and heathens; and the last would be the millennium, either followed or preceded by the Day of Judgment, depending upon how one interpreted John.

As William Haller has pointed out, this kind of chiliastic writing, widely disseminated through Protestant pulpit and press, increased remarkably just prior to the settlement of America and during the Cromwellian revolution.[11] The radical wing of Cromwell's following, styled the "Fifth Monarchists" because their timetable included five rather than the more orthodox seven stages, was so set upon realizing the earthly kingdom of Christ in their day that they took to fire and sword against Christ's enemies. But English Independency itself was characterized by extreme impatience for the great event, as indicated by Robert Browne's tract, "A Reformation Without Tarrying." As seen by its critics, Independency prided itself too much on being "a beginning, or at least a near antecedent of Christ's Kingdom upon earth." [12]

It is difficult to assess the extent to which the doctrine of the millennium and the Second Coming flourished among English Protestant leaders. Professor Perry Miller, in his studies of the background of colonial Protestantism, is inclined to stress its intellectual quality and hardheaded realism. Alan Simpson, on the other hand, stresses its emotional, millenarian flavor and in this respect does not distinguish the intellectual élite from the

---

[10] A useful guide to this jungle of literature is Le Roy E. Froom, *The Prophetic Faith of Our Fathers*, 4 vols. (Washington, D.C.: Review & Herald Publishing Assoc., 1946-1954), II, 159-579, *et passim*.

[11] Cf. William Haller, *The Rise of Puritanism* (New York: Columbia University Press, 1938), pp. 174-175, 269-287, *et passim*.

[12] In Benjamin Hanbury, ed. *Historical Memorials Relating to the Independents, or Congregationalists: From Their Rise to the Restoration of the Monarchy*, 3 vols. (London, 1839-1844), III, 140.

broad following. "Millenarianism, in one form or another," he writes, "was not confined to the common people. It lifts the hearts and be-devils the politics of the Center as well as the Left of the Puritan movement. Milton, Vane, Owen, Cromwell—all feel its spell." [13] This view would seem to be more nearly correct. The most painstaking examination of prophetic writing to date, Le Roy Froom's *Prophetic Faith of Our Fathers*, finds millenarianism dominant everywhere in the Reformation, highlighting "the whole colonial background." [14] We also have the confirming testimony of contemporaries who, without being advocates, were in a position to know the truth. Thus, Robert Baillie, an influential dissenting divine from Glasgow and member of the famous Westminster Assembly of 1643, expressed alarm that not only the Independents, but most of the chief Protestant divines "such as Twisse, Palmer, and many more, are express Chiliasts." He named others who were to carry great weight in the colonies: Joseph Mede, Thomas Godwin, John Archer, and Jeremiah Burroughs.[15] Finally, there is the evidence of millenarian writings by acknowledged leaders of the reformed churches in England.

The same would seem to be true of the colonies, though such historians of Colonial religious thought as Williston Walker, Perry Miller, Vernon Parrington, William Sweet, Kenneth Murdock, and Frank Foster have been virtually silent. Professor Miller treats the apocalyptic theme somewhat apologetically. The probability is that these historians have underestimated seriously the extent to which millennial fervor molded the motives of colonists, gave them their objectives, and controlled their conduct. We need to go back to some of the older historians if we are to correct the record. Thus, Edward Lambert, an early historian of the New Haven colony, held that a belief in the millennial kingdom was prevalent throughout New England.[16] But again the best evidence comes from the colonists themselves. We find the contentious Samuel Gorton, in 1646, sarcastically upbraiding the Massachusetts government of John

[13] Alan Simpson, *Puritanism in Old and New England* (Chicago: University of Chicago Press, 1955), p. 77.

[14] Froom, *op. cit.*, III, 23.

[15] From Robert Baillie, "A Dissuasion from the Errors of the Time," in Hanbury, *op. cit.*, III, 155-157; II, 554.

[16] Edward R. Lambert, *History of the Colony of New Haven* (New Haven, 1838), p. 50.

Winthrop, Thomas Dudley, Richard Bellingham, and Increase
Nowell for "looking after, and foretelling so much of the comming
of Christ, driving the day before you still for certaine years . . .
witnesse your prorogation thereof, if not to the descention of
Christ from heaven to the earth, to raign certain years, yet to the
calling of the Jews, (whom ye your selves are, according to the
flesh) and to the destruction of that man of sin. . . ." [17] In 1659,
Mary Dyer, the condemned Quaker, protested similarly against
laws framed by a people "that profess Christ come in the flesh."
One might be inclined to dismiss the evidence of hostile witnesses
such as these were it not confirmed in abundance by the ruling
powers.

Increase Mather, the foremost American Puritan for two generations, testified that the belief "that the Church of God shall
have a glorious time on Earth, after the Conversion of the Jews
and Destruction of *Antichrist,* and this for a *Thousand Years,* has
ever been received as a Truth in the Churches of *New-England."* [18] This doctrine was not controversial in the least, according to Mather; matters of controversy arose only in the spelling
out of details: whether the Second Advent of Christ followed or
preceded the millennium, whether the millennium was to be
purely spiritual or temporal or both, how to deal with false
prophets, etc. Mather himself would be slow to condemn "simple
Chiliasm," which he claimed the first and most famous pastors
of New England frequently insisted upon in their public ministry.
The only kind of chiliasm which did not get a favorable hearing
in New England, apparently, was the violent enthusiasm of the
Fifth Monarchists—and even some of them were granted asylum
in New Haven. The most popular doctrine in the colonies was
that America had been singled out, from all the nations of the
earth, as the site of the Second Coming; and that the millennium
of the saints, while essentially spiritual in nature, would be accompanied by a paradisiac transformation of the earth as the
outward symbol of their inward state. As Mather put it, "when

---

[17] Samuel Gorton, "Simplicities Defence Against Seven-headed Policy, Or
Innocency Vindicated," in Peter Force, *Tracts and Other Papers, Relating
Principally to the Origin, Settlement, and Progress of the Colonies in North
America,* 4 vols. (Washington, 1836-1846), IV, vi, pp. 28, 40.

[18] Increase Mather, "Preface," *A Discourse Concerning Faith and Fervency
in Prayer, and the Glorious Kingdom of the Lord Jesus Christ, on Earth,
Now Approaching* (Boston, 1710), p. i; also his *The Mystery of Israel's
Salvation, Explained and Applyed* (London, 1669), pp. 125-135, *et passim.*

this Kingdom of Christ has filled all the Earth, *this Earth will be restored to its Paradise state.*" [19] The jeremiads which accompanied periods of intense expectation of the coming kingdom, far from being merely propaganda devices for maintaining the power of the saints in the face of secularization, revealed a mass tendency toward purification, an inclination to devaluate the contemporary situation, which characterizes the myth of the eternal return. Jeremiah bewailed the sad declension of the times both as an obstacle to and a condition of man's restoration to paradise.

Richard Niebuhr, in his study, *The Kingdom of God in America,* claims that the utopian note struck during this early period of colonization by the announced hope of the restoration of a primitive paradise was a grace note, "sounded by some minor player in the orchestra, such as the author of *Wonder-Working Providence.*" [20] Edward Johnson is better likened to the popular performer in a band concert. His rustic trumpet, sounding loud among the common folk, echoed the finer trumpets of John Cotton, Thomas Shepard, Thomas Hooker, John Davenport, John Eliot, and many other respected leaders of the saints. Some of the first settlers, indeed, not waiting for a future transformation, fancied that the "howling" wilderness was paradise already. John Smith, sailing along the New England coast in the summer of 1614, compared it to Eden. Not many years later New England's lush summer beauty made the land "seem paradice" to Thomas Morton, who, to the consternation of the Plymouth worthies, behaved with the license of Adam.[21]

The land to the south of New England, by reason of its uniformly warmer climate, was more hospitable to the image of a paradise already regained. Imagery describing it as a paradise of material plenty connected it closely with economic motives and easy rewards. Such accounts of Virginia date, with mounting frequency, from the voyage of Captain Barlow in 1584. Thomas Harriot, taking leave of the ill-fated Roanoke colony, hated to depart "out of this paradise of the world." John Smith, who discovered Eve in the tribe of Powhatan, believed that "heaven and earth never agreed better to frame a place for mans habitation.

---

[19] Mather, *Discourse on Prayer,* p. 57.

[20] Helmut Richard Niebuhr, *The Kingdom of God in America* (Chicago: Willett, Clark & Co., 1937), p. 47.

[21] Thomas Morton, *The New English Canaan,* ed. Charles Francis Adams, Jr. (Boston: The Prince Society, 1883), p. 180.

. . . we chanced in a lande, even as God made it." For its climate, its verdant colors, woods, oils, fish, corn, minerals, its supposed spices, silks, and rubies, Daniel Price in a 1609 farewell sermon for the Virginia Adventurers called Virginia the garden of the world, "a good land, a land flowing with milk and honey." Overly enthusiastic subscription to such ideas, as Robert Beverly wrote, accounted both for the expectation that silk worms would thrive in Virginia and for the much-criticized indolence of the early inhabitants. "When man sets out for the Earthly Paradise, he anticipates felicity unlimited but not economic problems." [22]

The profound disillusionment and unkind abuse which resulted when economic reality failed to measure up to the settlers' dreams of felicity also afflicted other southern colonies whose settlement was promoted by the inflationary Edenic rhetoric. George Alsop advertised Maryland as the only "Terrestrial Paradice." Its very trees, plants, fruits, flowers, and roots spoke in "Hieroglyphicks of our Adamitical or Primitive situation," and their general effects and properties still bore "the Effigies of Innocency according to their original Grafts." A reckless philosophy of abundance was also encouraged by the promoters of that "future Eden" in Georgia. One writer thought it significant that Georgia lay "in the same latitude with *Palestine* herself, That promis'd *Canaan*, which was pointed out by God's own choice, to bless the Labours of a favorite People." Grandiose expectations became a major source of trouble in Georgia. Promotional hyperbole undoubtedly whetted economic motives for leaving Europe.[23]

----

[22] Arthur K. Moore, *The Frontier Mind: A Cultural Analysis of the Kentucky Frontiersman* (Lexington: University of Kentucky Press, 1957), p. 28. For other references in this paragraph see *Sir Walter Ralegh and His Colony in America* . . . (Boston: The Prince Society, 1884), pp. 121, 143, 185; *Narratives of Early Virginia, 1606-1625*, ed. Lyon Gardiner Tyler, Original Narratives Series (New York: Charles Scribner's Sons, 1907), pp. 81, 178; Alexander Brown, *The Genesis of the United States* . . . , 2 vols. (Boston: Houghton Mifflin Co., 1890), I, 314-315; Robert Beverly, *The History and Present State of Virginia*, ed. Louis B. Wright (Chapel Hill: University of North Carolina Press, 1947), pp. 298, 319.

[23] Cf. Louis B. Wright, *The Colonial Search for a Southern Eden* (Tuscaloosa: University of Alabama Press, 1953), pp. 40-62. Quotations in this paragraph are from George Alsop, *A Character of the Province of Maryland* (1666); reprinted in *Publications of the Maryland Historical Society*, no. 15 (Baltimore, 1880), p. 37; Sir Robert Montgomery, "Discourse Concerning the Designed Establishment of a New Colony to the South of Carolina . . . ," in Peter Force, *op. cit.*, I, vi, pp. 4, 6.

But for most of the chosen people in the early period of settlement, however opulent the writing of John Higginson and Edward Winslow in New England and of William Strachey in Virginia might envisage the green life of the New World, the land seemed a howling wilderness of sin, haunted by demonic powers; and they comforted themselves with eschatological dreams of a new heaven and a new earth under a *future* dispensation. The present time and condition, they were told in sermon after sermon, was a time of probation, a time of moral and spiritual trial, before entering upon their earthly inheritance. Both in New England and in the southern colonies, economic blessings were looked for, to be sure, but more often as a consequence, and not always as a necessary consequence, of righteousness, and the harvest time was postponed to the future.

Few millennial considerations did not entertain some notion of a literal transformation of the earth. Massachusetts was the place, according to the plain-spoken Edward Johnson, "where the Lord will create a new Heaven, and a new Earth." He would lead His people, like the Israelites of old, "through the great and terrible Wildernesse, from Egypt to Canaan." Thomas Hooker, who sighed for a deliverance from the Egyptian bondage and believed that the last days were rapidly approaching, led his flock through the wilderness to the promised land in the Connecticut Valley. What many look for as heaven, Samuel Hutchinson held, will be "a Heaven upon earth," because "they shall have no Devil to tempt them all that Thousand Years." Warning against carnal complacency, Thomas Shepard nevertheless insisted upon Christ's personal reign in the visible world: "We never looked for such days in New England."

Roger Williams, longing for the "bright appearance of the Lord Jesus" and "the Lamb's wife also, New Jerusalem," looked toward Rhode Island for "A Paradise in Paradise now worse/ Than Indian Wilderness." John Cotton informed those departing from England for Massachusetts that they had a patent from heaven, by reason of "the grand Charter given to *Adam* and his posterity in Paradise." Although his commentaries on Revelation did not deduce social and political consequences from his spiritualized millennium, he held out for a final utopia of the saints, who would rule bodily forever. Similar millennial hopes attached to the settlement of Virginia. Thus, Robert Johnson reminded the colonists of the "great wonders that should be wrought by Scots and English, before the coming of Christ." William Crashaw, in his farewell sermon, also told them that "thy God is coming towards thee." Insisting that the propagation of the gospel and not temporal gain was "the Principal and Maine Endes" of the Virginia settlement, the Governor and his Council, hardly aware that they protested too much, prayed for "the coming of the Kingdome of Glory."

By the time of the Great Awakening, which represented essentially a revival of millennialism from Virginia to New England, it was well established that the Second Advent of Christ, whether at the beginning or at the end of the millennium, brought with it a restoration to paradise. The glorious work begun here, Jonathan Edwards thought, "would make New England a kind of heaven upon earth." He believed that temporal blessings would follow from the spiritual reign of Christ. In that time, said Samuel Hopkins, who is usually considered a staunch foe of carnal chiliasm, men will have acquired skill "to cultivate and manure the earth in a much better and more easy way than ever before." There would be no poverty, and little labor would be needed to move great rocks and build houses, roads, bridges. The New Jerusalem was to be an engineers' paradise not very different from what we already know.[24] Religious salvation, like technological advance, gave access to material comforts.

We see here how easily millennialism lent itself to modern ideas of progress. The first step was to bring the heavenly paradise in touch with earthly possibilities, an inevitable step once the opportunities of the New World had made themselves widely felt. The next step would be to smooth out the millennial stages,

---

[24] For the content of the last three paragraphs see Johnson's *Wonder-Working Providence*, ed. J. Franklin Jameson (New York: Charles Scribner's Sons, 1910), pp. 25, 59; Thomas Hooker, Preface to "Survey of the Summe of Church Discipline," reprinted in *Old South Leaflets*, no. 55, pp. 2-6; Samuel Hutchinson's view in Froom, *op. cit.*, III, 102; *The Works of Thomas Shepard*, 3 vols. (Boston, 1853), II, 370-634, 375; the letter of Roger Williams in *Old South Leaflets*, no. 54, p. 6; the introductory verse to Williams' *A Key into the Language of America* (London, 1643); John Cotton, "Gods Promise to His Plantations" (1630), *Old South Leaflets*, no. 53, p. 6; John Cotton, *The Churches Resurrection . . .* (London, 1642), pp. 2-23, *passim;* "Nova Brittania" (1609), in Force, *op. cit.*, I, vi, p. 27; Brown, *op. cit.*, I, 339, 372; *The Works of President Edwards*, 4 vols. (Philadelphia, 1844), III, 334; Samuel Hopkins, *Works*, 3 vols. (Boston, 1854), II, 285.

omitting the period of declension which was to precede the
Last Days, until one was left with a steady evolutionary amelio-
ration.[25] But before this could happen, the saints of America had
to contend with the wilderness. In their eschatological aspirations, the wilderness became a type of the wilderness stand of the
Israelites after crossing the Red Sea, just as their condition in
England and Europe had been a type of Egyptian bondage.
Passage through the wilderness trials corresponded to the night
journey of the Rebirth archetype, which determined the vision
of paradise. The wilderness stood, at the same time, as a symbol
for iniquity. As Cotton Mather put it, "The Wilderness through
which we are passing to the Promised Land is all over fill'd
with Fiery flying serpents." It therefore served a moral purpose
in teaching the saints how to contend with the devil and acquire
virtue.[26] The virtues of modern "rugged individualism" were
bred in the eschatological Colonial jungles which interpreted
the meaning of frontier experience.

In 1690, Cotton Mather wrote that everything looked black, not
only from "inexcusable *Degeneracies* and *Apostacies*" of religion,
but from the advent of the Andros regime and the flowering
of witchcraft. It was as if "the Blessed God intend the Divel
shall keep *America* during the Happy *Chiliad* which His Church
is now very *quickly* Entering into." He wavered between two
contradictory opinions: one, that the supposed degeneration of
the times was but a prelude to the coming of a "Golden Age"
(Wasn't John led into the wilderness to see the destruction of
Rome?); two, that God's controversy with New England would
not terminate happily. The Massachusetts General Court leaned
to the latter view "if a speedy REFORMATION of our *Provoking
Evils* prevent it not." [27] If the saints had God in their hearts,

---

[25] Cf. Shirley Jackson Case, *The Millennial Hope* (Chicago: University of
Chicago Press, 1918).

[26] Cf. Alan Heimert, "Puritanism, the Wilderness, and the Frontier," *New
England Quarterly*, XXVI (September, 1953), 361-382. Mather is quoted
on p. 378. A similar typology followed the exiles to Holland. Reverend
Henry Ainsworth wrote in 1617, "When God calleth his 'people' out of
Babylon, it is not meant out of Rome only, or Italy, but Spain also, and all
other places, where popery reigneth. . . . The civil bondage of the Jews,
in the old Babylon, typed the spiritual bondage of God's 'people' in this new
Babylon," including the Church of England. Hanbury, *op. cit.*, I, 323.

[27] Cotton Mather, *The Present State of New England* (Boston, 1690), pp. 35,
48.

that is, there was something that they could do to insure the millennium. Increasingly, there were those without God in their hearts who thought by virtuous works to convert the wilderness into an earthly paradise without His direct intervention. But the point is that the strict regulation of morals and conduct in both Massachusetts and Virginia had as its chief objective the hastening the coming kingdom of God on earth as in heaven. Simonds D'Ewes wrote from his vantage point in England as a champion of the faithful in America, "Vices and sins are so severely punished amongst them, and the godly so countenanced and advanced, as in that respect it seems to be a true type of heaven itself." [28] The historian Richard Niebuhr has noted that belief in the kingdom of God on earth has been the distinctive note of American Christianity, differentiating it from religion in other lands. It is not surprising, therefore, that the American people have also been, as Tocqueville and Lord Bryce remarked, among the most moralistic people in the world, forever agitating for some reform or nostrum—social reform, political reform, or merely a new gadget or more practical way of doing things.

Millennial fervor entered into the mainstream of history primarily by polarizing significant experience in terms of good and evil according to eschatological views. A tremendous impetus was given the struggle for colonial empire when Rome and the Catholic nations were identified with Antichrist, upon whose destruction the coming kingdom absolutely depended. Also, the struggle for empire became, in part, a competitive race between the chosen peoples of the new European nations to propagate the gospel to the ends of the earth and convert the heathen in fulfillment of prophecy. That nation which succeeded in fulfilling the prophecies would alone merit the blessings of a chosen people. We have already seen the vacillating love-hate relationship to Rome which preceded the Reformation. Self-assertive energies were quickly channeled into the race for empire as a way of striking at the Romish Antichrist. Thus, stopping the flow of bullion from the New World meant to Richard Hakluyt, England's most influential champion of colonization, at once "to abate the pride of Spaine and of the supporter of the great Ante-

[28] *The Autobiography and Correspondence of Sir Simonds D'Ewes, Bart., During the Reigns of James I and Charles I,* ed. James Orchard Halliwell, 2 vols. (London, 1845), II, 116.

christe of Rome . . . touch him in the Indies, you touch the apple of his eyes." [29] Under each main heading of his classic *Discourse of Western Planting* (1584), he took note of the various benefits reaped in the New World by Spain and Portugal since the Donation of Pope Alexander VI, so that, essentially, each of the reasons he gave for England's planting colonies, usually considered materialistic reasons by historians, were corollaries of the first reason he gave, which was to propagate the true gospel.

This classic statement for colonization, repeated over and over again, was frequently accompanied by protests against the Pope's division of the New World between the Catholic nations, for this meant giving a wilderness which was now in Satan's possession over in partnership to the future dominion of Antichrist. Almost all of English colonial writing is concerned in one way or another with the invasion of America by Antichrist, threatening to rob the hopefuls of a glorious triumph for Christ. The first Virginia settlers, for instance, were careful "to carry thither no traitors, nor Papists, that depend on the Great Whore." "Suffer no Papists," William Crashaw admonished them, "let them not nestle there; nay let the name of the Pope or Poperie be never heard of in Virginea. Take heed of Atheists, the Devils Champions . . . let your lawes be strict, especially against swearing and other prophanenesse." "Before coming to details of this earthly Paradise," the author of *New Britain* took heed of Antichrist's work south of Virginia. John Winthrop considered the first duty of New England "to rayse a Bulworke against the kingdome of Antichrist, which the Jesuites labour to rear up in those parts." The main purpose of the New England Confederation in 1643, according to Edward Johnson, was to protect the purity of Christ's ordinances against foreign invasion, abetted by "inhumane and barbarous" Indian allies, and to assist Scriptural prophecies, "which so plainly prophecy the destruction of Antichrist and all Antichristian doctrines." Out of such reasoning was born the popular American conspiratorial theory of history which has been most recently exploited by Senator McCarthy. "If wars come against *New-England*," John Cotton wrote in 1656, "it will be from *Principalities and Powers*, and flesh and

---

[29] *The Original Writings and Correspondence of the Two Richard Hakluyts,* ed. E. G. R. Taylor (London: Hakluyt Society, 1935), II, 315.

blood will not be able to withstand them: They will be Principalities from Hell, or the great Beast, the Catholic Church. . . ." [30]

Such reasoning, continuing into the eighteenth century, helped to enlist the colonists in the European wars of empire. At the turn of the century, for instance, we find Samuel Sewall exercised by Las Casas' account of the Spaniards' barbarous cruelty in the New World: "*The Land was as the Garden of Eden,* or Paradise, *before them; and behind them a desolate Wildernesse.* They have fulfilled, and surpassed the Mischievousness of *Old Babylon.* . . ." A decade later, during Queen Anne's War, Increase Mather was similarly exercised about the French, who were converting the Indians not to Christ, but to Antichrist. "The Spanish Colonies, and the French Colonies are the Idolatrous Servants of Antichrist." During the War of Jenkin's Ear—so-called—Jonathan Edwards foresaw the coming millennium in the drying up of the fountains and streams of wealth flowing to Antichrist through the trade of France and Spain. He prayed that Protestants would "devote to the service of God the silver and gold they take from their Popish enemies." European Protestants read these events in much the same way. The Spanish invasion of England in Queen Elizabeth's time, said Edwards, backtracking, "was to suppress and root out the reformed religion." Indeed, the English hailed the defeat of the Spanish armada, in the main, as a deliverance from Popery. One example must here suffice to suggest the extent to which the English mind in its attitude toward the European wars was colored by eschatological considerations. The English man-about-town, John Chamberlain, wrote in 1609: "The Pope hath written to the French king complaining that our king misuseth him continually in table-talke and calls him Antichrist at every word." [31]

---

[30] For the content of this paragraph see Brown, *op. cit.,* I, 285-286, 263, 371; John Winthrop, "Conclusions for the Plantation in New England," *Old South Leaflets,* no. 50, p. 4; Johnson, *op. cit.,* pp. 36, 219-220; John Cotton, *An Exposition upon the Thirteenth Chapter of the Revelation* (London, 1656), p. 111.

[31] For this paragraph see Samuel Sewall, *Phaenomena Quaedam Apocalyptica, or, a Description of the New Heaven as It Makes to Those Who Stand upon the New Earth* (Boston, 1697, repr. 1727), p. 61; Mather, *Discourse on Prayer,* pp. 30-31; Jonathan Edwards, *op. cit.,* I, 464; II, 501-502, 503; *The Letters of John Chamberlain,* ed. Norman Egbert McClure, 2 vols. (Philadelphia: American Philosophical Society, 1939), I, 284.

The European rivalry for overseas empire was largely economic. There is little doubt about that. The paradise to be regained was a material and not a holy paradise. The rivalry
became acerbated, however, by a Christian eschatology which,
interpreting it as a cosmic conflict of good and evil, made men
more willing to venture their very lives for the outcome. The
savages who guarded the enormous wealth of the country were
accordingly given a special role in the cosmic drama. They were
alternately regarded as the descendants of Adam and the Ten
Lost Tribes of Israel or Satan's demons who would make America
the headquarters of Gog and Magog in the titanic holocaust
before the Last Days.[32] If the latter fate were to be prevented,
the Indians must at all costs be converted to God. Most of the
royal patents to Spanish, French, and English explorers included
a stipulation that an important objective was the propagation
of the gospel among the Indians in the fulfillment of prophecy.
The Spanish conquistadors, of course, felt justified in exterminating those Indians who refused to submit to Christian doctrine
on the ground that they were demons. Though these conquistadors did not want Catholic bishops back home interfering with
their employment of horses and firearms in executing their great
work, they were apparently sincere in their desire to convert the
natives and frequently requested Dominican or Franciscan friars
to assist them, that is, to leave them free to concentrate on
precious metals.

One of the earliest expressions of English interest in the conversion of the savages was John Rastell's "A New Interlude and
a Mery of the Nature of the Four Elementes," written about
1519. Rastell was the brother-in-law of Sir Thomas More and
familiar with the explorations of the Cabots. The letters-patent
of Henry VII, on the other hand, had made no mention of the
religious motive. It was some time before the Reformation generated this interest in English rulers. When it did come, the objective of converting the Indians was central. English explorers
and colonists inevitably coupled this mission both with millennial considerations and with the competitive efforts of the French
and Spanish to the same end. Thus, Edward Hayes, who de-

---

[32] Cf. Heimert, op. cit., p. 380; A. R. Anderson, Alexander's Gate, Gog and
Magog and the Inclosed Nations (Cambridge: Medieval Academy of America, 1932), pp. 59-62, 74.

scribed Sir Humphrey Gilbert's voyage of 1583, thought it probable "in this last age of the world" from the precedent attempts of the French and Spanish "that the countryes lying North of Florida, God hath reserved the same to be reduced unto Christian civility by the English nation." He thought that the gradual revelation of the new country would "prepare us unto a readinesse for the execution of His will against the due time ordeined, of calling those pagans unto Christiancy." [33] William Strachey, in 1612, coupled a prayer for the conversion of the heathen with an imprecation against Popery. From that time on, English missionary sentiment swelled, the more so as Indians were exploited for material advantage.

Among the many prominent colonists who seriously believed that the Indians were remnants of the Ten Tribes were Roger Williams, Richard Mather, John Endicott, John Oxenbridge, William Penn, Samuel Sewall, John Eliot, and Daniel Gookin. With the aid of the English Society for the Propagation of the Gospel, these people created a special mission among the Indians of New England and placed John Eliot in charge. This "Apostle to the Indians" was a millenarian who believed that the kingdom of Christ would come only after a conversion of all the Gentiles, and he thought of his mission as one with that of Oliver Cromwell, leading to the final destruction of Antichrist. His ideas were similar to those of other missionaries among the Indians up to the time of Jonathan Edwards' mission at Stockbridge. Eliot's successor, Daniel Gookin, once said that he was not ignorant that there were "some persons, both in Old and New England, that have low thoughts of this work, and are very prone to speak diminutively thereof; but I intreat it may be considered, that this frame of spirit is no new thing; for the servants of God heretofore have complained of it [i.e., the criticism], and with reference to the greatest and best tidings that ever was declared unto men." [34] These tidings had to do with the personal reign of Christ. Though the missionary enter-

---

[33] *Early English and French Voyages,* ed. Henry S. Burrage, Original Narratives Series (New York: Charles Scribner's Sons, 1906), pp. 180-182.

[34] Daniel Gookin, "Historical Collections of the Indians of New England . . . ," *Collections of the Massachusetts Historical Society,* Series 1, vol. I (Boston, 1792), p. 143. Gookin did not think that the theory that the Indians were a race of Israelites "greatly obtained," but he did not think on the other hand, that it was impossible or improbable. He thoroughly believed, however, that they were Adam's posterity.

prise had relatively little success and was little countenanced by the majority of the population, it nevertheless enhanced the prestige of the chosen people and condoned many sins. Thus, an address to the Princess of Orange in behalf of the restoration of the Massachusetts charter in 1689 boasted of Eliot's success in converting the Indians and ended with a reference to "the Almighty's most wonderful blessing and prospering *New England*, and his Gospel amongst the Heathen there, which to me looks like the Beginning of the fulfilling those many Prophecies in *Holy Writ* concerning them." It also suggested that since the most perfect Reformation was found not in old England, but in New England, New England's only enemies should be the Papists.[35] Up to the time of the American Revolution, a story calculated to inflame patriotic sentiment was current that the French taught the Indians that the Virgin Mary was a French lady.

Missionary work on the American frontier contributed greatly to what was to become an American superiority complex; it gave divine sanction to the nineteenth-century theme of "Manifest Destiny"; and it helped to make Americans great proselytizers all over the world of the "American Way of Life." Joined to millenarianism, it was part of the heritage of hope which attracted to these shores immigrants who themselves were made to feel missionary pressures of assimilation.[36] The Indians, as Roy Harvey Pearce has pointed out, presented a reverse image of European civilization which helped Americans to establish a national identity that was neither savage nor civilized in the European sense, but agrarian. Henry David Thoreau's bean field at Walden typifies this cultural midpoint.

Contact with the Indians also begot an idealized view of human nature, which since the Declaration of Independence and until quite recently has dominated an optimistic American world outlook. This last development grew out of a cult of nature which the early colonists, for the most part, did not espouse, and which is the subject of the next chapter. It could not come about on a wide scale until the struggle for empire had terminated successfully with the supremacy of the English-speaking peoples.

----

[35] "A Brief Relation of the State of New England from the Beginning of the Plantation to This Present Year, 1689," Force, *op. cit.*, IV, xi, p. 17.
[36] Rather similar conclusions about the importance of the millenarian tradition are reached by Ira V. Brown, "Watchers for the Second Coming: The Millenarian Tradition in America," *Mississippi Valley Historical Review*, XXXIX (1952), 441-458.

6

The American
Cult of Newness:
A Rebirth
Out of Hell

One short year after the discovery of America, the famous Papal Line of Demarcation sent Rome reaching out for the best parts of the New World. This act, as suggested, intensified the rivalry for colonial empire, insofar as Protestant England and Holland conducted a holy war against Catholic France and Spain to save the world for the true gospel. Prophetic Protestant faith, joined to economic self-interest and national pride, transformed French and Spanish adventurers into the minions of Antichrist. The apocalyptic image of the Antichrist, however, functioned as the supreme symbol of temporal authority against which Protestants rebelled. One might rephrase the words of the novelist Henry James to fit the historical context: for English Protestants, the Catholic Church—that was to say, the enemy, the monster of bulging eyes and far-reaching, quivering, groping tentacles—was exactly European society; exactly the multiplication of shibboleths; exactly the superfine discrimination of shades, tones, and classes; exactly the wicked old dungeons of inquisitorial Spain; exactly feudal Europe. The Antichrist, in its temporal aspect at least, represented all those barriers to worldly advancement, prestige, and power which hindered a rising class of people whose hopes for the future centered on America.

Those concerned with the English colonies as a bastion against
the domination of the world by Antichrist fixed upon its authoritarian repressive features, pointing to the feudal organization
of European society under Rome. Thus, the colonist John Cotton
fulminated against "earthly Pompious, stately Prelacy"; Edward
Johnson feared most in the French and Spanish threat to the
English colonies a transplantation of the Babylonian hierarchy
of "Popes, Cardinalls, Lordly-Bishops, Friars, Monks, Nuns, Semi-
nary-Priests, Jesuites, Ermites, Pilgrims, Deans, Prebends, Arch-
Deacons, Commissaries," and other officials; Thomas Hooker
warned against a "more than Egyptian bondage" under "the
tyranny and slavery" of Antichrist; William Symonds and others
referred to the "Babylonian captivity" which the colonists had left
behind. Joseph Bellamy summarized sentiments of long standing when in the 1700's he called Europe "a type of a fallen world
under the domination and tyranny of Satan."

The notion that Catholic Europe presented the spectacle of
a fallen world led to its depiction of a kind of Hell in contrast to the New World Paradise. John Cotton used the strongest
words to describe the transformation of early Christian Europe:
". . . all the garden of God was become a wilderness by an in-
undation of carnall people, Christians in name, but Pagans in
heart . . . when they took down the Pale, and let in all dogs and
swine that will come ine." He blamed Rome and the Turkish
empire for the murders, sorceries, fornications, and thefts that
had been let loose on Europe and wondered whether it would
not be wiser to banish all thrones as well as any "monarchicall
forme of Churchgovernment." When everything looked black
even in New England, Cotton Mather questioned whether the
next lodging place of the saints would be removal "to Heaven
or to Europe," that is, to Heaven or Hell. Jonathan Edwards
thought that the New World had been chosen as the site of
the Redemption because the old continent had Christ once, only
to slay him and then shed the blood of His saints and martyrs.
The colonial errand into the wilderness of America had as its
principal objective the redemption of man from the carnal sins
of a hellish Old World.[1] Europe has ever since, in one way or

----

[1] For Edward Johnson see *Johnson's Wonder-Working Providence*, ed. J.
Franklin Jameson (New York: Charles Scribner's Sons, 1910), p. 50;
Joseph Bellamy, *The Millennium* (1758); John Cotton, *The Powring Out of*

another, played the role of Hell in the American imagination. As long as the main poles of history described the conflict of Protestantism and Catholicism, England remained relatively immune to devaluation by the Colonial demonology. Beginning in the 1640's one finds, nevertheless, a strained love-hate relationship to English authority and example. English Protestantism under Cromwell, for instance, proved too tolerant for Colonial perfectionism. What appeared to be practical and literal reality in New England, as Herbert Schneider has said, was regarded as sheer fantasy in old England. On the one hand, Nathaniel Ward, the "simple cobbler of Agawam," would maintain as a patriotic Englishman that the Gospel never throve so well as in British soil, "nor is the like goodness of Nature, or Cornucopian plenty else-where to be found"; on the other hand, as an American Puritan, he would indulge in ferocious declamations against London fashions in dress and religion.[2] Edward Johnson, in the extremity of divided loyalty, prayed for England to follow the example of New England's "city upon a hill." The many expressions of Colonial cultural inferiority and desire to be treated at home as true-born Englishmen also hinted at a wounded pride that was to carry colonists far toward the pole of self-assertion, not against the European Antichrist merely, but against England herself.

The steps from a tender, mixed, almost adolescent love-hate relationship to parental authority, if England played that role, to outright rebellious assertiveness are easy to trace. They begin with the identification of English religious practices with Antichrist. By a principle of symbolic substitution, especially when the threat of France and Spain as authoritarian monsters began to subside, England took the place of Rome in Colonial imaginations. We find the process of substitution beginning very early, though not on a large scale, in the colonists' delusion of grandeur as a chosen people with a special mission, separate even from that of England. John Winthrop might urge, for instance, that

---

the Seven Vials (London, 1642), I, 11; IV, 11; V, 5; VI, 23; Cotton Mather, *The Present State of New England* (Boston, 1690), p. 35; *The Works of President Edwards*, 4 vols. (Philadelphia, 1844), III, 314; Perry Miller, *Errand into the Wilderness* (Cambridge: The Belknap Press of Harvard University Press, 1956), pp. 1-15.

[2] Nathaniel Ward, *The Simple Cobbler of Aggawam in America* (1647); reprinted in Force, *op. cit.*, III, viii, 18-19.

the great work upon which his people were embarking was a continuation of the English Reformation, but he also noted that England "growes weary of her Inhabitants, soe as man whoe is ye most pretious of all creatures is heer more vile & base then the Earth we Tread uppon. . . ." [3] Others after him would take the line that the English Reformation was an imperfect reformation: it stopped at the Episcopacy. Governor Thomas Dudley, for instance, rejected the idea of the divinity of the king of England as head of the Church, saying that Americans detested equally "the pageantry of a king, and the supercilious hypocrisy of a bishop." "You will find little difference between Episcopacy and Popery," John Cotton said, "for they are governed by Popish Canons." About the same time, the Remonstrant Major John Child was charging that the chief elders of New England were calling England "Egypt and Babylon." Such ideas prompted the humble Roger Clap to observe that the spirit of the Lord was working so efficaciously for a *"New Birth"* in America "that our Hearts were taken off from *Old-England* and set upon *Heaven*." [4] Clearly, England was becoming in Colonial imaginations the vestibule of the European Hell.

The chosen people of the American colonies increasingly looked upon their mission into the wilderness not merely as the continuation of something old, but as the beginning of something new: they were to usher in the final stage of history. They had inherited a new world in a physical sense, and in order "to vindicate the most rigorous ideal of the Reformation" they felt it necessary, in Jonathan Edwards' words, "to begin a new world in a spiritual respect." Their longing for a rebirth out of the European Hell was reflected in the change of emphasis which they gave to the conventional sun rhetoric which, as already noted, accompanied the westward expansion of Europe. In the symbolic language of spirit, they sometimes denied the westering sun of British empire its regular transit from east to west, and, instead had it hovering or rising for the first time over them, leaving all Europe in utter blackness. Thus, for Edward Johnson

---

[3] John Winthrop, "Conclusions for the Plantation in New England," *Old South Leaflets*, no. 50, p. 5.

[4] Dudley is quoted in Augustine Jones, *The Life and Work of Thomas Dudley, the Second Governor of Massachusetts* (Boston: Houghton Mifflin Co., 1899), p. 149; John Cotton, *The Churches Resurrection . . .* (London, 1642), p. 19; *Memoirs of Roger Clap, 1630* (Boston, 1848), pp. 19-20.

in 1653, the glorious reformation of the Church began in America, where Christ concentrated the "dazzling brightness" of His presence as in a magnifying glass which would then light up the dark corners of the world. Governor William Bradford of Plymouth caused a small candle to be lit as the prelude to greater things. In 1647, John Eliot, the Apostle to the Indians, was announcing "The Daybreaking if not the Sunrising of the Gospel . . . in New England." Regarding the New England planters as prophecy's Kings of the East, Samuel Sewall in 1697 hailed the morning star which would give "certain intelligence" that the Sun of Righteousness would rise over America. Increase Mather greeted the rising sun in the same year. "O New England," Samuel Willard hymned in a sermon of 1704, "thou art a Land of Vision; and has been so for a long time. The Sun for one day stood over Gibeon, so has the Sun of the Gospel been standing over us for Fourscore years together." The Sun of Righteousness, according to Jonathan Edwards, "*shall rise in the West,* contrary to the course of this world, or the course of things in the old heavens and earth." [5] Such language implied a break with the European past long before the Revolution. It is not surprising that Thomas Jefferson proposed as a seal of state for the new nation a representation of the children of Israel led by a pillar of light, or that the goddess of liberty on our coins is flanked by a rising sun.

Religious independency conditioned the colonists for political independence. This connection is readily seen in the fact that the overthrow of the hated Andros regime in 1689 was received as a rejection of Popery and reaffirmation of New England's special mission. The attempt of British imperial authority to bring all the colonies under a single command, ecclesiastical as well as political, beginning in 1675 with Edmund Randolph and ending in 1725 as the first serious threat of this kind until the revolutionary period, hastened psychological processes. Already we had

----

[5] Johnson *op. cit.,* pp. 49-50; William Bradford, *History of the Plimouth Plantation* (Boston: Massachusetts General Court, 1898), p. 332; John Eliot, *The Daybreaking if Not the Sunrising of the Gospel with the Indians in New England* (London, 1647); Samuel Sewall, "Dedication" to *Phaenomena Quaedam Apocalyptica . . .* (Boston, 1697); Willard as quoted in Perry Miller, *The New England Mind; from Colony to Province* (Cambridge: Harvard University Press, 1953), p. 178; Edwards, *op. cit.,* III, 316, 314-317 (italics are mine).

seen outbreaks of political independency growing out of the
religious differences between Colonial orthodoxy and Cromwellian toleration in the 1640's and again during the early Restoration period. Professor Morison has remarked that Robert Child's
charge of 1646 that New England looked upon herself as a free
state rather than "a colony or corporation of England" was substantially true. Child's charge was repeated by Captain Thomas
Breedon in 1661. In 1675, Edmund Randolph complained to the
king about Governor Leverett's declaration "that the laws made
by your Majesty and our Parliament obligeth them in nothing
but what consists with the interest of that colony; that the legislative power is and abides in them solely . . . by virtue of a
charter from your Majesty's royal father." Again and again, the
colonists were told that this patent was from God's direction and
likened to God's covenant with his Elect. When, in October of
1678, the Massachusetts General Assembly had the temerity to
tell the king that "the laws of England are bounded within the
four seas, and do not touch America," revolutionary precedent
was firmly established.[6]

Similar events and preconceptions provoked similar reactions
up and down the colonies, though New England took the lead.
Everywhere rebelliousness toward authority was central. As
the image of the material paradise supplanted that of the holy
commonwealth in response to the opportunities for land speculation and commerce, the popular assemblies throughout the
colonies set themselves against the royal governors and councils,
the frontier settlements against the older settlements, the country
against the towns, the poorer classes against an Anglicized
gentry, and in some areas primitive religion against a Colonial
Episcopacy, or the threat of it. Although English laws and economic exactions were not as burdensome as many colonists pretended, it cannot be said that the English at home dealt very
understandingly with tender Colonial pride. Condescending attitudes on the part of British officials toward Colonial co-operation
in the European wars in particular offended Colonial sensibilities.
Colonial troops were called bumpkins and bobtails and worse;
the Colonial pilots who assisted Admiral Walker in the difficult

---

[6] Cf. Samuel Eliot Morison, *Builders of the Bay Colony* (Boston: Riverside Press, 1930), p. 254; John G. Palfrey, *The History of New England,*
4 vols. (Boston, 1883), II, 201, 224.

navigation of the St. Lawrence were not trusted with the wheel; the efficiency of Colonial quartermasters in requisitioning provisions for British troops went unappreciated or was deemed tardy; and the colonies were constantly abused, though Colonial specie was in short supply, for not raising monies in their own defense. In 1711, for instance, Matthew Prior, the British diplomat and poet, attributed the entire miscarriage of the Tory Canadian expedition to the "Avarice or treachery of the godly at New England. . . . They are really such a race of men that the Palatins are more our countrymen than they." [7]

And this at a time when so many colonists whose loyalty could have been won forever were pathetically conscious of their Colonial status even as they were passionately proud of their English heritage. Almost every Colonial statement of grievances during this formative period included within it somewhere the plea that all that was desired were the undoubted rights of freeborn English citizens. Citizen John Saffin put this plea into the form of a general rule of conduct:

> I doe Endeavour allwayes, what I can
> To approve my Self a Reall Englishman. [8]

But the very vehemence of such pleas, like Saffin's adjective "Reall," expressed a deep sense of Colonial inferiority. Listen to John Cotton II on the inferiority of Colonial culture: "I cou'd not expect New-England cou'd compare with the Old, either for the Number of Authors, or the Excellency of their Parts and Endowments; New-England being only a Colony; and all their Learning but as springs from those two Fountains in Old England, Oxford and Cambridge. . . ." [9] Now hear the huffiness of Cotton Mather when he learned that the Colonial pretentiousness of his style of writing was not approved in England: "We should not be insensible, (having been very publickly inform'd of it) *That the style and Manner of the* New-England *Writers does not*

---

[7] In a letter to Sir Thomas Hanmer, *The Correspondence of Sir Thomas Hanmer, Bart.*, ed. Sir Henry Bunbury (London, 1838), p. 131. For a Colonial reaction to this charge see John W. Ford, ed., *Some Correspondence Between the Governors and Treasurers of the New England Company in London and the Commissioners of the United Colonies in America* . . . (London: Elliot Stock, 1897), pp. 96-97.

[8] *John Saffin His Book, 1665-1708*, ed. Caroline Hazard (New York: Harbor Press, 1928), p. ix.

[9] Quoted in John Dunton, *Letters from New-England* (Boston: The Prince Society, 1867), pp. 160-161.

equal that of the Europeans." [10] His only sin had been to try to write as he thought cultured Englishmen did. Think of the way in which the agents of the colonies had to fawn and bribe their way to the attention of the mighty at the Court of St. James, then to be sent out into a waiting chamber to cool their heels again. Think of the anxious manner in which the relatively well-to-do of Boston and Virginia tried to ape London fashions, sent their children abroad to embellish their minds, entertained visiting dignitaries, pursued family coats of arms, only to be regarded as inferior colonials after all. All this engendered mixed feelings which "salutary neglect" in the political sense did nothing to forge into an undivided loyalty. The step from injured pride to rebellious self-assertion was being taken long before the Revolution.

The series of Colonial wars, setting in motion tendencies toward united action by the colonies and giving Colonial assemblies the chance to exert themselves against royal authority, precipitated a significant crisis in the 1720's. This began in 1715 when the proprietary colony of Carolina petitioned to Parliament for relief from Indian spoliation on its frontiers. Parliament's reaction, directed mainly at the intransigency of Massachusetts, was to use this petition as a pretext for revoking all Colonial charters and making the colonies directly dependent upon parliamentary authority rather than loosely tied to the Crown. What the colonists tended to regard as patents from heaven—and indeed they were with respect to the wide latitude of self-government which they granted—Parliament regarded as no more legally binding than medieval corporation charters. Parliament was encouraged in its design by reports from the Board of Trade and from disaffected officials in the colonies. The Board of Trade reported in 1723, for instance, that "the Inhabitants, far from making suitable Returns to His Majesty for the Extraordinary Priviledges they enjoy by their Charter, are daily endeavouring to wrest the small remains of Power out of the hands of the Crown, and to become independent of their Mother Kingdom." [11]

The Board of Trade in turn received its information from people on the spot. John Jekyll, the collector of customs for New

[10] Cotton and Increase Mather, *Three Letters from New-England and* . . . (London, 1721), p. 8.
[11] Hardwicke Papers, British Museum Additional Manuscripts, 35908, fol. 56.

England, had written in 1720 that with the exception of the royal governor "everyman of the Council are New England men and as far as I can guess have their dear Idol ye Charter much at heart and a great love for independency in general." An anonymous writer believed to be a spy for Lord Carteret wrote from Boston a few years later, "We are all politicians yet have no will to forbear speaking of treason, of which I have heard more here in one day, than in all my life before. . . . Yet still His Majesty shall be heartily prayed for by us, as our titular King, but we ourselves must have the uncontroulable power, to act despoticily as we please." John Bridger, the unpopular surveyor of His Majesty's woods in America, added that "a great part of this I heave heard from their pulpits." News that the charters would be revoked only intensified Colonial resistance up and down the colonies and as far south as Barbados. But everywhere New England set the example by word and deed. The governor of Barbados thus reported that "this part of the world is infected with the maxims of the representatives in New England; they put themselves upon the very same foot with the Parliament in Great Britain." [12] From London, the New England agent, Jeremiah Dummer, and Harvard's benefactor, Thomas Hollis, warned that the colonists had few friends at home. In fact, plans were on foot to send troops to Boston; the situation seemed that desperate.[13]

The Colonial charters were not finally revoked because of rivalry within the British ministry between friends of the king and friends of Parliament. The new working relationship between king and Parliament since the Bloodless Revolution of 1688 had not yet been firmly established, and the king's royal charters remained intact until the American Revolution. But the point is that the state of opinion during the 1720's, in Massachusetts at least, was not very different from that which prevailed in the American Revolution, and the arguments used then were

[12] *Calendar of State Papers, Colonial Series, America and West Indies, 1719-1727*, ed. Cecil Headlam, 5 vols. (London: His Majesty's Stationery Office, 1933-1937), as follows: Jekyll in *CSP, 1720-1721*, no. 190; the anonymous writer in *CSP, 1722-1723*, no. 530; Bridger in *CSP, 1719-1720*, no. 274; and Governor Worsley in *CSP, 1726-1727*, no. 655.

[13] The plan to send troops is mentioned by the anonymous writer, above, and by Thomas Hollis in a letter to Benjamin Colman dated July 1, 1724, in the Hollis MSS (Harvard College Library, Cambridge).

repeated later. Jeremiah Dummer's masterly *Defense of the New-England Charters*, published in 1721, was reprinted several times in the Revolutionary period and may justly be considered, long before James Otis' famous speech, "the opening gun of the American Revolution." There were, of course, important differences. One was, as Professor Lawrence Gibson has pointed out, that fear of French encirclement was no longer a factor in Colonial allegiance to Britain, although Dummer had maintained in 1720 that the French "can't hurt us but [by] Surprizing our Frontier Setlements, and so preventing the growth of the Colonies. Their number is inconsiderable, compar'd with the British Subjects." [14] The second difference was the development of natural law theory side by side with the older theory of constitutional, or charter, restrictions upon Parliament's power. A third, and perhaps crucial, difference was the attempt to tighten British imperial authority over the colonies at a time when the French and Spanish threat no longer existed and the colonies had themselves grown powerful in population, wealth, and commerce.

All of these differences involved the shifting role of authority, both within and without the colonies. The appeal to natural law and natural rights arose, for instance, only as England took her place with France and Spain in the Colonial demonology and an Edenic image of natural felicity could be held up against the unrelieved hell of European civilization. But the Edenic image was generated with greater intensity by a growing division within the colonies between the older seaboard settlements and the frontier, between rural folk and town people, poor and rich: the pockets of apparent luxury in the commercial centers suggested the invasion of the colonies not merely by class-conscious English society, but by corrupt old Europe. Thus, a popular saying in early eighteenth-century America had it that "Simple Travellers not well Principled goe Abroad, and bring home Dutch Drunkeness, Spanish Pride: French Wantoness, and Italian Atheisme. As for their good Deeds . . . Those they leave behind them. But retaine their English Luxury." [15] How the increasing

---

[14] In Dummer's report to the Board of Trade, *Collections of the Maine Historical Society*, Second Series, X (Portland, 1907), 144.

[15] *John Saffin, op. cit.*, p. 139. One often meets similar sentiments in Colonial folklore and popular writing.

identification of the vices of part of the native population with the invasion of America by hellish Europe came about again has its origin in the religious imagery of the first settlers. This is so because the Protestant Reformation, while usually thought of as a civilizing movement, had regressive features which came to the fore when transplanted to America.

The Protestant Reformation was fundamentally a religious revolt against authority—easily transferred to the political or economic—in the name of a fancied restoration of the primitive Church. Colonial clergymen insisted upon this. They came to this country in the first place, as Jonathan Edwards said, because although the Protestant religion was then established in England by law, "yet there were very severe persecutions by those in authority, who symbolized in many things with the Papists." Roger Williams claimed that the word "plantation" to describe the earliest settlements referred to the first plantations of the primitive Church. Colonization itself was held to repeat the act of Creation, and the setting up of a church edifice or cross on new, uncultivated land dedicated the country to a "new birth," commemorating the resurrection of Christ. Colonists were often explicit and detailed in developing the imagery of planting, especially since many of them were an agricultural people familiar with nature. They were planting the seed of the posterity of a new Adam and Eve in the rich, virgin soil of a new Eden, warmed by the Sun of Righteousness. They were tilling a vineyard which would produce the fruit of blessedness, raising a regenerate people out of sin. Do not rest in a reformation, John Cotton urged; continue on to a resurrection: return to the purist, primitive Churches of Christ. Satan was raising wars against the saints since the Reformation in Europe, William Bradford thought, for fear lest "ye churches of God reverte to their anciente puritie, and recover their primative order, liberties, and bewtie." "Let the matter and forme of your Churches," Edward Johnson urged, "be such as were in the Primitive Times (before Antichrists Kingdom prevailed). . . ." Cotton Mather foresaw in New England a return to the first ages of Christianity; "In short, the *first Age* was the *golden Age:* to return unto that, will make a man a *Protestant,* and I may add, a *Puritan.*" Increase Mather wrote that the restoration of primitive Christianity would turn the earth into Paradise.[16]

The chief virtue of the primitive Church was held to be simplicity—simplicity of ordinance, moral conduct, manner, dress, speech. The more simplicity, as John Cotton put it, the "more evident witness to the truth of God." Simplicity of thought and speech in particular recommended the cause of truth. This belief continued in America the strain of anti-intellectualism which flourished during the Renaissance. John Cotton put it plainly: "The more learned and witty you bee, the more fit to act for Satan will you bee. . . . take off the fond doting . . . upon the learning of the Jesuites, and the glories of the Episcopacy, and brave estate of the Prelates. I say bee not deceived with these pompes, and empty shewes, and faire representations of a goodly condition before the eyes of flesh and blood, bee not taken with the applause of these persons. . . ."[17] To the devil's capacity for deception as displayed in the temptation of Eve and seduction of Adam, Cotton added false prophecy. But, above all, the devil accomplished his wiles in the guise of a princely gentleman—suave, sophisticated, cultured, aristocratic, accustomed to power and authority. The chief enemy of simplicity, then, was the habitude of authority. Colonists increasingly contrasted a natural simplicity and freedom with compulsion, restraint, artificiality, and self-seeking, and associated the vices of authority with intellectualism, worldly extravagance, irreligious lasciviousness, indolence, dilettantism, drunkenness, and deceit. Massachusetts and Virginia passed strict laws against such vices as part of the campaign to restore a condition of primitive innocence.

These laws were especially severe in dealing with the gentlemanly sin of worldly extravagance in fashion and dress. In 1634, for instance, the Massachusetts General Court passed laws against "new and immodest fashions," "great, superfluous, and unnecessary expenses," lace, slashed sleeves, and the wearing of gold

---

[16] For this paragraph see Mircea Eliade, *The Myth of the Eternal Return* (New York: Pantheon Books, Inc., 1954), pp. 10-11, 69-70. Roger Williams' letter to Winthrop (1637) in *Old South Leaflets*, no. 54, p. 6; John Cotton, *The Churches Resurrection*, p. 23; Johnson, *op. cit.*, p. 25; Bradford, *op. cit.*, p. 3; Cotton Mather, *Magnalia Christi Americana* . . . , 2 vols. (Hartford, 1820), I, 25; Edwards, *op. cit.*, I, 466.

[17] John Cotton, *Seven Vials*, VI, 39-40.

and silver trinkets.[18] Economic necessity, of course, prescribed many of these laws, but the mission of regeneration weighed more heavily in Colonial thinking. That this was true is indicated by the general tenor of Nathaniel Ward's *Simple Cobbler of Aggawam*, which in 1647 contrasted the plain living and high morals of the colonists with the corrupt manners of England as evidence of progress toward the paradisiac state of the primitive Church. In it he also thanked God that he lived in a colony of many thousand Englishmen for twelve years; yet "never heard but one Oath sworn, nor never saw one man drunk, nor ever heard of three women Adultresses. . . . I would not be understood to boast of our Innocency. . . . But. . . ." [19] His sarcastic denunciation of aristocratic refinement carried in it a note of self-righteousness which was to characterize American attitudes toward the Old World, particularly in the conduct of foreign policy, for much of United States history. The assumption of moral superiority by Americans was not something bred of the Revolutionary struggle in 1776 or born with the new republic of 1789; rather, it was already in existence from the early days of settlement, swelling and intensifying the tide of nationalism.

During Colonial days the collective self-righteousness of a covenanted people often hid an inferiority complex, as the colonists tried to ape the ways of their mother country. In their secret hearts, nursing convictions of a divinely appointed mission, they never doubted their moral superiority over the English; they felt inferior only in respect to their dress, their manners, their culture. Compensating for a deep sense of cultural inferiority, they made plain dress and natural expression positive virtues. The popular contrast between morals and manners, between simple, virtuous American democrats, uncouth in their speech and dress, and suave but unprincipled European aristocrats, which dominated nineteenth-century American thought, thus had its native roots in the Colonial experience. The first American "common man" was not Jefferson's or Crèvecoeur's sturdy yeoman farmer, who stuck to the saw and axe and the common virtues, or even Benjamin Franklin's printer's apprentice, who contrasted his rise in life to a position of middle-class superiority with his humble origins. Rather, it was Nathaniel Ward's simple cobbler of Aga-

---

[18] Cf. Jones, *op. cit.*, pp. 186-187.
[19] Ward, *op. cit.*, p. 43.

wam, who lectured the English gentry for their vain and immoral fashions as early as 1647. Ward's was one of the first statements of the classic American fable of East and West which, at one end of national existence, would constitute the polar terms of Royal Tyler's patriotic drama, *The Contrast*, and in the latter part of national existence would structure the international novels of Henry James and direct the pilgrimages of Scott Fitzgerald's heroes.

The American, "this new man," was early conceived in relation to civilized Europe, if not to the savage frontier, as a primitive. This was clear, too, in the increasing association of vice with the centers of authoritarian civilization—first the great cities of Europe and later the towns and cities of the colonies. Ward's animadversions had been directed, after all, against London *city* fashions. This association of evil with cities had precedent in a conventional Christian symbolism growing out of the Old Testament and which, as represented by Dante's *Inferno*, depicted hell in the image of a crowded underground city. Rabelais had made Paris the home of sin; Protestants, Rome. A Protestant Colonial people whose civilization rested upon rural foundations, surrounded by great forests, was naturally disposed to such symbolism. Such preconceptions, related to the expansion of settlements along the frontier, gradually took the celestial city out of the center of paradise and either located it farther west as an ideal yet to be realized or consigned it to hell with existing temporal cities. Winthrop's and Bulkeley's temporal "city upon a hill" always disappointed expectations. Thus, the clergyman Daniel Price told the Virginia Adventurers, speaking of the city of London: "It should be Jerusalem the City of God, and it is become Murder's sloughterhouse, Thefts refuge, Oppressor's safety, Whoredom's stewes, Usury's Bank, Vanity's stage, abounding in all kind of filthiness and prophaneness. O! remember that sins have been the pioneers of the greatest cities, and have not left one stone upon another." Similarly, William Bradford attributed the Pilgrims' difficulties in Holland to an avaricious city culture, "Espetially seeing they were not acquainted with trads nor traffique . . . but had only been used to a plaine countrie life, and ye inocente trade of husbandrey." [20]

---

[20] For Price see Alexander Brown, *The Genesis of the United States* . . . , 2 vols. (Boston, 1890), I, 315; Bradford, *op. cit.*, p. 16.

The rise of towns in the colonies, bringing with them an un-accustomed luxury and social stratification, not only hastened the decline of religion, but more importantly in the long run fixed in American minds the notion that the American paradise was being infiltrated by diabolical powers whose ancestral home was urban Europe. In 1739, Rev. Thomas Allen of Charleston, near Boston, was called to account by his parishioners for having paint on his dwellings, on the ground that he "was encouraging the tendency to showy, aristocratic ways of living that would en-danger the morals of the community." "The Sea swallows up the land," Josiah Cotton cried about the same time, "by which means and an extravagance of living beyond our selves we are forc'd to be beholden to other parts. . . ." He bewailed not only a servile dependency upon Europe, but also the relative decline in the status of farmers as compared to the merchant class of the towns. There were similar complaints of the aristocratic way of life of the tidewater planters to the south. Long before Jefferson or Franklin, as Clinton Rossiter has said, Americans were warning that the result of "clustering into Towns, is Luxury; a great and mighty Evil carrying all before it, and crumbling States and Empires, into slow, but inevitable Ruin." Long before John Taylor of Caroline, they were announcing that "Agriculture is the most solid Foundation on which to build the Wealth, and . . . the political virtue of a Commonwealth." [21]

The supposed invasion of America by urban European civi-lization (by feudal artistocracy in the case of the southern plant-ers) raised new centers of authority about which revolved internal divisions and dissensions comparable to the transatlantic tensions. By the process of symbolic tranference with which we are familiar, the polarization of America and Europe, para-dise and hell, nature and civilization became internalized. The resulting internal pressures hastened the settlement of the West, where the old mixed love-hate, submissive-rebellious relation-ship to authority was repeated. These forces were already at work in the first great migration into the rich Connecticut Val-

---

[21] For this paragraph see the Allen indictment as quoted by Mrs. S. P. Wetherill, "Samuel Wetherill and the Early Paint Industry of Philadelphia," *Philadelphia History*, II, no. 1 (1916), 11; Josiah Cotton, "Memoirs" (Ms in the Massachusetts Historical Society Library), p. 291; and the Colonial newspapers cited by Clinton Rossiter, *Seedtime of the Republic* . . . (New York: Harcourt, Brace & Co., 1953), p. 146.

ley, one of the many interior Canaans which beckoned to those frustrated or disappointed with the results of coastal civilization: Cambridge was thus too small a town to hold two such assertive individualists as Thomas Hooker and John Cotton. "Besides the need for fresh soil, it was thought that the personal ambition of Hooker, the pastor of Cambridge, made him eager for greater freedom and authority than he could enjoy in Massachusetts."[22] The earliest as well as the latest of the many great American land manias represented self-assertive energies directed to the relocation of Eden, variously interpreted.

Internal conflicts were never—or almost never—simple East-West or North-South conflicts in a geographical sense, nor simple rural-urban, rich-poor conflicts in the sociological sense, because the key was a relationship to authority which cut across these lines. Moreover, viewing the country as a whole in relationship to the rest of the world, one could always belabor or praise all sections and classes of the country equally, as the current urgency of America's world mission seemed to dictate. Thus, Cotton Mather could simultaneously call New England "the almost only garden" in the world, heap abuse upon her, and longingly look for "a more goodly countrie" within the continent. When he did the last, his perspective was not international, but local. Viewing America solely from within, Solomon Stoddard of Northampton was a spokesman for a frontier community and frontier religion, but thinking on the plane of world destiny, he could rebuke both frontier and coastal towns for not living up to the obligations of the covenant. Nevertheless, several broad lines of conflict coinciding with lines of force, or authority, begin to emerge. The great revivals, for instance, usually began on the frontier and only later touched the cities. In the cities, they were more popular with the poor than with the educated and well-to-do.[23] Carolina and Virginia frontiersmen were more lukewarm to Revolutionary sentiment than the tidewater planters because they had been resisting the tidewater aristocracy, which favored the Revolution, for more than a hundred years. On the

----

[22] Jones, *op. cit.*, p. 210.
[23] Cf. Edwin S. Gaustad, *The Great Awakening in New England* (New York: Harper & Bros., 1957), pp. 42-44; Timothy L. Smith, *Revivalism and Social Reform in Mid-Nineteenth-Century America* (New York: Abingdon Press, 1957), pp. 47, 59.

other hand, tenant farmers in the Hudson Valley ardently espoused the Revolution in opposition to their semifeudal landlords, who remained Tories. The Loyalists tended to come from the well-to-do classes which had enjoyed privileges and authority under the Crown. Antislavery sentiment was precipitated by displaced elites in the North with a strong sense of national mission who feared that slavery was "a road lying open to the same degeneracy [as in Europe], in some parts of this newly settled land." [24]

The decline of religion was spelled out in the many diatribes against urban vices. Americans have tended to exalt as peculiarly American the virtues of sobriety, frugality, industry, honesty, chastity, and the like not merely because they have inherited these as part of the Protestant ethic most congenial to frontier conditions, but because these virtues were, almost from the beginning, opposed to the urban vices of indolence, drunkenness, extravagance, lewdness, deceit—which were, in turn, held to be the characteristic vices of a leisured aristocracy originating in Europe. The many crusades of the nineteenth century were launched by the often unconscious fear that America, the land of destiny, the land of nature and God, was going, after all, to hell, the way of Europe. The decline of religious piety, the rise of rural-urban tensions, the imaginative transfer of England to the status of hell with other European nations, and the feared invasion of America by Europe all combined to produce in American thought the long-lived reign of nature and natural law. John Wise, whose *Vindication of the Government of New-England Churches* (1717) contained one of the earliest significant developments of American natural law theory, was a clear-cut spokesman for the American farmer in opposition to the crafty merchants of the budding Colonial metropolis. "In his sentences," Professor Perry Miller writes, "first clearly appears that contrast between the natural felicity of America and the miseries of artificial Europe which Crèvecoeur, Tom Paine, and Thomas Jefferson were to make the main theme of American literature." [25]

To American colonists, the bursting of conventional bonds

----

[24] In this quotation I anticipate myself, but it happens to have been written during the Colonial period and comes from John Woolman's *Journals*.

[25] Miller, *op. cit.*, p. 300.

and authoritarian restraints which their exodus from Europe to America signified seemed to promise a rebirth into a new life. Their first accounts of the New World were accordingly fresh with the dew of the creation, glowing with the abundance of new life, sparkling as from the waters of a fountain of youth. The very atmosphere was claimed in one promotional tract to restore the body to physical and spiritual health, "for a sup of *New-Englands* Aire is better than a whole draft of old *Englands* Ale." It was a land "farre more excellent than Old England in her proper nature," "more like the Garden of Eden," growing partridges so heavy that they couldn't fly, turkeys the size of sheep, and (delightful horror) mosquitoes as large as birds.[26] Such grandiose conceptions of the prodigality of life in contrast to degenerate Europe begot the characteristically American tall tale, anticipated Franklin's story of the whale which leaped Niagara Falls, underlaid Jefferson's resentment of the Frenchman Buffon's supposedly scientific diminution of American animals, laid the psychological foundation for a national jingoism, and, above all, makes understandable the national preoccupation with size, number, quantity. The celebration of the physical dimension of the new country concealed or expressed an elect people's longing for moral and spiritual grandeur among the world of nations.

Hailing the rebirth of a new life out of the old, colonists named their habitations Canaan, *New* England, *New* York, *New* Haven, Virginia. Virginia was named after the virgin queen Elizabeth because it was "a Virgin Countrey, so preserved by Nature out of a desire to show mankinde fallen into the Old age of the Creation, what a brow of fertility and beauty she was adorned with when the World was vigorous and youthfull, and she her selfe was unwounded with the Ploughshares. . . ." [27] The ploughshares might one day despoil the country, but it was hoped and expected that they would first engender a new Adam and Eve. William Byrd half-humorously named the newly explored land south of Virginia "Eden" after Virginia's Governor Eden and maintained that old people who migrated there would be

---

[26] Cf. John Higginson in Force, *op. cit.*, I, xii, 10-11; Morton, *ibid.*, II, v, 42; William Symonds in Alexander Brown, *op. cit.*, I, 289. Examples such as these are too numerous to document.

[27] From E. W., *Virginia, Truly Valued* (1650) in Force, *op. cit.*, III, xi, 19; see also *The New Life of Virginea* (1612), *ibid.*, I, vii, pp. 8-17.

rejuvenated. The pamphlet which contained Samuel Sewall's passionate dithyramb on Plumb Island ended with testimony to the curative powers of the land by calling attention to the longevity of such of "the saints in light" as Peregrine White, John Alden, and his wife Elizabeth. Cotton Mather's monumental *Magnalia Christi Americana* was essentially an attempt to hasten a millennial rebirth by restoring to life the inspired example of early New England saints. In a dedication to it, Timothy Woodbridge wrote:

> The *dead ones* here, so much alive are made,
> We think them speaking from bless'd *Eden's* shade.[28]

Some of the saints could not wait for the Second Coming to inaugurate the millennial rebirth. In 1640, Governor Winthrop of Massachusetts had to banish one Hugh Bewett for declaring himself free from original sin.[29] The famous Antinomian controversy similarly arose from premature convictions of the inward-dwelling presence of Christ.

The newness of the country, the expectation of some kind of rebirth or beatitude in the near future, and the eternal promise of future blessings associated with the land produced a distinct emphasis on youth in America. As each successive generation fell short of its appointed mission, it concentrated its hopes for futurity on the next generation. As the physical frontiers gave way to industry and mechanized agriculture in what seemed to many a process of corruption following the invasion of America by Europe, Americans sought their lost innocence increasingly in their children. A psychic primitivism of youth replaced or accompanied geographical and cultural primitivism. The youth of America, representing her future, accordingly became at once the most glorified and the most lectured youth in the world.[30] Classic American literature, which surely expresses the most deeply rooted emotional attitudes of the society, is full of the symbolic innocence of youth.

The cult of newness followed the pioneers westward; it forti-

---

[28] Cotton Mather, *Magnalia Christi Americana*, I, 18.

[29] Cf. *Winthrop's Journal "History of New England," 1630-1649*, ed. James Kendall Hosmer, Original Narratives Series, 2 vols. (New York: Charles Scribner's Sons, 1908), II, 17.

[30] Cf. Clyde Kluckhohn, *Mirror for Man* (New York: Whittlesey House, 1949), p. 238.

fied bumptious individualism in its never-ending contests with authority; it contributed to a characteristically American disrespect for tradition and history; it minimized fatally the large contribution which European civilization has made to our culture; it served as an important basis for criticism of the "new" industrial order and supplied the moral and intellectual framework within which it was to operate. Finally, it continued to haunt the American mind long after, conceivably, it should have reached maturity. As Mark Twain said in his *Life on the Mississippi*, "The world and the books are so accustomed to use, and over-use the word 'new' in connection with our country, that we early get and permanently retain the impression that there is nothing old about it."

7

The Art

of Virtue:

Franklin

and Jefferson

Counteracting the New World accent on newness, an accent which, according to the astute French observer Tocqueville, made some Americans talk as if they belonged to a distinct species of mankind, was the activity of those natives who recognized a cultural community with Europe and who longed for the creation of a true Atlantic civilization which would extend beyond the ocean bounds. Since early Colonial days, Americans have gone to Europe for reasons of business, education, travel, scientific study, ancestral tidings, and sexual holidays. Others have been responsive to overseas influences while remaining at home. But, until lately, these cosmopolitans have formed a distinct minority both in numbers and in public esteem. Moreover, from the beginning, as even Professor Sachse admits in his study of American colonists in Britain, Americans who turned toward Europe came largely from the upper classes in eastern urban centers and the tidewater South.[1] Historians of our international cultural ties seldom point out that these were the very people who represented to "grass-roots" America the invasion of America by Europe!

---

[1] William L. Sachse, *The Colonial American in Britain* (Madison: University of Wisconsin Press, 1956), pp. 3-4.

Large numbers of these people were Tories and Loyalists during the American Revolution. Far from impeding the Revolutionary cause, they unwittingly intensified Revolutionary fervor as scapegoats and ever-present reminders of the menace from abroad. Jefferson and Franklin were among the few Americans in this period who combined a cosmopolitan outlook with provincial patriotism. In any event, whether we emphasize the real contribution of Europe to the formation of the new nation or whether we wishfully minimize the European origins in deference to the Turner hypothesis, the fact remains that a majority of Americans voluntarily separated themselves from England and for a hundred years self-consciously pursued a course of political, economic, and even cultural isolation from Europe. A major cause along with economic necessity, political tyranny, and the influence of the frontier was a tender pride long nursed in the school of salutary neglect which magnified slights according to an Edenic conception of national mission borrowed originally from Europe and later turned against Europe.

In the American Revolution, the common man asserted himself against British imperial authority, which had hurt his pride even more than his pocketbook, in order to revert to a simpler, freer existence symbolized by the image of Paradise—or a state of nature. The influence of the frontier worked imaginatively on minds already predisposed to the Paradise-Hades archetype. The Colonial love-hate relationship to authority compounded attitudes of infantile regression or servility with rebellion. It was individualistic, self-assertive, and aggressive in order that it might finally make its peace with the Atlantic community. It looked back at the same time as it looked forward. It fought the American Revolution of 1776 with the ideas of the English Revolution of 1688.[2] In trying to restore the simplicity and freedom of primitive days, conceived as a state of mind, it founded a nation dedicated to the idea of progress.

----

[2] Clinton Rossiter, in his book *Seedtime of the Republic* (New York: Harcourt, Brace & Co., 1953), p. 440, writes: "Conservatism, we are told, is the worship of dead revolutionists. If this is true, then Americans are conservatives twice over." I do not wish my interpretation to be construed, however, as a plea for neoconservatism. We already have in this country many more conservatives than we need, and I have no wish to become one of Mr. Rossiter's disciples.

The myth of newness, as part of the imaginative complex, contributed significantly to the cause of separation. That it did so was not merely owing to its focus upon the physical attributes of the country, but more importantly to its emphasis on a moral and spiritual rebirth in conjunction with the country. By the middle of the eighteenth century, American nature seemed pregnant with implications for ethical betterment. As piety gave way to moralism, the blessings discovered in natural law were conferred upon it. The beneficence of nature which survived the displacement of God from the center of creation seemed best realized in it. In its workshop nature best exhibited that marvelous harmony which wedded the "is" and the "ought." The morality to be derived from nature, moreover, continued to express the original sense of mission. Just as the early frontier hardships had been held to be a test of the fitness of an Elect people in their incessant warfare against sin, so success in subduing the wilderness was tantamount to entering the kingdom of heaven on earth and seemed to demonstrate a direct causal relationship between moral effort and material reward. The opportunity for advancement and freedom afforded by this land of promise was contrasted to the static caste system of a Europe still fettered by feudalism. America's answer to Europe was now to rise in the economic scale by an application of industry, sobriety, frugality, and the like, to make the wilderness, which at least in its primitive state suggested Paradise, more hospitable to that image by converting it into a pleasing land of rural villages, small shops, churches, and tilled fields [3]—in short, to establish a superior civilization in which modest prosperity was a mark of especial virtue.

The process of moral regeneration was to be, indeed, a civilizing process, but, as opposed to the supposedly corrupt urban culture of Europe and in response to the attraction of newness, the new American civilization would hew to its agrarian basis. Thus, the peculiar virtues of America came to be associated with the cultivators of the soil and with the regenerating powers of nature. Throughout the nineteenth century the United States

---

[3] Cf. Alan Heimert, "Puritanism, the Wilderness, and the Frontier," *New England Quarterly*, XXVI (September, 1953), 370. Also my article, "The Garden of America," *Modern Review*, Calcutta, India, XCII (July, 1952), 24-25.

was more or less dominated by what David Riesman has called "inner-directed moralists," who, while turning to industrial techniques in the development and exploitation of natural resources, still followed an ethical code which emphasized visible works, glorified the ascetic virtues of industry, and interpreted most problems as moral ones. The mission of regeneration, as will be seen, was never wholly abandoned in the shift from agriculture to industry. Both ways of salvation, moreover, gave access to abundance.

The image of Paradise in the American myth of Eden has had its greatest development in the moral sphere. The superiority of the United States in quantitative achievements and political skills has consistently been blazoned forth in moral terms. Perceptive foreign observers such as Alexis de Tocqueville and James Bryce have called Americans as a whole the most moralistic and religious people in the world. The philosopher George Santayana once remarked that to be an American "is of itself almost a moral condition, an education, and a career," and, similarly, the expatriate Logan Pearsall Smith complained that Americans acted as if "America were more than a country, were a sort of cause." "No people," a noted American anthropologist has said, "moralizes as much as we do. The actual pursuit of power, prestige, and pleasure for their own sakes must be disguised (if public approval is to be obtained) as action for a moral purpose or as later justified by 'good works.' " [4] Of the many Americans who have helped to establish the United States as a land of virtue in the public mind, none has played a more prominent part than Jefferson and Franklin.

It would be rather easy to show that Benjamin Franklin was the product of eighteenth-century urban culture extending from Europe to Colonial Boston and Philadelphia, that Franklin's "Poor Richard" had an affinity with the *Compleat Tradesman* of Daniel Defoe's England, and that therefore Franklin's moral virtues were broadly middle class rather than peculiarly American. It has been argued, for instance, that Franklin's ethics were those of a tradesman and that the eighteenth-century con-

---

[4] George Santayana, *Character and Opinion in the United States* (New York: Charles Scribner's Sons, 1920), p. 168; Logan Pearsall Smith, *Unforgotten Years* (Boston: Little, Brown & Co., 1939), p. 280; Clyde Kluckhohn, *Mirror for Man* (New York: Whittlesey House, 1949), p. 233.

cept of tradesman was English in origin.[5] At the same time, an English writer, D. H. Lawrence, has found Franklin's moralism to be archetypally New World, and Herbert Schneider has written that, as a moralist, Franklin was "a child of the New England frontier." [6] The truth is that the individualistic virtues of industry, frugality, and sobriety—taught, if not always practiced, by Franklin—were adaptable to both the tradesman and farmer, hence the American note. Like the middle-class tradesman, the pioneer farmer was in fact if not in myth a small entrepreneur and capitalist, a speculator in land, "a cultivator," as Veblen has said, "of the main chance as well as of fertile soil." The career of Daniel Defoe, who died in obscurity and poverty, shows that Defoe spoke for a single class which was not yet able to break through the cramping restrictions of class and caste. Franklin spoke for a whole nation of middle-class *arrivistes*, but addressed himself particularly, after the native tradition, to the "Cultivators of the Earth" in opposition to the urban dwellers of the Colonial city and of the European metropolis.

A. Whitney Griswold has shown that Franklin's thirst for moral perfection was a distillation of the Protestant ethic taught by Puritan ministers in Franklin's home town of Boston. Franklin himself acknowledged the influence of Cotton Mather's "Essays to Do Good." But, as already noted, the Protestant ethic taught in America had a localized application and significance. Though the Colonial urban culture opened to Franklin the opportunities for advancement beyond what he might have expected on a farm, gave him access to the scientific and philosophical ideas of the Enlightenment, and enlisted him in projects for civic improvement, his moral vision was colored by the presence of the frontier. Cosmopolitan though he was, Franklin dreamed of a

[5] For these views see Stuart P. Sherman, "Franklin and the Age of Enlightenment," *Americans* (New York: Charles Scribner's Sons, 1922), pp. 28-62; Carl and Jesse Bridenbaugh, *Rebels and Gentlemen: Philadelphia in the Age of Franklin* (New York: Reynal & Co., 1942), ch. I; Gladys Meyer, *Free Trade in Ideas* (Morningside Heights: King's Crown Press, 1941); Vernon L. Parrington, *Main Currents in American Thought* (New York: Harcourt, Brace & Co., 1927), I, 166.

[6] D. H. Lawrence, *Studies in Classic American Literature* (New York: Thomas A. Seltzer, 1923), pp. 13-31; Herbert W. Schneider, *The Puritan Mind* (New York: Henry Holt & Co., Inc., 1930), p. 256.

great agrarian utopia in which to preserve America's "glorious public virtue."

As early as 1753, when he was preoccupied with problems of Indian defense, he proposed, as a means both of enriching himself and strengthening the British empire, to settle a wilderness colony on the banks of the Ohio. "What a glorious Thing it would be," he wrote on that occasion, "to settle in that fine Country a large strong Body of Religious and Industrious People!" But his imperialistic vision of a greater England in the West, to be cemented by the Albany Plan of Union, reserved a special destiny for Americans which overshadowed the role of the mother country. Reflecting a typical Colonial ambivalence, he expressed both British pride and incipient American patriotism in the sun and light imagery common to the rhetoric of westward expansion. "'Tis said the Arts delight to travel Westward," he once remarked. He was long of the opinion "that the *foundations of the future grandeur and stability of the British empire lie in America.*" Half-playfully, he attributed a cosmic significance to the work of spiritual pioneering: "by *clearing America* of Woods," Americans were "*Scouring* our Planet . . . and so making this Side of our Globe reflect a brighter Light to the Eyes of the Inhabitants in *Mars* or *Venus.* . . ." [7] Franklin early identified the frontier with opportunity and tended to measure moral and spiritual progress by progress in converting the wilderness into a paradise of material plenty.

A city-dweller—by profession a printer and tradesman— Franklin nevertheless located the true source of virtue in agricultural pursuits. "There seem to be but three ways for a nation to acquire wealth," he wrote, with an eye to the widening breach between England and the colonies. "The first is by *war,* as the Romans did, in plundering their conquered neighbors. This is *robbery.* The second by *commerce,* which is generally *cheating.* The third by *agriculture,* the only *honest way* wherein man receives a real increase of the seed thrown into the ground in a kind of continual miracle. . . ." This was more than physiocratic economic doctrine; it was a program to keep a chosen people

[7] *The Writings of Benjamin Franklin,* ed. Albert H. Smyth, 10 vols. (New York: The Macmillan Co., 1905-1907), III, 72-73, 339; IV, 4, 194. For a similar treatment of Franklin's attitudes toward the extension of the British empire, see Henry Nash Smith, *Virgin Land: The American West as Symbol and Myth* (Cambridge: Harvard University Press, 1950), pp. 7-8.

on the path of righteousness and prepare them for the moral
and spiritual leadership of mankind. He made it clear that public
morality was his chief concern when he wrote after independence had been secured: "The vast Quantity of Forest Lands
we have yet to clear, and put in order for Cultivation, will for a
long time keep the Body of our Nation laborious and frugal." [8]
He repeatedly contrasted the vices of Europe and England with
the "glorious public virtue" of America and habitually bestowed
upon American farmers the ennobling title of "Cultivators of
the Earth." By an outstanding example of good works, by his
Almanacks and *Autobiography*, by his proposed *Art of Virtue,*
and by other writings, Franklin constituted himself a guardian
of the national conscience.

American moralism implied a repudiation of sophisticated
European culture and of urbanism, though not a denial of the
civilizing process—as Franklin himself testified in borrowing the
best which Europe had to offer. His cultural indebtedness often
did not square with the mythology. As the Revolution drew near,
Franklin exaggerated the differences which he found abroad.
From England, still smarting from the abuses of Attorney-
General Wedderburn, he wrote to Joseph Galloway, who longed
for a reconciliation, "When I consider the extream Corruption
prevalent among all Orders of Men in this old rotten State, and
the glorious publick Virtue so predominant in our rising Country,
I cannot but apprehend more Mischief than Benefit from a closer
Union." Political and military necessity demanded a smiling
compliance with the ways of the world in Paris, where among
the powdered heads he wore his fur cap as a native emblem. It
must be admitted that he took genuine delight in urbane repartee
with the court ladies—for if Europe was hellish, it also provided
by the very virtue of its hellishness, as will be seen, a release
for repressed desires. Franklin was also flattered by the attention
of the *philosophes,* but always he had private reservations about
the state of French culture. And occasionally his moral obsessions
led him to flirt with a primitivism akin to the sentimental cult
of the noble savage. Thus, returning from a tour of Ireland and
Scotland, he wrote:

. . . if my Countrymen should ever wish for the honour of having
among them a gentry enormously wealthy, let them sell their Farms

[8] *Ibid.,* V, 202; IX, 245.

and pay rack'd Rents; the Scale of the Landlords will rise, as that of the Tenants is depress'd, who will soon become poor, tattered, dirty, and abject in spirit. Had I never been in the American colonies, but was to form my Judgment of Civil Society by what I have lately seen, I should never advise a Nation of Savages to admit of Civilization: For I assure you, that, in the Possession and Enjoyment of the various Comforts of Life, compar'd to these People every Indian is a Gentleman. . . .[9]

But taking the American colonies as his model, Franklin was able to recommend a virtuous agrarian civilization. In identifying prosperity with virtue, however, Franklin remembered that the covenant promise was with a whole people, not merely the few, and he wanted, as he said, "a general happy Mediocrity of fortune."

To be an American was to be a "backtrailer to a more sophisticated society," in itself a moral condition. An aristocracy of wealth based on commerce and land speculation blossomed in the larger seaport towns of America. Rich Boston merchants thirsted after London much as London aspired to Paris. Like Jefferson and many other Americans imbued with a sense of mission, Franklin did not want to see Colonial urban centers emulate the class patterns of European society, and he too sometimes wished for an "ocean of fire" between the Old World and the New. He transferred some of his animus against Europe to the coastal towns. "The people of the Trading Towns," he wrote at the end of the Revolution, "may be rich and luxurious, while the Country possesses all the Virtues, that tend to private Happiness and publick Prosperity. Those Towns are not much regarded by the Country; they are hardly considered as an essential Part of the States . . . we may hope the Luxury of a few Merchants on the Seacoast will not be the Ruin of America." [10] Franklin felt apprehensive about the social dislocations and misery caused by the new factory system in Europe. No more than Jefferson did he want to see Americans "twirling a distaff" in factories. Though he was the prophet of American technological efficiency, he did not anticipate industrialism. It may be supposed that his response to such urban problems as fire-fighting, poor street-lighting, pauperism, and improper sanitation was

---

[9] *Ibid.*, V, 362-363; the preceding quotation is from VI, 311-312.
[10] *Ibid.*, IX, 245-246, 248.

unconsciously motivated by a patriotic desire to avoid or mitigate the worst evils of urbanization.

Franklin's whole moral fiber was geared to raising a new man and a new society in the world of nations. Viewed in this light, his *Autobiography* is a great moral fable pursuing on a secular level the theme of John Bunyan's *Pilgrim's Progress*. There is little doubt of the serious moral intent underlying either the *Autobiography* or the creation of "Poor Richard." He wrote the *Autobiography*, as he said, to acquaint his posterity with the means of his success, "as they may find some of them suitable to their own situations, and therefore fit to be imitated." [11] After breaking off the work, a friend persuaded him to continue it on the grounds that it would be useful to millions and would "lead the youth to equal the industry and temperance of thy early youth." [12] Another friend urged its continuation "in conjunction with your Art of Virtue (which you design to publish) of improving the features of private character, and consequently of aiding all happiness, both public and domestic." [13] Franklin began *Poor Richard's Almanack* to make money, but, more importantly, to convey "instruction among the common people." He filled the calendar spaces "with proverbial sentences, chiefly such as inculcated industry and frugality, as the means of procuring wealth, and thereby securing virtue." [14] Of late it has been popular to say with Robert Spiller that "Poor Richard" was a humorous creation, never intended to be taken seriously. But Franklin's very humor was a vehicle for serious moral instruction, and also expressed his sense of special destiny. Thus, his tall stories of sheep with tails so heavily laden with wool that they needed trailer-carts to carry them and of the whale which chased salmon up Niagara Falls were Franklin's way of whittling the urban sophisticate and European down to size and telling him, in effect, that things grew bigger and better in God's country. This moral exuberance remained the essence of Western frontier humor.

The *Autobiography* is not simply a formless record of personal

---

[11] Benjamin Franklin, *Autobiography*, ed. Dixon Wecter (New York: Rinehart & Co., Inc., 1948), p. 1.

[12] *Ibid.*, p. 71.

[13] *Ibid.*, p. 73.

[14] *Ibid.*, pp. 97-98.

experience, or just a charming success story. Consciously or unconsciously, it is a work of imagination which, by incorporating the "race" consciousness of a people, achieves the level of folk myth. Franklin's biographer, Carl Van Doren, tells us that Franklin had no model for his kind of autobiography.[15] This is not quite true. As a report on Franklin's spiritual progress in the new heaven on earth, the *Autobiography* in its basic dramatic form parallels Bunyan's great allegory. Franklin merely substituted, to use the phrase of Carl Becker, the secular story with a happy ending for the Christian story with a happy ending. *Pilgrim's Progress* was a best-seller in New England during the latter part of the seventeenth century.[16] It admirably fitted the situation of a people whose feet were planted on the path to worldly success, but whose heads were still filled with visions of the Celestial City. Franklin's first book was *Pilgrim's Progress,* and his favorite author was John Bunyan. Franklin absorbed from the pages of *Pilgrim's Progress* lessons in artistry as well as confirmations for the New World theme of moral regeneration. According to Franklin, Honest John was the first author whom he had met "who mixed narration and dialogue, a method of writing very engaging to the reader, who in the most interesting parts finds himself, as it were, brought into the company and present at the discourse." [17] Franklin regarded Defoe's works as imitations of Bunyan in this respect. Franklin also combined narrative and dialogue in his *Autobiography* in order to convey the felt immediacy of his experience, but in relating Bunyan's theme to the details of his new environment he created an allegory of American middle-class superiority.

Franklin states his central organizing theme at the outset: his emergence "from the poverty and obscurity" in which he was born and bred "to a state of affluence and some degree of reputation in the world." [18] He gives to this secular "rise" a moral and spiritual meaning discoverable in the special blessings of

[15] Carl Van Doren, *Benjamin Franklin* (New York: The Viking Press, Inc., 1938), pp. 414-415.

[16] See the book lists in Daniel Henchman's "Account Book" (MS in the Boston Public Library). Also Thomas G. Wright, *Literary Culture in Early New England, 1620-1730* (New Haven: Yale University Press, 1920), p. 123. Franklin expressed his debt to Bunyan in his *Autobiography*, pp. 10, 21.

[17] Franklin, *Autobiography*, p. 21.

[18] *Ibid.*, p. 1.

God. The boy entering Philadelphia with three loaves under his arm is obviously the prototype of Bunyan's Christian beginning his toilsome ascent to the Heavenly City. Franklin heightens the drama of his struggle upward against odds in his more worldly pilgrimage by reiterating the contrast between his humble beginnings and his improved station in life. Three times he halts his narrative at conspicuous points in order to recall to his readers the pathetic picture of his first arrival in Philadelphia. He frames the Philadelphia anecdote as carefully as if he were deliberately setting out to create an immortal legend. "I have been the more particular," he writes, "in this description of my journey, and shall be so of my first entry into the city, that you may in your mind compare such unlikely beginnings with the figure I have since made there." [19] He would have the reader believe that his future wife, Deborah Read, happened also to be present on that occasion to observe his unlikely beginnings.

Since his marriage is one of convenience contributing to his rise in life, he associates the episode of the rolls with his courtship of Miss Read. Once established as an up-and-coming printer, he notes for the reader's attention that he "made rather a more respectable appearance in the eyes of Miss Read than I had done when she first happened to see me *eating my roll* in the street." [20] Though his success story is a triumph of moral individualism and personal salvation, he identifies it with the rise of a whole people. His rise in life thus parallels the growth of Philadelphia. After he has bought out his partner Meredith, there is a building boom: "whereas I remembered well, that when I first walked about the streets of Philadelphia, *eating my roll*, I saw most of the houses in Walnut Street . . . with bills on to be let. . . ." [21] When, finally, he achieves world-wide fame by his electrical experiments, he confesses to being flattered by the honors heaped upon him: "for, *considering my low beginning*, they were great things to me." [22] By now he has no need to mention the symbolic rolls.

Franklin's confessed *errata* are analogous to Christian's bundle of sins and to the giant Despair, over which he must prevail in

[19] *Ibid.*, p. 23.
[20] *Ibid.*, p. 27. Italics are mine.
[21] *Ibid.*, p. 65. Italics are mine.
[22] *Ibid.*, p. 123. Italics are mine.

order to gain the Heavenly City. Carl Van Doren has said that Franklin owed his success to "natural gifts of which Poor Richard could not tell the secret." [23] But Franklin was not altogether without a sense of sin, and he believed that good works were the necessary means to personal salvation, or success. Obversely, as his attitude toward charity in the *Autobiography* indicates, he felt that failure to rise in life was the result of moral turpitude. Accordingly, in one of the most famous passages of the *Autobiography*, about the year 1728 Franklin "conceived the bold and arduous project of arriving at moral perfection." [24] The important point is not that he failed, but that he tried and that the program of good works which he outlined here and elsewhere, in effect, completed the long process of dismantling the Celestial City. A tale by Nathaniel Hawthorne, "The Celestial Railroad," suggests an ironic inversion of Bunyan's original allegory. Franklin, in his pilgrimage toward the Heavenly City, sends his baggage ahead by postal service and sets up signposts for other travelers. He fills the Slough of Despond with Philadelphia cobblestones and almanacs. He lights the Valley of the Shadow of Death with street lamps. He smites Apollyon with a thunderbolt. He throws a bridge over the River Styx.

In the spiritual drama of a chosen people lay the source of that economic romanticism, so frequently confused with materialism, by which so many Americans have assumed a God-given right to the fruits of an Edenic tree. As Franklin said, "The Divine Being seems to have manifested his Approbation . . . by the remarkable Prosperity with which He has been pleased to favour the whole Country." [25] Americans after Franklin would merely inherit the earth by presumption and without waiting for Divine Approbation. Franklin's motives for land speculation were not sordidly pecuniary, but included, as did his enthusiasm for science, a poetic conception of national destiny. Thus, he called his proposed colony on the Ohio the future "paradise on earth." [26] The outbreak of the Revolution ended his petition to the Crown for western lands, but Americans came into a larger inheritance. To a great degree the American passion for liberty was an ex-

---

[23] Van Doren, *op. cit.*, p. 118.
[24] Franklin, *Autobiography*, p. 83.
[25] *Writings*, VIII, 614.
[26] Quoted by Van Doren, *op. cit.*, p. 592.

tension of the passion to possess the earthly inheritance. This passion was not essentially economic, for Americans felt that they were enacting a spiritual pilgrimage in their westward trek toward light.

The spiritual longing of the colonists prepared the psychological foundations of the nineteenth-century concept of Manifest Destiny, which sanctioned American imperialism. Thus, Nathaniel Ames, Franklin's competitor in almanacs, predicted in 1758 that "as the celestial light of the gospel was directed here by the finger of God. . . . So arts and sciences will change the face of nature in their tour from hence over the Appalachian Mountains to the Western Ocean."[27] After Franklin's death Americans who were disappointed with the results of coastal civilization pursued their special destiny inland, continuing to read the promise of American life in the westward cycle of the sun. At the height of westward expansion in the nineteenth century, Fourth of July orators often recaptured the old millennial fervor and were typically lyrical in sun worship: "Christianity, rational philosophy, and constitutional liberty, like an ocean of light are rolling their resistless tide over the earth. . . . Doubtless there may be partial revulsions. But the great movement will . . . be progressive, till the millennial sun shall rise in all the effulgence of universal day."[28] Americans refashioned for their own use a conventional rhetoric of spirit which had antedated the voyage of Columbus.

Such sentiments inspired Jefferson's acquisition of Louisiana. Indeed, almost everything that has been said of Franklin applies as well to Jefferson. Although Jefferson was not a Puritan, his southern Protestant background (there is to this day a broad streak of Puritanism in southern Methodism and among southern Baptists) gave him a strong sense of mission. "Those who labor in the earth," he wrote in a famous passage from his *Notes on Virginia* in 1782, "are the chosen people of God, if ever He had a chosen people, whose breasts He has made His peculiar deposit for substantial and genuine virtue." In his first inaugural

---

[27] In Moses Coit Tyler, *A History of American Literature, 1607-1765* (Ithaca: Cornell University Press, 1949), p. 372.

[28] The previous quotation, typical of a great many in the literature of nineteenth-century westward expansion, is taken from Ralph H. Gabriel, *The Course of American Democratic Thought* (New York: The Ronald Press Co., 1940), p. 36.

address of 1801, which contained the seeds of modern isolationism, he thanked Providence for separating the chosen country
"by nature and a wide ocean from the exterminating havoc of
one quarter of the globe." He devoted his life to preserving
the garden land from infiltration by a devilish European aristocracy of kings, nobles, and priests whose conspiratorial centers
were the cities of Europe. So long as agriculture remained our
chief object, he thought, we should remain virtuous: "When we
get piled upon one another in large cities, as in Europe, we shall
become corrupt as in Europe, and go to eating one another as
they do there." [29]

In the cities of Europe one found the best opportunity to
observe the exploitation of the many by the few. Again and again
he attacked this concentration of privilege, which during his
embassy he saw at first hand. On several occasions he warned
against sending American students to Europe for fear that they
would acquire a "fondness for European luxury and dissipation,
and a contempt for the simplicity of [their] own country." Above
all, he feared that they would contract a "partiality for aristocracy or monarchy" and look with abhorrence upon "the lovely
equality which the poor enjoy with the rich" in their own country.
He shuddered at the misery produced by European manufacturing, which, instead of extending the comforts of life to all
classes, further debased the masses and strengthened the hand
of privilege. He welcomed the French Revolution accordingly
as a continuation of the American struggle in behalf of the rights
of man. When this revolution failed, he was depressed but
blamed its failure and excesses primarily upon the "canaille of
the cities of Europe" who had been too long perverted by the
"tinsel-aristocracy" to be capable of virtuous self-government.
"The mobs of great cities," he said on another occasion, "add
just so much to the support of pure government, as sores do
to the strength of the human body." [30] Cities, like manufacturing and like aristocracy, were a product of artifice and therefore
unnatural and evil. To preserve her virtue, America must remain
a land of nature.

- -

[29] *The Complete Jefferson; Containing His Major Writings, Published and
Unpublished, Except His Letters,* ed. Saul K. Padover (New York: Duell,
Sloan & Pearce, Inc., 1943), pp. 678, 385, 123.
[30] *Ibid.,* pp. 1056, 286, 679.

Was there anything America could learn from Europe? Strangely, there was. On the negative side there was the spectacle, in each country's politics and courts, of humanity acting like beasts of prey, cautioning a patriotic avoidance of similar behavior. On the positive side, agriculture, the lighter mechanical arts, and manufactures might be worth a "superficial view." Of the nobler arts, those of architecture and gardening were particularly useful and instructive. Europe's gardens were especially worthy of the attention of Americans, "because [America] is the country of all others where the noblest gardens may be made without expense." But, on the whole, the risk of weakening the virtues of the heart—that is, the generous passions inculcated by nature—through oversophistication in the courts and inns of Europe outweighed the advantages to be gained. One did not want the aid of foreign travel to render oneself precious to his country. Jefferson's stay in Europe, in the main, merely confirmed his image of America. When he called the French the most benevolent people he had ever known and France his second choice among the nations, he was thinking not of "the man of the old world, crowded within limits either small or overcharged, and steeped in the vices which that situation generates," but of the new France, which during his stay promised to be the first of European nations to respond to America's world mission of regeneration. What attracted Jefferson's sympathy was the stirring of the same hopes in the French masses and among French intellectuals like Lafayette that kindled the American Revolution.[31]

Living through the period of partisan political struggles from within and of repeated military threats from without which followed Franklin's death, Jefferson was more concerned than Franklin with the supposed invasion of America by European civilization. He saw the beginning of this invasion in the cities of the eastern seaboard. He was accordingly dubious about sending his grandson to Philadelphia for his education and in this connection wrote to his friend Dr. Wistar, "I am not a friend to placing growing men in populous cities, because they acquire there habits and partialities which do not contribute to the happiness of their after life." He lectured both his daughter and grandson on such upper-class vices as indolence, dissipation,

---

[31] For this paragraph see *ibid.*, pp. 820-821, 1192.

and novel-reading. Above all, he viewed the cities and the eastern states—by which he generally meant the northeastern states, including New York—as the breeding ground of diabolical plots to foist European privilege in the form of monarchy or artistocracy upon the American people. He thought, for instance, that Massachusetts and Connecticut were further advanced in the principle of hereditary privilege than Virginia. Hamilton's "monarchical cabal" of 1787 was hatched in the eastern states. Attempts to sabotage his Embargo and Non-Intercourse Acts originated with "good citizens" in the East who were "dupes" of England. The strongholds of Federalism, which was infected with English principles of government, were the eastern cities.[32]

Jefferson was frequently explict in identifying Federalism with the transplantation to America of European aristocracy. He regarded the issue of aristocracy versus democracy as the great issue of his day, to be settled only with the demise of Federalism. The Federalist stress upon a strong executive government seemed to prove to him a love of monarchy, and he never tired of repeating the view that Colonel Hamilton and his friends wanted a king and a house of lords. Such Federalists, moreover, used devilish European methods of deceit and deception. Afraid to wear their true name of monarchists, he said, "they creep under the mantle of federalism." Their manipulation of finances and the public debt, for instance, was a species of swindling like the French Mississippi Bubble, and their appointment of the "Midnight Judges" was a highhanded piece of treachery designed to circumvent the will of the people. They also had direct ties with Europe, particularly with England, through their commercial interests and wealth. The English and the French, he wrote bitterly to Elbridge Gerry in 1797, "have wished a monopoly of commerce and influence with us; and they have in fact obtained it."

When we take notice that theirs is the workshop to which we go for all we want; that with them centre either immediately or ultimately all the labors of our hands and lands; that to them belongs either openly or secretly the great mass of our navigation; that even the factorage of their affairs here, is kept to themselves by facti-

---

[32] *Basic Writings of Thomas Jefferson*, ed. Philip S. Foner (New York: Wiley Book Co., 1944), pp. 672, 553-554, 755; *The Complete Jefferson*, pp. 280-285, 559, 1211-1213, 1273.

tious citizenships; that these foreign and false citizens now constitute the great body of what are called our merchants, fill our sea ports, are planted in every little town and district of the interior country, sway everything in the former places by their own votes and those of their dependants, in the latter, by their insinuations and the influence of their ledgers; that they are advancing fast to a monopoly of our banks and public funds, and thereby placing our public finances under their control; that they have in their alliance the most influential characters in and out of office; when they have shewn that by all these bearings on the different branches of government, they can force it to proceed in whatever direction they dictate, and bend the interest of this country entirely to the will of another; when all this, I say, is attended to, it is impossible for us to say we stand on independent ground, impossible for a free mind not to see and to groan under the bondage in which it is bound.[33]

Federalism, in other words, was not simply a party program; it was a gigantic European conspiracy to subvert America. Jefferson attributed its ultimate failure to the character of the American people, which was different from that of the French rabble.

As a barrier to "creeping monarchy," Jefferson advanced his preference for a strong legislative branch, advocated a bill of rights, and emphasized the role of the separate states in resisting "executive usurpation." The Jeffersonian attitude that "that government is best which governs least," which grew out of early fears of foreign tyranny has, as part of American tradition, been transferred to the often irrational distrust of one's own democratic government, which Americans have managed remarkably to disassociate from themselves. And they have tended to regard their own representatives at the seat of the government as "politicians," with all the connotations of corruption and lurking criminality once reserved for European political authority. But Jefferson's chief answer to the threat of "creeping monarchy" was to elevate the standard of nature which he associated with the peculiar character of his country. Thus, men possessed the right of self-government by virtue of their receiving it "from the hand of nature." From the precepts of nature he derived many of his practical measures for containing the growth of aristocracy. It was incompatible, he thought, for a people "surrounded by so many blessings from nature" to be loaded with

---

[33] *Basic Writings*, pp. 637, 800; *The Complete Jefferson*, pp. 280, 321-322, 367, 377.

misery by "kings, nobles and priests, and by them alone." He struck at a native priesthood with his Virginia statute for religious freedom, which, he said, followed nature's "standard of reason." He advised against the formation of the Order of the Cincinnati on similar grounds and wiped away the legal basis in Virginia for the creation of an artificial aristocracy by having laws passed against the Entail. He hoped that America would produce for its leadership a natural aristocracy of virtue and talent. His University of Virgina was intended to contribute to that end.

For Jefferson, one of the cardinal precepts of nature, once liberty was assured, was simplicity. Accordingly, when in public office, he encouraged a simplicity and frugality of government which extended from the management of public expenditures to rules of etiquette and the style of state papers. He frequently contrasted the Republican simplicity of a virtuous agricultural nation with the complex machinations of monarchists at home and abroad. Aristocratic oversophistication corrupted language as well as morals. For this reason, he was glad to be able to trace the roots of the American language to the "primitive felicity and simplicity" of Anglo-Saxon usages, and he criticized those Americans who were "seduced" too much by Greek and Latin structures with their multiplication of rules and distinctions. In this respect, he was particularly critical of "monarchical writers" like Hamilton. Hamilton's object from the beginning, he thought, was to throw the accounts of the United States into forms which would be "utterly undecypherable." If Mr. Gallatin, to be the new Secretary of the Treasury, would put them in a form as simple as they would admit, he would merit "an immortal honor." "The accounts of the United States," said Jefferson, unconsciously echoing More's *Utopia*, "ought to be, and may be made as simple as those of a common farmer, and capable of being understood by common farmers." [34] The cult of the simple, carried to much greater lengths than Jefferson himself would go, makes understandable a traditional American impatience with speculative thought, with rigorous analysis, with precise use of terminology and language as tools for communication, with difficult new art forms, with efforts to understand

[34] Quoted in Gilbert Chinard, *Thomas Jefferson; the Apostle of Americanism* (Boston: Little, Brown & Co., 1933), p. 310.

increasingly complex public issues and governmental operations on other than moral grounds.

Simplicity of manner and institutional functions was for Jefferson synonymous with moral integrity. His reason for this relationship was, first, that unobstructed nature as designed in the act of creation worked for moral ends, and, secondly, as a corollary, that nature had implanted in man a moral instinct which sprung from the unstudied promptings of the heart. Jefferson's whole idea of virtue assumed this. belief; the Enlightenment faith in the perfectibility of man depended upon it. The purpose of education, which Jefferson gave a high pre-eminence, was not so much to improve upon nature as to fortify the moral sense in its eternal conflict with self-love.[35] But, in the main, as much as Jefferson valued reason, especially natural reason, and employed the conceptual tools of reason, he still tended to distrust the head. He considered the head an instrument of that calculating self-love which begot all entrenched privilege, and he valued the heart as the seat of humanitarian impulses. Thus, he made the heart the heroine of his dialogue between the head and heart. To his friend Mrs. Cosway he wrote, "Morals were too essential to the happiness of man, to be risked on the uncertain combinations of the head. [Nature] laid their foundation, therefore, in sentiment, not in science. That she gave to all, as necessary to all; this to a few only, as sufficing with a few." [36] Jefferson's virtual abandonment of the earlier Puritan view of unregenerate man and his emphasis on sentiment looked forward to the creation of an American Adam by romantic nationalism; it also had much in common with the earlier Renaissance vogue of the fool.

The main difference between Jefferson and Franklin is that Jefferson's progressive impulses were almost wholly measured by the regression to nature, while Franklin's mediated between a similar primitivism and the forward thrust of civilization. One seldom hears in Jefferson, for instance, the soft shuffle of success, because he already belonged to an established élite. But even in this respect the lifelines of Franklin and Jefferson tended to converge in time, as both identified their careers with a "rising

---

[35] Cf. *The Complete Jefferson*, pp. 1032-1034. Jefferson's speculation about the moral sense was influenced, of course, by the Scotch moralists.
[36] *Ibid.*, p. 829.

nation" and Jefferson lived long enough to change his mind
about certain things. Both were drawn to scientific study and
experimentation—first by their enormous respect for and curiosity about nature and secondly by their desire to "do good" in
the pragmatic sense of discovering useful truths. Since nature
reconciled the "is" and the "ought," each believed that the art
of virtue could be practiced in science as in other things. Jefferson defined usefulness as that "which contributes to fix in the
principles and practices of virtue." Their dedication to "natural
philosophy" delivered both from the backwoods of America to
the most civilized centers of Europe. Jefferson alone protested
this unholy alliance through science. "As for France and England, with all their pre-eminence in science," he wrote to John
Adams in 1812, "the one is a den of robbers, and the other of
pirates. And if science produces no better fruits than tyranny,
murder, rapine and destitution of national morality, I would
rather wish our country to be ignorant, honest and estimable, as
our neighboring savages are." [37] Jefferson nevertheless remained
a friend of science.

The application of scientific principles to business enterprise
spurred the rise of urban industrialism. Franklin felt more at
home than Jefferson in an urban environment, but even Franklin's acceptance of urban culture was conditioned upon its modification in America by civic improvements whose objective was
to harmonize material and moral progress. The myth of newness after all demanded that the garden land must not be contaminated in a moral sense. Jefferson was from the beginning
opposed to manufacturing on moral grounds. During his administration, however, enterprising New England merchants,
without his knowledge, imported the English technicians who
were to launch the industrial revolution in America. Jefferson's
own embargo of 1808 unwittingly encouraged the development
and consumption of home manufactures. He finally had to bow
to a *fait accompli*, though he had to satisfy himself, as will be
seen, that manufacturing *could* be moral in its effects upon the
public character. Experience taught him too that "manufactures
are now as necessary to our independence as to our comfort . . .
how are circumstances changed!" [38] His efforts to stave off the

----

[37] *Basic Writings*, pp. 506, 702.
[38] *Ibid.*, pp. 744-745.

inevitable nevertheless resulted in the opening to settlement of vast new western territories where the myth of the Garden of Eden might yet be realized.

The conception of America as a land of virtue was largely responsible for a national compulsion which tended to confuse material and moral progress by seeing an identity between them. It was also responsible for the waves of criticism which first greeted the new industrial order. The orgies of self-criticism have not been less patriotic than the shouts of progress, however, functioning very much like the early New England institution of the jeremiad, recalling a chosen people to righteousness. Liberals and conservatives alike have been moralists, forever pitting themselves, as Richard Hofstadter has remarked, against the fancied evils of life, forever demanding changes, improvements, cure-alls. Since Colonial days, in fact, there has been a marked tendency to regard America as having greater moral obligations than other nations and therefore to consider her sins more heinous than those of other nations.[39]

An unfortunate result has been much exaggeration of America's deficiencies by patriotic citizens and an equally unfortunate exaggeration of her innocence and uniqueness in terms of moral (material, political, economic) superiority. By their great prestige as culture heroes, Franklin and Jefferson contributed significantly to a national superiority complex which alternated between an isolationism which would retreat behind a *cordon sanitaire* of protecting oceans to a hermetically sealed paradise in the Mississippi Valley, and a messianic internationalism which would make the world over in the American image. Above all, they helped to ease the coming of the industrial revolution by insisting that useful improvements are the handmaid of civic virtue. The old antithesis between primitivism and progress was to be transcended by the promise of still greater material abundance without a corresponding lapse in public morals. The garden image thus accommodated itself to the image of a scientific paradise.

----

[39] Cf. Perry Miller, *The New England Mind: From Colony to Province* (Cambridge: Harvard University Press, 1953), pp. 33-34.

8

National

Self-consciousness

and the Concept

of the Sublime

A dominant characteristic of the fifty-year period following the American Revolution was the rise of national self-consciousness, reflected by patriotic experiments in literature, in fine arts, in science, and in other areas of culture. Cultural nationalism was whetted by the War of 1812, and by the end of the period had made its way into foreign policy with the Monroe Doctrine and into domestic policy with Henry Clay's American system of protective tariffs and internal improvements. Celebrating the grandeur of native scenery especially fulfilled the psychological needs of a nation thirsting for greatness. National pride in the rude native scene as contrasted to the supposedly effete European civilization helped produce our first school of landscape painting, Cooper's evocation of the ideal American as a frontier type, and the nature philosophy of Bryant, Emerson, and Thoreau.

It also stimulated our first significant contributions to science. Jefferson expected that the acquisition of Louisiana would result in the enlargement of scientific knowledge, and he instructed Lewis and Clark to take careful note of the country's soil, rivers, mountains, minerals, vegetation, and animals. The notable achievements of the Bartrams in botany, of Jedidiah Morse in geography, William McClure in geology, Thomas Say in entomology, and Alexander Wilson and John Audubon in ornithology were closely connected with explorations and travels in the wilderness. That these travelers were motivated in large part by a patriotic love of the American landscape is indicated by the fact that they did not restrict themselves to exact scientific measurement and description, but were also poetical, sprinkling their letters and journals liberally with expressions of admiration for the picturesque and romantic.[1] One Dr. James DeKay noted in 1826 that exploration of American forests had awakened a widely diffused feeling of nationality among our naturalists—"a feeling which has impelled them to study and examine for themselves, instead of blindly using the eyes of foreign naturalists, or bowing implicitly to the decisions of a foreign bar of criticism." Dr. Daniel Drake, who founded a medical college in Cincinnati, acknowledged the inspiration of American nature in attempts to establish a cultural pre-eminence when he wrote: "Let the architects of our national greatness conform to the dictates of science; and the monuments they construct will rise beautiful as our hills, imperishable as our mountains, and lofty as their summits, which tower sublimely above the clouds."[2]

A significant word in Drake's rhapsody, marking a transition between eighteenth- and nineteenth-century views of nature, is "sublimely." The word "sublime" was commonly reserved in this period of national development for the more awe-inspiring aspects of the landscape such as the spectacle of crocodiles locked in mortal combat, the passage of the Potomac through the clefts of the Blue Mountains, the cascade of Niagara, the vast stretch of the Mississippi through limitless prairie plains, and, of course, the majestic forests and mountains. Jefferson though it "worth a voyage across the Atlantic to see these objects; much more to paint, and make them, and thereby ourselves, known to all ages." How sublime it was, he thought, "to look down into the workhouse of nature, to see her clouds, hail, snow, rain, thunder, all fabricated at our feet!" He considered Virginia's Natural Bridge "the most sublime of nature's works": "If the view from the top

---

[1] Cf. Mary E. Woolley, "The Development of the Love of Romantic Scenery in America," *American Historical Review*, III (1898), 56-66.

[2] DeKay and Drake are quoted in Merle Curti, *The Growth of American Thought*, 2d ed. (New York: Harper & Bros., 1951), pp. 252-253.

be painful and intolerable, that from below is delightful in an equal extreme. It is impossible for the emotions arising from the sublime to be felt beyond what they are here; so beautiful an arch, so elevated, so light, and springing as it were up to heaven! the rapture of the spectator is really indescribable!"[3] Jefferson's concern here was not with nature as a logical concept or even as a substantive reality demonstrating logical concepts, but with nature as an object of human feeling. His emotional intensification of nature had more in common with romantic poetry than with the eighteenth-century veneration for a harmonious universe governed by natural law.

In England the sublime had been a principal ingredient in the late eighteenth-century vogue of Gothic terror and in the popularity of the savage landscapes painted a century before by the European painters, Salvator Rosa and Claude Lorraine.[4] An influential formulation of the concept of the sublime for Americans was Edmund Burke's *Philosophical Inquiry into the Origin of Our Ideas of the Sublime and Beautiful*, first published in England in 1756.[5] Burke revived Longinus' concept of the sublime from antiquity in protest against the uninspired formalism of much English neoclassical literature, which imitated the balance and formal perfection of classical literature without heeding Aristotle's injunction to imitate nature and which found pleasure in the typically symmetrical eighteenth-century garden rather than in mountains.[6] By reinstating the sublime, evocative of awe and terror, Burke intended that literature and, to a certain extent, painting (which actually came nearer to the classical meaning of *mimesis*), should be measured by their

---

[3] *The Complete Jefferson; Containing His Major Writings, Published and Unpublished, Except His Letters,* ed. Saul K. Padover (New York: Duell, Sloan & Pearce, Inc., 1943), pp. 581, 826.

[4] The influence of these two painters on English taste is the subject of Elizabeth W. Manwaring, *Italian Landscape in Eighteenth Century England* (New York: Oxford University Press, 1925). The standard treatment of the sublime in eighteenth-century English aesthetics is Samuel H. Monk, *The Sublime* (New York: Modern Language Assoc., 1935).

[5] Edmund Burke, *A Philosophical Inquiry into the Origin of Our Ideas of the Sublime and Beautiful* (Philadelphia, 1806). I find ten different American editions of this work issued between 1800-1856.

[6] Cf. Irving Babbitt, *The New Laokoön* (Boston: Houghton Mifflin Co., 1910), pp. 9-27; Myra Reynolds, *The Treatment of Nature in English Poetry* . . . (Chicago: University of Chicago Press, 1909), p. 15.

sheer power in stirring emotions. Burke's treatment enthroned
subjectivity and helped the romantic artist to free himself from
the neoclassical aesthetic of imitation.

It doubly helped the American artist, who had to contend
not only with an enslaving aesthetic, but also with charges of
cultural imitativeness. American poets and painters turned to
the sublime for emotional intensification of American scenery
both to assert personal freedom as romantic artists and to assert
their cultural independence of Europe as Americans. European
in origin, like so many other unacknowledged importations, the
concept of the sublime in the hands of American artists wedded
native creativity to native subject matter. Thus, William Cullen
Bryant's lectures on poetry in 1825, which issued a declaration
of independence for American poetry, coupled a defence of
native materials with a sharp denial that poetry was an imitative
art. Like Burke, Bryant emphasized the view that emotion was
the mainspring of poetry.[7] Washington Allston performed a similar service for American painting in lectures which were to
bear fruit for Thomas Cole, the father of American landscape
painting. The chief departure from Burke in these lectures, a
typically American difference, was the insistence that the passions released into art by the sublime be harnessed to lofty
spiritual ends commensurate with a land of virtue whose highest
genius was dedicated to the redemption of mankind.

Patriotic sentiment centered in the sublime made the religion
of nature virtually a national religion. Foremost among early
American artists who fostered such a conception of nationality
were the poet William Cullen Bryant and the painter Thomas
Cole.[8] Cole's attraction to the American landscape usually com-
bined sentiments of piety and patriotism as in the following
statement, productive of his trip to Europe: "The painter of
American scenery has, indeed, privileges superior to any other.
All nature here is new to art. No Tivolis, Ternis, Mont Blancs,
Plinlimmons, hackneyed and worn by daily pencils of hundreds;

---

[7] William Cullen Bryant, *Prose Writings,* ed. Parke Godwin, 2 vols. (New
York, 1884), I, 5ff.

[8] Professor Perry Miller first made me aware of this connection. Donald A.
Ringe, "Kindred Spirits: Bryant and Cole," *American Quarterly,* VI (Fall,
1954), 233-244, describes their moral and religious feeling for nature without noting its national coloration or indebtedness to the concept of the
sublime.

but primeval forests, virgin lakes, and waterfalls . . . hallowed
to his soul by their freshness from the creation. . . ."[9] Similar
sentiments informed his "Essay on American Scenery," published
in 1836, in which he quoted lines from his friend Bryant's poems,
"The Prairies" and "Autumn Woods." Painter and poet in this
period often collaborated in attempting to establish a distinctively
native art. But it was more difficult for painters than for poets
to free themselves from the aesthetics of imitation. Even Burke
had set limits on the capability of painting to convey a sense of
the sublime. He considered it ridiculous, for instance, for painting to cultivate obscurity, which was an important source of
the sublime, and thought that the passions were best aroused
by words.[10] In line with this reasoning, in 1766, the influential
German critic, Lessing reaffirmed the almost forgotten Renaissance distinction between the ends of poetry, which were to
express human actions and emotion, and the ends of painting,
which were to be purely descriptive. He seemed to excuse the
plastic artist from the need to invent.[11] Thus, Bryant's declaration of independence for poetry, adhering to the convention,
extolled poetry at the expense of the plastic arts: "There is no
propriety in applying to poetry the term *imitative* in a literal
and philosophical sense, as there is in applying it to painting
and sculpture. . . . The truth is, painting and sculpture are, literally, imitative arts. . . ."[12]

The romantic painter in America naturally found such limitations intolerable. As one critic of the period said, "He will try
language, perhaps, and write poems, because the poem does not
pretend to imitate, only to celebrate the beauty of the universe."[13] With other limners Thomas Cole aspired to write poetry

---

[9] Cole's journal entry for July 6, 1835, in Louis Legrand Noble, *The Course
of Empire and Other Pictures of Thomas Cole, N. A. Life and Works* (New
York, 1853), p. 202.

[10] Burke, *op. cit.*, pp. 83-89.

[11] Gotthold E. Lessing, *Laocoön, an Essay upon the Limits of Painting and
Poetry*, trans. E. Frothingham (Boston, 1874), pp. 73-75.

[12] Bryant, *Prose Writings*, I, 5-6.

[13] Philip G. Hamerton, "Transcendentalism in Painting," *Thoughts About
Art* (Boston, 1888), p. 91. Among American artists of this period who turned
to creative writing or illustrating books were Washington Allston, the
sculptor William Wetmore Story, William Dunlap, George Harvey, A. B.
Durand, Thomas Doughty, and Daniel Huntington. Horace's *ut pictura
poesis* ("in painting as in poetry") was an important credo at this time.

and short stories as well as to paint; he also consciously tres-
passed on poetry's domain of the sublime in his canvases. "He
who has no such conceptions," Cole explained, "no power of creation, is no real painter. . . . His works ought not to be a dead imitation of things, without the power to impress a sentiment, or
enforce the truth." [14] He felt that the national ideal in art was
being daily betrayed by a host of copyists, portraitists, genre
painters, and by a public which purchased pictures as if they
were palpable things like merchandise. "Would you know what is
going on here in the way of art?" he asked a friend. "It is difficult
to say, except that Tom has painted a portrait which shames the
old masters; Dick has just finished a red herring to the very
life; and Harry has completed his grand historical picture of
the Pig-Killing." [15] Cole greeted the daguerreotype as the symbol
of a degenerate mechanical age—as if, he said derisively, "the
poor craft of painting was knocked on the head by this new
machinery for making Nature take her own likeness. . . . The
art of painting is a creative, as well as an imitative art." [16] With
such ideas it was almost inevitable that Cole should turn to
nature symbolism and allegory in his painting, vying with the
poet.

Another alternative might have been some form of expres-
sionism, but he was barred from this by his moral predilections
and by those of his society. Even so, in certain phases of their
discovery of the sublime, influenced by Burke and the German
Sturm und Drang, both Cole and Bryant occasionally reveled in
the wild, tumultuous aspects of nature which they associated
with the "wild grandeur peculiar to our country." Thus Bryant
recorded in delicious detail "a brief moment of astonishment and
terror" while watching a whirlwind advance upon the summits
of a forest.[17] With Byronic abandonment, Cole described a
Catskill storm in which he thought himself "careering, in a
chariot of rock, through airy wastes beyond the reach of gravi-
tation, with no law but my own will." He said, "I shouted—sung
—whistled for the very horror of the thing." [18] Some of these mo-

---

[14] Noble, *op. cit.,* pp. 116, 356.
[15] *Ibid.,* p. 339.
[16] *Ibid.,* p. 282.
[17] Bryant, *Prose Writings,* I, 172 ("The Whirlwind").
[18] Noble, *op. cit.,* pp. 69, 77.

ments of wild emotional unheaval Cole transferred to canvas, particularly in those pictures in which diminutive human figures stood in foregrounds of awesome scenic violence, dwarfed yet ennobled by the elements. One such picture, called "Salvator Rosa Sketching Banditti," plainly revealed that Cole's emotional response to nature owed much to the concept of the sublime. With the discovery of sublime nature, prints of Salvator Rosa and Claude Lorraine had multiplied in America, and literary allusions to them abounded. For their treatment of nature Washington Allston had advised Cole, leaving for Europe, to study Claude Lorraine and Salvator Rosa, "together with Turner." [19]

The canvases of Claude Lorraine, as distinguished from those of Salvator Rosa, captured nature in moments of quiet repose and therefore were better described by Burke's concept of the beautiful than by that of the sublime. Vying with one another in their ability to distinguish between the beautiful and the sublime in American art and literature, American critics frequently took Lorraine and Rosa as their aesthetic standard. Thus, Rufus Griswold referred to the "Claude-like beauty of Mr. Prescott's descriptions," and William Ware compared Allston's painting of "Elija in the Desert" to the sublimity of Salvator Rosa.[20] Critical controversy over the beautiful and the sublime caused Thomas Cole to lament, "The world requires much of us that was not demanded of the artist of antiquity. . . . He probably speculated little . . . on the sublime and beautiful. His faith was fixed." [21] But a graver cause of controversy was the moral and metaphysical issue which allusions to the two European artists revealed. The hero of Washington Irving's story, "The Painter's Adventure," recollected apropos of his plight, "that Salvator Rosa in his youth had voluntarily sojourned for a time among the banditti of Calabria, and had filled his mind with

---

[19] Jared B. Flagg, *The Life and Letters of Washington Allston* (New York, 1892), pp. 203-207. Allston also recommended Nicholas Poussin, Francesco Mola, and Titian.

[20] Rufus W. Griswold, *The Prose Writers of America* (Philadelphia, 1846), p. 19; William Ware, *Lectures on the Works and Genius of Washington Allston* (Boston, 1852), pp. 89-90. Other influential American critics who employed this terminology included Margaret Fuller, Henry Tuckerman, Ralph Waldo Emerson, Gulian C. Verplanck, James J. Jarves, Hugh S. Legare, Edgar Allan Poe, George T. Tucker, Charles Lanman, and Richard H. Dana.

[21] Noble, *op. cit.*, p. 379.

savage scenery and savage associations by which he was surrounded."[22] The presence of banditti surrounded by savage
scenery, featured also in Bryant's poem, "The Robber," suggested that the sublime tended to celebrate the lawlessness of
man in collusion with blind, amoral forces in nature.

This was a view of nature and man which many Americans associated with the fallen Old World. The concept of the beautiful,
on the other hand, with its accent on a gentle, regular beauty
was much more in harmony with the supposed morality and
beneficence of American nature. "Beauty," Emerson wrote, "is
the mark God sets upon virtue." The distinction between the
concepts of the beautiful and the sublime also corresponded in
a cultural sense to the distinction which Henry Nash Smith has
found between the agrarian image of cultivated nature and the
opposing image of the wilderness. The beautiful in American art
commonly described gentle, rolling countryside with glimpses
of cultivated fields and pastures, while the sublime represented a
radical withdrawal into primitive wilderness. The one reflected
progressive, the other regressive, tendencies. But in order to
maintain the fiction of America as an unspoiled garden in contrast to Europe and in the face of increasing urbanization and
industrialism, American writers and artists tried to merge the
two images of rural earth and sublime nature into a single image.
The reason was that the rural earth by itself was not quite wild
enough and sublime nature was too wild.

The kind of emotional self-indulgence released by the sublime
led the historian of the sublime in England, Samuel Monk, to
call the English development "a sort of Methodist revival in
art."[23] For Americans, it might have been revivalism, but it
certainly did not correspond to their ideas of Methodism, and,
on the whole, they were inclined to reject it as an immoral and
atheistic European importation. Thus American critics rejected
the chief English poets of the sublime—Godwin, Shelley, Keats
—and only partially accepted Byron, some of whose poems
were characterized as "the poetry of hell," or "of unsound moral
fibre." One critic, H. J. Brent, protesting the "fulsome and un-
discerning adulation" of Byron in certain quarters, compared

---

[22] Washington Irving, *Works*, 27 vols., Knickerbocker ed. (Philadelphia,
1870-1871), XVIII, 381-382.
[23] Monk, *op. cit.*, p. 235.

Byron invidiously with Salvator Rosa.[24] At the same time, Americans had need of the sublime to celebrate what they felt was peculiar and unique about American scenery, which the concept of the beautiful was incapable of expressing. What could be done, therefore, to salvage the sublime for patriotic service? The most popular solution was to substitute for the "false sublime," as Washington Allston called it, the "true sublime," a modification of Burke by the Scotch moralists—chiefly Kames, Blair, and Alison—which united sentiments of the sublime to a great moral idea assumed to exist in and behind nature. True sublimity, the influential critic James Jackson Jarves told American artists, being rightly joined only to things "imbued with the Divine essence or will," represented "the highest manifestation of those qualities which constitute Beauty." [25] The true sublime, then, was to be regarded in the light of an extension of the concept of the beautiful, which had long been associated with the ideas of the true and the good. This formula enlisted passion on the side of virtue.

What this meant in actual practice is again best illustrated in the works of Bryant and Cole. It meant in the first place that every manifestation of nature from the most gentle to the most terrifying was a moral symbol inspiring a reverential awe of deity. The true sublime now measured the terrible distance between God and man, as in Cole's description of Mt. Etna: "Sublime thou art!—a resting place for thought,/Thought reaching far above thy bounds; from thee/To HIM who bade the central fires construct/This wondrous fabric; lifted thy dread brow/To meet the sun while yet the earth is dark." [26] But more impor-

---

[24] William Ellery Leonard, *Byron and Byronism in America* (New York: Columbia University Press, 1907), pp. 102-103, 105-106; William Charvat, *The Origins of American Critical Thought, 1810-1835* (Philadelphia: University of Pennsylvania Press, 1936), pp. 40-46, 58. An amusing example of this filtering process is Washington Allston's denial of Burke's belief that feminine beauty depends in some measure upon sexual attraction. Allston argued that beauty in the female body depended upon moral virtue.

[25] James Jackson Jarves, *Art-Hints; Architecture, Sculpture, and Painting* (New York, 1855), p. 82.

[26] Thomas Cole, "Sicilian Scenery and Antiquities," *Knickerbocker Magazine,* XXIII (1844), 110. Cole paraphrases Bryant's "Oh God! Whose Dread and Dazzling Brow" and lines from Bryant's "A Hymn of the Sea." Cole once wrote to his friend Ver Bryck, "Pray give my best regards to Mr. Bryant . . . and tell him, that when I look at the mountains, I often think of him."

tantly, perhaps, the true sublime supplied a language of symbolism which better enabled the painter to compete with the poet. Cole was aware of the technical difficulties in trespassing upon poetry, in representing on canvas correspondences between the visible world and the moral, spiritual world. "The poetical conception of a subject may not be difficult," he wrote, "for it is spontaneous; but to imagine that which is to be embodied in light, and shadow, and colour,—that which is strictly pictorial— is an accumulative work of the mind." [27] Edmund Burke in his treatise on the sublime had recommended to painters of the sublime dramatic transitions from light to dark and favored the dark side of the spectrum over the "warmer" values of red, yellow, and green. Cole's forte became a clashing chiaroscuro, the moral significance of which made his canvases a battleground for the warfare of good and evil. At one side of his palette was white and at the other end black, between whose limits, like Winston Churchill, a more recent warrior in paint, he generated his power. Dramatic contrast was particularly noticeable in such allegorical "narratives" as "Past" and "Present," "Departure" and "Return," and "The Voyage of Life." Of his painting, "The Expulsion from the Garden of Eden," he wrote: "I have introduced the more terrible objects of nature, and have endeavoured to heighten the effect by giving a glimpse of the Garden of Eden in its tranquillity." [28]

The premonition of evil contained in this last picture typified a whole generation's fear of being dispossessed from paradise by the swift changes overtaking society and transforming the landscape of both America and Europe. But in America the bastion of nature had not yet been surrendered to industrial civilization. Where in Europe there remained only a few isolated pockets of wilderness for the poet and landscape painter, in America the wilderness stand backed up much the greater part of the nation. Looking across the continent, Cole observed that nature has spread for us "a rich and delightful banquet." "Shall we turn from it?" he asked. "We are still in Eden; the

---

Bryant and Cole in a sense revived the earlier Puritan attitude toward the inscrutable deity who manifested His secret will in the "remarkable providences" of nature.

[27] Noble, *op. cit.*, p. 276.

[28] *Ibid.*, p. 94.

wall that shuts us out of the garden is our own ignorance and folly." [29] His landscapes alternated between tranquil images of the beautiful designed to rekindle his countrymen's feelings for nature and images of terrifying sublimity which pronounced a judgment upon their ignorance of nature and their folly for departing from it.

The main tension in the work of both Bryant and Cole came from the polarity of nature and civilization. In their drama of good and evil the dark, violent sublimity of nature now served as a salutary warning against the ravages of civilization. Thus, storms symbolized "the clash of arms and pools of blood," against which "the earth has stood aghast." The calms which followed storms, when "on all the peaceful world the smile of heaven shall lie," were sometimes emblematic of the desire for peace after centuries of Old World strife.[30] Cole expressed this sentiment in paint by a stream of light from a patch of blue heaven on an otherwise darkened canvas, as in "The Tornado" or "View near Ticonderoga." "In the pure blue sky," he once wrote, "is the highest sublime. . . . There we look into the uncurtained, solemn serene—into the eternal, the infinite—toward the throne of the Almighty." [31]

But Bryant and Cole also turned to nature as a symbol of reassuring permanence amidst change, a restorative and refuge from a frenetic, utilitarian civilization. In such moods they found a quieter language, a gentler style, which sentimental convention accorded to the beautiful. At such times, the mountain wind played the role of a healing balm. It "stooped" (because emanating from on high) to "kiss" or "caress" the "fair bosom" of earth. What Cole could not convey by impersonation on his canvas, he tried to convey through suggestion by means of color, line, selection and arrangement of detail. He represented the soft, the fresh, the healing in nature by the warm colors of "tender green," red, and yellow.[32] He used line to contribute to

---

[29] Cole, "Essay on American Scenery," *American Monthly Magazine*, second series, I (1836), 12.

[30] The quotations are from Bryant's poem, "After a Tempest," but could be matched by a number of Cole's statements. In writing Cole habitually rendered storms in the metaphors of military conflict.

[31] Noble, *op. cit.*, p. 376.

[32] This is Cole's own exposition of semiology. See Noble, *op. cit.*, p. 274. The personification in the passage referred to compares with that in Bryant's "Mountain Wind."

the atmosphere of restfulness, stressing the panoramic sweep of horizon melting into the soft mist of distant mountain and sky, as in "River in the Catskills." His "quieter mood" filtered out such discordant notes as jagged rocks and precipices, gnarled Salvatorean trees, cascades, storm clouds, woodchoppers, laborers, villages, and cities in preference for gentle, rolling countryside opening on cultivated fields and pastures through which meandered peaceful streams lined with feathery foliage and flowers.[33] His tiny human figures, everywhere subordinate in interest to the features of the landscape, were, in the main, engaged in leisurely contemplation and enjoyment of the scene before them.

Such evocations obviously reinforced the Jeffersonian dream of rural bliss and, as idealizations having little to do with agrarian reality, had special appeal for weary city-dwellers. Indeed, many of these pictures were commissioned by them. It would be misleading to suggest, therefore, that the American dream of paradise was a monopoly of an agricultural people. The irony is that sophisticated urbanites could cherish dreams of rural bliss and at the same time display attitudes of condescension toward the rude life of the farmyard and pioneer clearing. Their refined contempt for manual labor confirmed the nativist suspicion that America was being invaded by the European aristocracy. Thousands of pioneers went west, as Hamlin Garland once put it, "to get a start where the cursed European aristocracy hadn't got a holt on the people." [34]

At Cole's death, some of his friends, remembering only his gentler moods, felt that his life was an affirmation of the joy of living. Reverend Orville Dewey, for instance, believed that he belonged "to the earth and the sky, to the serene day, the lovely sunset, the living verdure, the soft, warm, breathing air, not to the grave. He was a son of morning." A recent critic has said that Cole "voiced the faith and optimism of an America looking forward a hundred years ago." [35] But this is to miss the

[33] Cf. Kenneth J. LaBudde, "The Rural Earth: Sylvan Bliss," *American Quarterly*, X, no. 2, Part 1 (Summer, 1958), p. 149.

[34] Hamlin Garland, *Main-Travelled Roads* (New York: Harper & Bros., 1899), p. 139.

[35] Dewey's letter to Bryant in Bryant, *Prose Writings*, II, 34; Esther I. Seaver, *Thomas Cole*, Exhibition Catalogue (Hartford: Wadsworth Atheneum and Whitney Museum, 1949), p. 15.

melancholy which pervades all his work in the felt juxtaposition of American forests and cities. One has only to consider Cole's treatment of trees. In fact, both Bryant and Cole, in their senti-mental regard for nature, reserved a special role for trees. Cole said they were "like men, differing widely in character," and he took particular pains in their delineation. Bryant noted Cole's care with trees, seeing in it "a robust vigour of hand . . . and a diversity of character which seems to me almost boundless." [36] The first victims of industrial progress, trees symbolized most forcibly for them nature's losing fight with civilization. They mourned to see trees fall before the axe, leaving "ghastly wounds" in the "green bosom of the woodland." On the other hand, they admired the spirit of defiance in lone gaunt, gnarled survivors of battles with the elements. Hence the attraction of sublime Salvatorean trees.

Cole always returned from his beloved Catskills to the city "with a presentiment of evil." He said, "What is sometimes called improvement in its march makes us fear that the bright and tender flowers of the imagination shall be all crushed beneath its iron tramp. . . ." He added that intercourse with men was daily deadening "that sense of the beautiful in nature which has been through all my early life such a source of delight." [37] Bryant also spoke of the primal curse which affected the "jostling crowd," and just as sorrowfully wrote in his poem, "Stanzas":

I have mixed with the world, and its follies
have stained me,
No longer your pure rural worshipper now.

Yet, like other romantic artists whose melancholy was in part a sentimental pose, they found that return to the wild seldom failed to refresh their spirits.

Their fear of industrial and social change delivered them to a morbid preoccupation with the passage of time. Yet, with other romantics, they discovered in nature's inner rhythms a great moral idea which helped to reconcile them somewhat to change. This was the principle of mutation of all things—again best illustrated for them by trees. "In the American forest," Cole wrote, "we find trees in every stage of vegetable life and decay

---

[36] William Cullen Bryant, *Orations and Addresses* (New York, 1873), p. 7.
[37] Noble, *op. cit.*, pp. 132, 191; Thomas Cole, "Essay on American Scenery," p. 3.

—the slender sapling . . . the giant in his prime . . . the hoary patriarch of the wood—on the ground lie prostrate decaying trunks that once waved their verdant heads in the sun and wind. . . ." [38] And Cole painted such trees, carefully, for their moral import. They exhibited the continuous miracle of life in its successive stages, periodically returning to nothingness, but promising a rebirth and novelty in a world increasingly circumscribed by science, which Bryant and Cole rendered in images of iron and steel. Bryant's poem, "Mutation," advised:

> Weep not that the world changes—did it keep
> A stable, changeless state, 'twere cause indeed
>   to weep.

Similarly, Cole wrote, "I sigh not for a stormless clime." [39] Yet weep and sigh they did, for their acceptance of mutation seemed to incline them neither to their society's roseate faith in progress nor to a tragic acceptance of less perfect states of being, including their personal extinction. The recurring cycles delivered them individually to what Norman Foerster has called "the somber certainty of the grave." They read their own fates in the natural history of a tree, and Bryant's lifelong fear of death was matched by Cole, through whose journals stalked the spectre-figure immortalized in Emerson's poem, "Days," and in Young's "Night Thoughts."

The single great theme of Bryant and Cole was the passage of time, charged with premonitions of the evil which would overtake their country if the people strayed from their original mission. Together they parceled the universe into packages labeled, with due regard for the mystery of their contents, Past, Present, Future, Life, Death, Eternity. In the minds of each the Past was represented symbolically by a place, a chamber, a cavern, out of which the enigmatic stream of life issued, as in the first picture of Cole's series, "The Voyage of Life," or in Bryant's poem, "The Past." Not having much sympathy with present trends or the future march of progress, they sought their country's present greatness in unspoiled nature or in legends of the past and fantasies of the future. The romantic Past appeared in Bryant's Indian legends and in such paintings by Cole as: "The Dream of Arcadia," "Past" and "Present," "Scene from the

---

[38] *Ibid.,* p. 9.
[39] Noble, *op. cit.,* p. 193.

Last of the Mohicans," "Chocura's Curse." The longing for the distant, the remote and faraway, was also expressed in Cole's nature landscapes by haze-filled aerial perspectives into which, as Bryant said, an arrow could be shot out of sight.

The faraway reminded them of the future, which the promise of American life assured Americans could be nobler and better than the present. During the agonies of the Civil War, the pen of the aging Bryant was busy with futurist fantasies. During this period, too, he reviewed Cole's paintings before the National Academy of Design. One poem written in this phase, "Castles in the Air," held Cole in sentimental retrospect. The "region in the clouds" recalled the aerial mirage in Cole's second picture of "The Voyage of Life," even to the colonnades, the architecture suggestive of "stately palaces, Gothic or Greek,/Or such as in the land of Mohammed/Uplift the crescent, or, in forms more strange,/Border the ancient Indus. . . ." The poem's fair guide with magical powers alluded to Cole's guardian angel in the same series. The bright vision of the poem then faded, giving way to the more tragic one of Cole's "Course of Empire," a position antithetical in the thinking of both poet and painter, who saw only decay in advanced stages of civilization— in this case, the blight of civil war. In the last two stanzas of the poem Bryant longed for "Nature's grander aspects" and returned in memory to a forest dwelling, similar to Cole's Catskill lodge, where "a glimpse was given/Of canvas, here and there along the walls."

For allegorical presentation Bryant and Cole symbolized Life by a flowing river, a journey, a pilgrimage, in which individuals, trees or human beings, participated briefly. These images belonged to the journey pattern of the rebirth archetype. Their central image for the flow of time was a stream, as in Cole's "The Voyage of Life." The introduction of temporal sequence into pictorial art, however, posed a special problem for Cole. He solved it by painting related series of pictures. Bryant considered the conception of the **series** for "The Voyage of Life" a "perfect poem." [40] In a sense **more** literal than Bryant perhaps realized, it was a poem, for Cole **was** quite aware that by painting progressive scenes in a series he was competing with poetry. "Poetry and Painting," Cole said, "sublime and purify thought,

---

[40] Bryant, *Orations and Addresses*, p. 25.

by grasping the past, the present, and the future." [41] Series such as "The Voyage of Life," he confessed to a prospective client, gave him "more scope for poetical invention, and are, perhaps, more capable of sentiment than subjects requiring only a single canvas." [42] He originally visualized "The Voyage of Life" as a poem, for in composing a poem from the canvas in memory of his friend, Ver Bryck, he devoted a "canto" to each picture.

Bryant and Cole were very similar in their allegorical development of the journey pattern. A few examples may throw further light on the problem of parallelism between the arts. Bryant's poem, "The Stream of Life," utilized the literary seasons, as did Cole in his painting, to mirror the different stages of human destiny. His poem, "A Lifetime," omitted the stream metaphor, but presented word pictures divided roughly into scenes representing infancy, youth, manhood, and old age, and corresponding to the stages of Cole's voyage of life series. "The Flood of Years" was pre-eminently a voyage of life à la Cole: an allegory with tragic overtones, told in a series of pictures, and ending on a note of religious hope suggestive of the archetypal rebirth. In the last part of the poem, beginning line 108, Bryant recast the allegorical figures borne beneath the flood into stages of youth, manhood, and old age. He associated the first stage with the "brood of Hope" and with flowers upon the bank, reminding one of the guardian angel, the flowers, and expanding horizons of Cole's first two pictures. The "brood of Hope" were replaced in the second stage by "forms of grisly aspect," corresponding to the "demon forms" of Cole's gloomy third picture.[43] In the final stage Bryant's flood passed a "dismal barrier," a "belt of darkness," to broaden into the Sea of Eternity and, hopefully, immortal life. Cole, too, in his final picture reached the Sea of Eternity, seen dimly beyond a dismal cloud and barrier of rocks. Cole injected his own intimation of immortality into the painting by revealing to the broken traveler an angelic being and by leading the spectator's eye from the intense chiaroscuro of the boat detail to a burst of light in the upper heavens.

In such grandiose allegorical conceptions of the passage of

----

[41] Cole, "Essay on American Scenery," p. 1.

[42] Noble, *op. cit.*, p. 251.

[43] It is possible here to make a rather precise comparison, because Cole once explained his symbolism for this series. Cf. Noble, *op. cit.*, pp. 287-290.

time Cole believed that he had achieved the "sublimest of the sublime." His venture beyond landscape into allegory had dated roughly from his European study trip, 1829-1832. Viewing his allegories and missing their intended relevance for American society, many Americans felt that he had lost that "earlier, wilder image" of his native forests and somehow betrayed his country. Thus, Charles Lanman's review of "The Course of Empire," a series conceived in Europe which sketched the rise and decline of a great civilization in a succession of lurid, violent scenes, displayed a curious blend of native pride and patriotic condescension: "He [Cole] has but set a noble example, which ought to be extensively followed. Mind, we do not mean by this that his subjects ought to be imitated. Far from it, because they are not stamped with a national character, as the production of all painters should be. Excepting his actual views of American scenery, the paintings of Cole might have been produced had he never set foot upon our soil." [44] With more justice another critic, Richard Henry Dana, attacked the strained, wooden quality in much of Cole's allegorizing. But Bryant was quick to defend his friend's allegorical turn against these critics, underscoring his preference for the "bolder manner" which Cole had brought back from Rome. In his funeral oration for Cole in 1848, he pointed out that such an allegorical series as "The Cross and the World" exemplified Cole's position "that landscape painting was capable of the deepest moral interest" and exclaimed of the third picture in the series, "The idea is Miltonic." [45] The critic Lanman could not know, as Bryant did, that Cole merged all his allegorical figures in landscapes which he got at first hand from close study of actual scenes, or that the moral themes of such allegories as "The Course of Empire" had application to the course of the American democracy.

The principle of mutation in nature—the birth, flowering, and decay of trees—taught Bryant and Cole a cyclical theory of human history in which great empires flourished and passed away. At the same time nature's slower rhythms pronounced a judgment on man's "feeble strife with time, and childish strug-

---

[44] Charles Lanman, "Cole's Imaginative Paintings," *Democratic Review*, XII (1843), 602-603. Lanman repeated this remark in the *Southern Literary Messenger*, June, 1849, p. 356.

[45] Bryant, *Orations and Addresses*, p. 33-34.

gles on the bosom of his mother earth." Symbol of permanence in change, Bryant's oak tree in his poem "Among the Trees" outlived "flitting generations of mankind." For Bryant as for Cole, a waterfall represented unceasing change and everlasting duration.[46] Cole's picture, "Mount Etna from Taormina," which Bryant hailed for its sublimity, contrasted the evanescent work of man in the ruins of the foreground with the enduring work of God. Bryant's poem, "The Fountain," remarked a similar contrast. The visible signs of mortal defeat amidst the permanent things of nature inevitably reminded Bryant and Cole of the theme for the Course of Empire. This theme, joined to that of mutation, appeared in dozens of Bryant's poems. Almost always, as in "The Prairies" or "A Walk at Sunset," his subject was the rise and decline of Indian nations. The last three lines of "A Walk at Sunset" anticipated "The Savage State" of Cole's epic:

> States fallen—new empires built upon the old—
> But never shalt thou see these realms again
> Darkened by boundless groves, and roamed by savage men.

Taking nature for its norm, the Course of Empire theme expressed both a warning against complacency to a modern civilization overconfident in its use of techniques and the hope that, in Bryant's words, "a nobler growth and a nobler age than ours" would win a triumph for the power of good "in the eternal strife between Evil and Good."

Cole conceived his idea for "The Course of Empire" amidst the ruins of Italy, where both he and Bryant, who visited Italy later, were fearfully impressed by what Bryant called "the tremendous warfare waged 'twixt good and evil." [47] They read in their European experience a lesson for America: America must avoid the mistakes of the corrupt, old European civilization. Thus, Cole, in his poem, "Lament of the Forest," dreamed of a paradise in the New World, remote from the destructive forces of Europe. But already, he noted, the work of desolation was beginning here, the skies "darkened by ascending smoke . . ./An altar unto Mammon":

---

[46] Cf. Cole's "Essay on American Scenery," p. 8. The preceding quotation of Cole's is from Noble, *op. cit.*, p. 154.

[47] From Bryant's poem, "Earth," written in Italy. Bryant's hope for a nobler future, quoted above, comes from "Among the Trees."

A few short years!—our ancient race shall be,
Like Israels', scattered 'mong the tribes of men.[48]

Cole's painting, "The Course of Empire," was a direct result of
this concern for the welfare of his country, particularly as it was
affected by the rising gospel of progress. His picture "Destruction" in that series was as much a reminder to the boastful young
republic which liked to compare itself to the glory that was
Greece and the grandeur that was Rome, as Turner's painting,
"The Decline of Carthage," was a warning to the conqueror of
Napoleon. Cole's motto for the series read: "First freedom, and
then glory; when that fails,/Wealth, vice, corruption." [49]

Bryant and Cole drew upon literary conventions, attitudes,
and themes common to many romantic artists both in America
and Europe and, as Americans, made them peculiarly their own.
In his use of nature symbolism and subjective coloring Cole was
of the school of Emerson, Thoreau, Hawthorne, and Melville.
He combined Emerson's regard for the pulsing life beneath the
rind of things with Hawthorne's knowledge of evil. Like Melville, he suffered some loss of reputation when he ventured into
allegory. Above all, Cole belonged to that great company of
American heroes and mythmakers who, in opposition to Europe,
wanted to simplify life and establish a garden of innocence in the
forests and plains of the New World and whose idea of progress
was retrospective and nature-centered.

In 1829, Bryant wrote an ode, "To Cole, the Painter, Departing for Europe," imploring him not to lose that "earlier, wilder
image" of his native forests. When Bryant reviewed Cole's
works in the midst of the Civil War, he passed over the allegories
in favor of the landscapes, which symbolized the lost innocence
of former days. The national guilt of civil war was the more
grievous, because many Americans, holding before them a contrasting image of Europe's urban culture, unconsciously assumed
that the vast tracks of virgin wilderness, already diminishing,
somehow guaranteed America's moral and spiritual sanctity.
Bryant and Cole, by infusing their art with such sentiments,
helped to foster this conception of nationality. In an idyllic
scene called "Kindred Spirits," the painter Asher B. Durand char-

---

[48] Cole, "Lament of the Forest," *Knickerbocker Magazine*, XVII (1841),
518-519.
[49] Noble, *op. cit.*, p. 226.

acteristically located Bryant and Cole together on a jutting spur of rock, dwarfed and all but engulfed by the precipices, crags, hanging woods, and silent, empty spaces of *sublime* American forest. If the cultural influence of Franklin and Jefferson helped to ease the transition from a largely agrarian to an industrial America, that of Bryant and Cole aggravated the tensions it produced.

9

The Intellectual Origins

and New-Worldliness

of American Industry

Sublime nature in American art during the early nineteenth century flourished side by side with the classical revival. Patriotic Americans in this period liked to think of the American Revolution as an epic struggle upon whose outcome hung the destinies of mankind for ages to come, and, ransacking history for parallels to this momentous event, they often came up with the conclusion that Americans were the Greeks and Romans of the modern world. They clothed the statuary of their Revolutionary heroes in Roman togas. They discovered an historical archetype for the embattled farmers in Cincinnatus. They affixed to public letters such names as Decius, Portius, Agricola. They named their new frontier cities after Troy, Syracuse, Athens, Rome. They founded Greek-letter fraternal societies. They struck the Hellenic note in architecture, and in literature they tried to write epics. It would be difficult to exaggerate the extent of the classical influence during this heroic phase of American culture. One scholar has remarked that it was as hard to find a building that was not Greek in 1827 as it was to find a skirt that was not short in 1927.

But the classical revival was only a phase of nationalism which ended by offending national pride. A patriotic craftsman expressed his indignation by smuggling native ears of corn into the decorative intertwining of acanthus leaves which graced the Greek pillars of the capitol at Washington. Davy Crockett in 1834 protested against a statue of General Washington because "they have a Roman gown on him, and he was an American. . . . He belonged to *this country*—heart, soul, and body: and I don't want any other to have any part of him—not even his clothes." [1] The classical revival, insofar as it marked the rise of an aggressive, expanding civilization with antecedents in Europe, came into conflict with the American religion of nature. One hears in the words of Davy Crockett, who was an embodiment of Leather-stocking and even before his death a national symbol, the judgment of the American Adam. That the classical revival was able to exist on the scale that it did, however, suggests that it did not altogether conflict with the dominant mythology, but rather accommodated itself to it. The theme of the regression to nature was evident, for instance, in the many references to Attic simplicity, Spartan economy, and republican virtue: the sturdy yeoman farmer was supposed to live in Attic simplicity; his government to emulate a Spartan economy; and the chief end of his civilization, like that of Greece and Rome, to establish a moral order for the world. Classical architecture was believed to embody these ideals, and the movement as a whole envisaged the restoration of a Golden Age.

The classical revival in America thus contained within itself elements both of provincialism and cosmopolitanism, intimations of a glorious civilization of the future and the reversion to a more primitive civilization of the past. But in the main it expressed the American recognition that the course of empire had at last, for better or worse, made its way to this country. This revelation coincided with a related development in the transit of civilization which has had far-reaching consequences and which may be justly regarded as the central event of our national history, the coming of the industrial revolution. The revolutionary technological changes which have come to typify modern society, transforming the face of the landscape and upsetting traditional ways of life, were first felt in the New England textile industry. The American zeal for useful improvements that greeted the indus-

---

[1] In Warren S. Tryon, *A Mirror for Americans; Life and Manners in the United States 1790-1870 as recorded by American Travelers*, 3 vols. (Chicago: University of Chicago Press, 1952), I, 140.

trial revolution was counterbalanced, however, by patriotic fears that the ill effects of European manufacturing would be repeated here. The textile manufacturers who introduced the factory system into the United States early in the nineteenth century found it necessary, in order to win a full measure of public support and secure workers in a land where labor was dear, to demonstrate that "the moral standards of the community would not be impaired." [2] Industrialism, like the classical revival, had to be adapted in some measure to paradisiac images of America. It accommodated itself more readily, however, to agrarian dreams of a rich material abundance than to the requirements of republican simplicity and virtue.

The factory pioneers had to profess in their great debate with the Jeffersonians a patriotic concern for the effects of manufacturing upon the public character. They were also often obliged to embody their professions of morality in philanthropy and a paternalistic regard for the welfare of factory operatives by establishing schools, churches, carefully supervised boarding houses, and some working restrictions for women and children, who constituted their main supply of labor. As a result, although exploitation was inevitable, the worst horrors of the industrial revolution in England were avoided here. The moralizing impulse which surrounded the introduction of the factory system in New England and to a somewhat lesser extent later in Pennsylvania and the South has been an important characteristic of American industry, distinguishing it from its European counterparts. [3]

The thinking of both the critics and champions of the new factory system took place within a limiting, moralistic framework. Like hundreds of other Americans following a variety of different callings, the industrial pioneers conceived of themselves, for the most part, in the role of principal agents in an American world mission. They shared with poets, painters, re-

---

[2] Caroline F. Ware, The Early New England Cotton Manufacture (Boston: Houghton Mifflin Co., 1931), p. 8.

[3] The evidence of such foreign observers as Charles Murray, David Thomas, Harriet Martineau, Anthony Trollope, James Montgomery, and William Scoresby would seem to be conclusive. The kind of materialism which Charles Dickens attacked was essentially a moral materialism. A work emphasizing the element of exploitation in this early period of the industrial revolution is William A. Sullivan, The Industrial Worker in Pennsylvania, 1800-1840 (Harrisburg: Pennsylvania Historical and Museum Commission, 1955).

formers, professional men, and pioneer farmers the pervasive American hope of redeeming men and society from the sins of a supposedly corrupt Old World and achieving a new heaven on earth. The early industrialists differed from their critics mainly in wanting to effect this happy transformation by manufacturing rather than by agriculture, through a political élite leadership rather than through the democratic leavening.

Convinced, on the whole, of an identity between moral and material progress, these industrialists, while not averse to profits, were conscious of making a patriotic contribution and of trying to establish a pattern in manufacturing for the nation. Public-spirited as a group and strongly Federalist in politics, many served the government as elected representatives, as consultants, diplomats, and so forth. The leading spirits of New England enterprise were George Cabot, Francis Cabot Lowell, Patrick Tracy Jackson, the Appleton brothers, Kirk Boott, and Amos and Abbott Lawrence—all closely related by family and marriage ties.[4] To these names must be added those of Moses Brown and Samuel Slater, instrumental in establishing the Rhode Island system; Alexander Hamilton, the influential Secretary of the Treasury, who promoted the industrial undertaking at Paterson, New Jersey; Tench Coxe and Matthew Carey of Pennsylvania, the foremost propagandists for manufacturing; and William Gregg, who later introduced the New England pattern into the South. Analysis of their family letters, business correspondence, and other writings, including materials not directly related to manufacturing, reveals unmistakably the imprint of the American myth of Eden.

The pioneers of modern industrial enterprise employed the familiar rhetoric in defence of manufacturing. The European pole of thought continued to dominate their thinking. "The strongest and most lasting prejudice [against American manu- facturing]," Caroline Ware writes, "rested on a horror lest the factory system in America should degrade the worker as it had

---

[4] I have compiled this listing primarily from *The Dictionary of American Biography* and checked it against the many cross-references in the source materials examined. But see also the list of original promoters in Ware, *op. cit.*, pp. 320-321. Other members of the group who are occasionally referred to in this book include Israel Thorndike, Samuel Batchelder, and Edmund Dwight, as well as close family relatives who may be assumed to share their basic attitudes.

in England and become a menace to American social and political ideals."[5] Oddly enough, American industrialists disliked the manufacturing system of Europe almost as much as did Jefferson and the agrarians—and for much the same reasons. Or at least they said they did. Few were willing to state a case for economic self-interest as nakedly as had Hamilton in his *Report on Manufactures*.

In 1800, Dr. George Logan, a friend of Jefferson, but an early advocate of American industry from Pennsylvania, appealed for the encouragement of domestic manufacture because the products of foreign manufacture "were threatening to destroy the American character." Before embarking upon textile manufactures Nathan Appleton went to Europe in 1810, avowedly to find the answers to two questions: first, did it make for general prosperity or degradation and "secondly, was labor demoralized under its influence or improved?" He was appalled by the "misery and poverty" of the people he saw in the industrial sections of Durham and Dunbar, near Liverpool, but was favorably impressed, as was Francis Cabot Lowell about the same time, by the Lanark industrial experiment of Robert Owen, who had also felt the impulse of New World idealism. In his essay *Labor*, Appleton later presented the case for American protective tariffs primarily as a defense against the competition of the "cheaper and more degraded labor of Europe." The southern industrialist, William Gregg, habitually contrasted the happy state of American manufacturing with European depravity: "Look at the wages of England, and consider that her operatives are but scantily fed, and are without fuel sufficient to keep them comfortable in cold weather. . . ."[6] Were it not for the need to borrow European technicians and techniques, American manufacturers would seem to be nearly as disposed as Jefferson to wish for an "ocean of fire" between the Old World and the New.

---

[5] Ware, *op. cit.*, pp. 7-8.

[6] For Dr. Logan see Samuel Rezneck, "The Rise and Early Development of Industrial Consciousness in the United States, 1760-1830," *Journal of Economic and Business History*, IV (August, 1932), 798; Frances W. Gregory, "Nathan Appleton, Yankee Merchant, 1779-1861" (unpublished doctoral dissertation, Radcliffe College, 1949), pp. 199-200; Nathan Appleton, *Labor, Its Relation in Europe and the United States Compared* (Boston, 1844), p. 14; William Gregg, *Essays on Domestic Industry: Or, An Enquiry into the Expediency of Establishing Cotton Manufacturing in South Carolina* (Charleston, S.C., 1845), p. 46.

The rising tide of nationalism stimulated by the American Revolution and the War of 1812 made it popular to justify American manufacturing on the ground of economic independence.[7] Such pleas for a national economic independence, however, usually pointed to the horrifying alternative of a moral and spiritual as well as economic prostration at the feet of the manufacturers of Europe. Though these public pronouncements may have functioned consciously as convenient rationalizations of economic interest, their authors were sometimes taken in by their own propaganda, for the same ideas appeared again and again in their private letters and journals, when they had no need for propaganda. To them European manufacturing, on the whole, not only seemed degrading to character; it was presided over by a devilish class of aristocrats and hatched in an atmosphere of conspiracy. To them, it must be said, Europe—with some reservations—represented the same hellish inferno, or fallen garden, which the colonists had rejected.

These manufacturers instinctively looked to Europe for patriotically instructive examples of aristocratic corruption, immoral leisure, extravagance, intellectual cunning, and degrading poverty, and in their travels frequently were not disappointed. Writing from Bordeaux, France, in 1795, young Francis Cabot Lowell, later the humanitarian architect of Waltham, had to reassure his father that the streets were safe and the people just as religious as ever. His wife wrote home about the degeneration of the London stage.[8] Amos Lawrence warned his junior partner leaving for Europe to preserve his native virtue: ". . . the scenes of another land may be more than your principles will stand against." [9] John Lowell, the brother of Francis Cabot, satisfied his Puritan moral sense by contrasting the beggars of Rome with the "Rich and Proud Cardinal . . . wrapped in his double folds of purple, arrayed with proud magnificence," who, "accompanied with his princely train of liveried domestics [,] rolls along

---

[7] The publicity given this argument is reviewed by Samuel Rezneck, *op. cit.*, pp. 784-811; but see also *Industrial and Commercial Correspondence of Alexander Hamilton*, ed. Arthur H. Cole (Chicago: A. W. Shaw Co., 1928), pp. 42-43, 49-50, 122, 261-265.

[8] Ferris Greenslet, *The Lowells and Their Seven Worlds* (Boston: Houghton Mifflin Co., 1946), pp. 128, 175.

[9] Amos Lawrence, *Diary and Correspondence; with a Brief Account of Some Incidence in His Life*, ed. William R. Lawrence (Boston, 1855), pp. 48-49.

unheeding these objects of horror which meet him on every side. . . ."[10] A similar spectacle of pomp and iniquity, extravagance and wretchedness, greeted the eyes of a cousin of Nathan and Samuel Appleton. William Appleton accused a Roman bishop of pilfering charities. He also noted that the European nobility had a poor opinion of mercantile men, "unless they can make something of them." He took no pleasure in viewing the "fallen greatness" at Kenilworth, made invidious comparisons between English and American railroads, and save for the occasional magnificence of European scenery, was glad to get home to the American paradise.[11]

The patriotic contrast of American morals and European manners, central to the American myth of Eden, made such things as fashionable dress, intellectualism, leisure, and often art into foppish instruments of the devil and at the same time elevated the ascetic virtues of simplicity of dress and manner, plainness of speech and thought, modesty, sobriety, manliness, and industry. William Gregg, whose trip to Europe also produced jibes at Catholic potentates, observed: "The men of the country are soldiers, priests, monks, sculptors, painters, etc. Indeed, [if] the labor . . . so employed [were placed] in productive pursuits, they would make the country rich." Much like the archetypal American of Henry James' novels, he looked upon the Colosseum as a symbol of European decay. He was prudish about naked figures in statuary and frescoes. With other American manufacturers he taxed his countrymen on moral as well as economic grounds for their extravagant importation of European fashions during the period between wars before American industry was well established.[12] Amos Lawrence, who was glad that his wife had the "infinite advantage of good sense and good principles over the merely elegant accomplishments of fashionable education," wrote to his eldest son in Paris: "Bring home no foreign

---

[10] Greenslet, op. cit., p. 122.

[11] Selections from the Diaries of William Appleton, 1786-1862, ed. Susan M. Loring (Boston: privately printed, 1922), pp. 19, 24, 29, 78. William Appleton was a merchant and banker rather than industrialist, but he invested money in his cousins' factories.

[12] Broadus Mitchell, William Gregg, Factory Master of the Old South (Chapel Hill: University of North Carolina Press, 1928), pp. 237-239; Gregg, op. cit., pp. 10-11.

fancies which are inapplicable to our state of society." [13] Indeed, a widespread fear of the invasion of America by Europe helped to reconcile Americans to native industry. None but Tories were clothed in purple and fine linen, they were told; only domestic manufactures could appease the "untimely passion for European luxuries."

This intensely American, Protestant stereotype of Europe, an adumbration of Mark Twain's *Innocents Abroad,* was incomplete without a devil. Early American manufacturers almost took for granted in Europeans, especially in the aristocracy and ruling hierarchies, a conspiratorial cunning directed at contaminating the American garden. Thus, even though the Prince of Aci might appear superficially to be a democrat, there was "much of the cunning of the Sicilian in his countenance." It occurred to George Cabot that the European manufacturer would gladly suppress the patriotic efforts which he and his friends were making to establish a cotton manufactory at Beverly. He strongly disagreed with the plan of Alexander Hamilton, the most European in sympathies among American promoters, to employ foreign laborers at Paterson, on the ground that they were not to be trusted. Of them he wrote to Hamilton, "[We are] misled by every pretender to knowledge." He was satisfied from experience "that we must at last depend on the people of the country *alone* for a solid and permanent establishment." [14] Americans were inclined to overlook their own connivance in bringing the basic design for the power loom to America and in persuading Samuel Slater to migrate from England contrary to English law forbidding technicians from leaving the country. Indeed, Samuel Slater's first biographer took pains to disprove a popular American belief "that the British government employed a person to assassinate Mr. Slater, by means of an infernal machine." [15]

Belief in the existence of a conspiratorial European devil led

----

[13] Lawrence, *op. cit.,* pp. 43, 90.

[14] Appleton, *op. cit.,* p. 20; Cabot's letters in Robert S. Rantoul, "The First Cotton Mill in America," *Historical Collections of the Essex Institute,* XXXIII (1897), 39-41.

[15] George S. White, *Memoir of Samuel Slater, the Father of American Manufactures. Connected with a History of the Rise and Progress of the Cotton Manufacture in England and America, with Remarks on the Moral Influence of Manufactories in the United States,* 2d ed. (Philadelphia, 1836), p. 97.

also to the patriotic contrast of honestly made American manufactures with reputedly fraudulent European goods. An 1815 memorial to Congress from Massachusetts cotton manufacturers which helped to pass the protective tariff of the following year argued, for instance: "The articles, whose prohibition we pray for, are made of very inferior materials, and are manufactured in a manner calculated to deceive rather than to serve the consumer." [16] William Gregg later enumerated some of the deceptive materials. The English put "pot metal" instead of iron into their rails. "The English cheat the whole world; they make good articles for home consumption, [and] inferior for every other people. Such goods in appearance as [our] Graniteville are loaded with clay sizing until 25 per cent is added to the weight of cotton." [17] The dumping of supposedly inferior foreign goods and luxuries upon the American market after the wars was publicized as an economic as well as a moral and spiritual threat.

The European devil of the American imagination commonly brewed his concoctions in urban centers. Jefferson held in 1805 that his animus against manufacturing was meant to apply "only to the great cities of Europe and not to this country at the present time," when American manufacturers were "as much at their ease, as independent and moral as our agricultural inhabitants." [18] Many of the merchants who turned their energies to industry had agrarian roots or rural connections. Amos and Abbott Lawrence were sons of a Groton farmer, whose country connections made their dry-goods business prosper. The father of Nathan and Samuel Appleton was a well-to-do farmer in New Ipswich. Both sons tried their hand at farming and once ran a country store. George Cabot and Israel Thorndike kept country seats in Beverly. The Dwights brothers were reckoned "the most extensive country traders that came to Boston." [19] The Lowells and the Jacksons came from Newburyport, as well known for its opulent green fields as for its flourishing commerce. Though these people eventually gravitated to Boston, their memories were often nos-

---

[16] Quoted in [Friends of Domestic Industry], *Report on the Production and Manufacture of Cotton* (Boston, 1832), p. 8.

[17] Mitchell, *op. cit.*, pp. 150, 304n.

[18] Rezneck, *op. cit.*, p. 799.

[19] *The Aristocracy of Boston; Who They Are, and What They Were, by One Who Knows Them* (Boston, 1848), p. 15.

talgic. William Gregg, who lived most of his life in Charleston, South Carolina, inherited an agrarian bias from the planting aristocracy.

For the most part, their animadversions against cities echoed those of American farmers who were afraid to trust their daughters in manufacturing towns. Attributing the degradation of European industrial workers to urban conditions rather than to manufacturing alone, many American manufacturers sought to locate their factories in the outlying countryside, creating conditions similar to village life. "A cotton factory should not be located in a city," said William Gregg; "there it would be impossible 'to control the moral habits of the operatives, and to keep up a steady, efficient, and cheap working force.'" His Graniteville, modeled upon Lowell and Waltham, proved to the South that "there need be no fear of overcrowding in manufacturing towns, with attendant lapse of morals." [20] Patrick Tracy Jackson reported for a committee of northern manufacturers in 1832: "In Europe, manufactures are established in large cities, the business is followed from parent to child, and wages are so miserably low, that few families can be supported without parochial aid. One consequence of this abject poverty is, that children are set to work at a very tender age, and have no time allowed for education, literary or moral. In the United States, manufactories are dispersed through the country." [21] An extensive poll of American manufacturers by a clergyman in 1835 suggests not only that many factories were, for moral as well as economic reasons, located in rural areas, but that the introduction of grog shops and taverns was forbidden; in many cases family plots of land were provided for keeping gardens, cows and pigs, and so forth.[22] These precautions, together with the erecting of attractive boardinghouses or cottages, schools, and churches, succeeded, as Freeman Hunt observed in his *Lives of American Merchants,* in gaining the confidence of the rural population, from whence the operatives came. In 1817, Jefferson, Adams, and Madison officially capitulated to moral American manufacturing by accepting honorary membership in the American Society for the Encouragement of Domestic Manufactures.

----

[20] Mitchell, *op. cit.,* pp. 107, 141.
[21] [Friends of Domestic Industry], *op. cit.,* p. 13.
[22] See the queries and answers in White, *op. cit.,* pp. 125-142.

Americans tended to consider the rise of urbanization in the United States at this time a more serious indication of the invasion of America by European culture than either native manufacturing or the consumption of foreign goods. The manufacturers did not disagree. "It is chiefly in the town," Tench Coxe wrote in 1787, "that this madness for foreign finery rages and destroys. . . . Our farmers, to their great honor and advantage, have been long in the excellent oeconomical practice of domestic manufactures. . . ." [23] The biographer of Samuel Slater thought that swindling was caused chiefly by flooding the *cities* with foreign imports. He held up to American youth the example of Slater's virtuous conduct in the city of London. There was a part of Boston in which Amos Lawrence never set foot, because he "not only wished to keep clear of the temptations common in that part, but to avoid the appearance of evil." He told a young man, "It is on account of so much leisure, that so many fine youths are ruined in this town." [24] Lawrence and his fellow manufacturers exalted the virtues of sobriety, industry, and the like in part as the means of salvation for urban sinners.

The identification of American cities with an European invasion was clear also in some manufacturers' reactions to the foreign wars. These Federalists charged the Jeffersonians with "the cursed foul contagion of French principles." But, said George Cabot, the few "disaffected, seditious people" of New England resided "chiefly in the town and vicinity of Boston." The disease —note the imagery—spread through the country from the urban centers. Cabot rhetorically disapproved a "secret" political deal which brought Tennessee into the Union: "With what exultation may the ministers of monarchical governments expose the secret movements of our pure republican system, when the public good is *supposed* to be the constant spring of action!" He compared Governor Hancock of Massachusetts to a foreign king, swallowing the "gross flattery of servile citizens." [25] Ironically, the Jeffersonians brought substantially the same charges against the Federalists: the Federalists were lovers of monarchy, or artistocracy,

---

[23] Tench Coxe, *An Address to an Assembly of the Friends of American Manufactures* (Philadelphia, 1787), pp. 24-25.

[24] White, *op. cit.*, pp. 38, 120; Amos Lawrence, *op. cit.*, pp. 78, 126.

[25] Henry Cabot Lodge, *Life and Letters of George Cabot* (Boston, 1877), pp. 96, 158, 160, 232, 238.

infected with *English* principles. Both sides tended to distrust urban centers. Both sides agreed that America was being betrayed by some insidious foreign ideology. The Federalists traced the trail of supposed sedition in their land back to rabble-rousing French Jacobinism, the Republicans to England. Thus, partisan rhetoric used the same ideological language, merely reversing the tags.

The political sympathies, as well as commercial self-interest, of the budding manufacturers lay naturally at this time with England. They wanted war with France in 1798 and broke with their president, John Adams, on that issue. They did not want war with England in 1812, and were among the leaders of a separatist movement, as Jefferson and Madison had been in 1798. In 1814, the merchant-manufacturer, George Cabot, was elected president of the Hartford Convention, strongly supported by the Lowells and other future manufacturing families. Thus, on both sides the European tie was a complicated love-hate relationship. Although manufacturing finally won an acceptance in the American community, in many respects a patriotically enthusiastic acceptance, it was a conditioned acceptance among some elements, particularly the agrarian, laboring, and professional groups. As the manufacturers consolidated their position, as the advent of the immigrants with their cheap labor supply made it no longer necessary to secure community respect and guarantee the workers' social welfare, these disaffected groups fastened the label of an European-type aristocracy on the business community. This symbol transference was facilitated by traditional fears of the invasion of America by Europe.

In 1835, the French observer, Tocqueville, warned Americans against the rise in their midst of a manufacturing aristocracy. In the next year an organization of workingmen, remembering that "foreign tyranny" had found a limit in 1776, watched "with painful solicitude" "the rapid advance of inequality in our beloved country." In 1844, Parke Godwin, lawyer, writer, and reformer, expressed alarm at "the rapid and powerful constitution of a new Aristocracy, of a commercial and financial Feudality, which is taking the place of the ancient aristocracy of nobles and warriors." Many of the errors on this point seemed to Wendell Phillips in 1847 "to proceed from looking at American questions through European spectacles, and transplanting the eloquent complaints against capital and monopoly, which are well-grounded and well-applied there, to a state of society here, where they have little meaning or application. . . ." [26] However misapplied such symbol transference may have been, it helped to organize a patriotic suspicion of the manufacturing and business community which expressed itself in the political reform movements of the late nineteenth and early twentieth centuries. It helped to reawaken in the business community, notorious for its late nineteenth-century "robber barons," a new sense of social and civic responsibility. And it introduced into American society not only an aggravation of existing political tensions, but a national sense of guilt which hinged upon the question whether material progress and prosperity functioned as a reward for virtue for an elect people living in a scientific paradise or as evidence of corruption in a society rapidly going the way of Europe. As Bishop William Lawrence, a grandson of Amos Lawrence, put it: "There is a certain distrust on the part of our people as to the effect of material prosperity on their morality. We shrink with some foreboding at the great increase of riches, and question whether in the long run material prosperity does not tend toward the disintegration of character. [The] history [of Tyre and Sidon, Babylon, Rome, Venice, and the great nations of Europe] seems to support us in our distrust." [27] The Edenic myth of newness thus continued to generate criticism of the industrial order well into the twentieth century.

Although, as has been suggested, the pioneer manufacturers' tie with Europe was a complicated one—and was still more complicated for American artists, writers, and intellectuals—Europe, taken as a whole, held up to them a reverse image of America. American manufacturers, with the possible exception of their friend Hamilton, never felt altogether easy in their link with England. George Cabot, for instance, wished on several

----

[26] Alexis de Tocqueville, *Democracy in America* (New York: Alfred A. Knopf, Inc., 1946), II, 161; the labor view and statement of Wendell Phillips in John R. Commons *et al.*, ed., *Documentary History of American Industrial Society*, 10 vols. (Cleveland: Arthur H. Clark Co., 1910-1911), V, 363; VII, 221; Parke Godwin, *Democracy, Constructive and Pacific* (1844), in Willard Thorp *et al.*, ed., *American Issues*, 2 vols. (Philadelphia: J. B. Lippincott Co., 1944), I, 414.

[27] William Lawrence, "The Relation of Wealth to Morals," *World's Work*, I (January, 1901), 286.

occasions that England were less "haughty." They protested that they did not intend by the Hartford Convention to break up the Union. As the biographer of Israel Thorndike has observed, when the chips were down, patriotic considerations had the edge. Although smuggling was rampant from 1807 to 1814, there is some evidence in the Appleton papers that the merchant-manufacturers studied here tried to pursue the neutral trade within the limits of American law. Nathan Appleton himself opposed the Jeffersonian duties, opposed the Embargo, nonintercourse, and the War of 1812, but he waxed eloquent over the sinking of the "Guerrière," which, he said, "must raise the Yankee character a little," and he finally joined the militia.[28] The European pole of thought, as part of the Colonial intellectual inheritance, was responsible for the reforming sense of mission with which these merchants turned to manufacturing after the War of 1812.

They were frequently explicit, almost poetic, about their divine mission in America. Amos Lawrence, who glorified the American landscape as a "transcript of the beautiful scenery around Jerusalem," wrote to his son in France, "God has given us a good land and many blessings. . . . We shall be called to a strict account." Nathan Appleton wrote about his part in the industrial revolution, "Ours is a great novel experiment. . . . Whatever the result, it is our destiny to make it. It is our mission —our care should be to understand it and make it succeed." William Gregg spoke of his mission to restore the South from a blighted wasteland caused by depressed conditions in cotton and tobacco into a "garden spot." Amos and Abbott Lawrence, William Appleton, and others deemed themselves "stewards of the Lord" with a civic responsibility for the nation's moral and spiritual welfare. All were distinguished for philanthropy.[29]

The American mission to establish a cultural pre-eminence was held to include the mechanical arts as well as the fine arts. John

---

[28] Lodge, *op. cit.*, p. 227; J. D. Forbes, *Israel Thorndike* (New York: Exposition Press, 1953), p. 117; Gregory, *op. cit.*, pp. 303, 307-310; Nathan Appleton MSS, Massachusetts Historical Society, Vol. I.

[29] Amos Lawrence, *op. cit.*, pp. 20-21, 100, 155-156; Nathan Appleton, *op. cit.*, p. 9; Mitchell, *op. cit.*, pp. 20, 73; Gregg, *op. cit.*, pp. 7-8, 14-17, 137; for the concept of the "stewardship" see, for example, William Appleton, *op. cit.*, pp. 31, 33, 39, 47, 49, 107-108, and Frank Ballard, *The Stewardship of Wealth . . . as Illustrated in the Lives of Amos and Abbott Lawrence* (New York, 1865), pp. 3-16.

Lowell wrote to Francis C. Lowell with reference to the impending Waltham experiment:

As to the mechanical arts, and even the fine arts it may be truly said that we have a great natural turn for them, and that we excel in them as much as could be expected considering the degree of encouragement they receive or could receive in a new country.

We have invented more useful machines within twenty years than have been invented in all Europe, and we need but mention our Wests, Copleys, Stewarts, Trumbulls, Alstons, etc., to convince any liberal foreigner that the Fine Arts do not refuse us their aid. . . .[30]

American manufacturing, moreover, was to be adapted to *American* conditions. The industrial pioneers were as much offended as American poets and artists of the sublime by charges of cultural imitation. Nathan Appleton wrote, "The attempt at imitation, which sometimes prevails, is a mistake and a blunder." "Are we forever to be the dupes of European influence . . . ?" Samuel Slater's biographer asked in 1835: "Let us rather assume a national character, a national costume. If we are to be guided by fashion, let that fashion be American; the produce of American evil, of American invention and skill, and of American industry and enterprise. The day is past and gone, when any of our citizens will think it best to have our *work-shops* in Europe. . . ." He went on to picture Slater as a great savior, delivering a chosen people from Old World despotism, following the example of Christopher Columbus and Martin Luther in "exhibiting a mighty spirit of reformation."[31] But his reference to "American evil" suggests secret misgivings in coupling business enterprise with the Protestant Reformation.

These servants of the Lord professed to be setting a national example of manufacturing morality and skill and were indeed

---

[30] Greenslet, *op. cit.*, p. 140. An informed estimate of Francis Cabot Lowell's idealism and sense of mission is William R. Bagnall, "Contributions to American Economic History (Unpublished Materials): Sketches of Manufacturing Establishments . . . ," 4 vols. (Carnegie Institute, 1908 [typed MS in Baker Library, Harvard University]), III, 2007-2008, 2022. Bagnall also testifies to the patriotism of Uriah Cotting, the Thorndikes, and other promoters. Thorndike, however, was not as liberal a public donor.

[31] Nathan Appleton, *op. cit.*, p. 9; White, *op. cit.*, pp. 14, 24. White's reference to "American evil" in this passage is an indication of what Leo Marx, Bernard Bowron, and Arnold Rose have called "covert culture." See their article, "Literature and Covert Culture," *Studies in American Culture*, ed. Joseph J. Kwiat and Mary C. Turpie (Minneapolis: University of Minnesota Press, 1960), pp. 84-95.

often generous in encouraging the establishment of rival factories. Regarding New England as the "seat of influence to the vast multitude of millions who are to people this republic," Amos Lawrence urged the South to embark on manufactures. Abbott Lawrence wrote to the southerner, William C. Rives, "We have not [sic] jealousy, whatever, concerning the establishment of manufactories in all parts of the country. . . ." George Cabot expected that New England operatives would "diffuse their knowledge and skill through all the States in the Union where manufactories can be carried on." Francis Cabot Lowell fostered the growth of manufacturing elsewhere by letting out his patents for the power loom on easy terms. The New Hampshire pioneer, Samuel Batchelder, joined his fellow New Englanders in recommending to southerners the establishment of cotton factories where the raw product grew, in the South: New England would specialize in the finer fabrics, the South in the coarse cloth.[32]

New England missionary zeal bore fruit in Pennsylvania and in the South. The historian of the Philadelphia textile industry, for example, professed to find more paternal characteristics there than in such places as Lowell, where the employers were large corporations. "Some of the [Pennsylvania] manufacturers," he wrote, "are men who are distinguished for benevolent effort . . . where the factories are remote, schools and churches have been specially established by factory proprietors." Colonel Breithaupt, an early industrialist of South Carolina, enthusiastically advertised "the improvements of the Northern States, and the liberality of their citizens." William Gregg, who introduced the New England pattern into the South, taunted an unsuccessful fellow manufacturer: "Why did you not follow the patriotic example of the Lowells, Bootts, Jacksons, Appletons, and Lawrences, of Boston?" He tried to enlist John C. Calhoun, Langdon Cheves, and William Lowndes "in the great cause of reforming the habits of your countrymen." "God speed on the glorious result," he said, "that may be anticipated from so great a change, in our indus-

[32] Amos Lawrence, *op. cit.*, pp. 103-104, 79-80, 169, 258; Rantoul, *op. cit.*, p. 38; *Letters from the Hon. Abbott Lawrence to the Hon. William C. Rives of Virginia* (Boston, 1846), p. 19; Lowell's letter in Jonathan T. Lincoln, "Beginnings of the Machine Age in New England: Documents Relating to the Introduction of the Power Loom," *Bulletin of the Business Historical Society*, VIII (1933), 7-9; Samuel Batchelder, *Introduction and Early Progress of the Cotton Manufacture in the United States* (Boston, 1863), p. 8.

trial pursuit." [33] One of the great results which he hoped, prematurely, would follow was the erasing of differences between North and South.

Manufacturing not only was *not* evil; it was productive of positive good in rescuing labor from indolence, drunkenness, pauperism, and vice, and in initiating habits of industry, learning, and religious piety. This was the central theme and gospel by which the manufacturers defined their conception of progress toward the paradisiac state. They identified technological progress with moral and spiritual improvement through the agency of the factory and a benevolent paternalism. Thus, Amos Lawrence forced an overzealous factory superintendent to close down on Sundays: "I am a firm believer in the doctrine that a blessing will more surely follow those exertions which are made with reference to our religious obligations." In preaching the morality of industry to the South, Abbott Lawrence advised a foundation in the "pure precepts of the Gospel." [34] The Gospel of Wealth was completely formulated long before Andrew Carnegie made it the cornerstone of his defense of capitalistic enterprise.

"Nor are the mechanical arts and agricultural industry alone fostered," Patrick Tracy Jackson told the nation. "The village steeple is an unfailing companion to the water-wheel. . . ." He was seconded by the practical Kirk Boott. Matthew Carey compared the moral phenomenon of industry to that "of Niagara in the natural world." For Slater's biographer, the locomotive was a more fitting symbol for mechanical progress, but he tried to wrench images from bountiful, paradisiac nature, again revealing hidden doubts. Comparing machine improvements to a mighty swelling river, he wrote, "And the same feeling of reverential gratitude, which attached holiness to the spots whence mighty rivers sprung, also clothes with divinity, and raised alters in honour of, the inventors of the saw, the plough, the potter's wheel, and the loom." By the middle of the nineteenth century, American concepts of progress and regeneration centered as much in manufacturing as in geographical westering, and Benjamin

---

[33] Edwin T. Freedley, *Philadelphia and Its Manufactures in 1857* (Philadelphia, 1858), p. 252; Commons, *op. cit.*, II, 333; Gregg, *op. cit.*, pp. 8, 17, 35.

[34] Amos Lawrence, *op. cit.*, p. 202; Abbott Lawrence, *op. cit.*, p. 6.

Franklin, to whom the manufacturers sometimes alluded, became a national archetype to stand for both ways of salvation.[35]

Nathan Appleton tried to sum up the whole meaning of American industry in a retrospective essay on the origins of Lowell and the power loom. In it he credited himself, Lowell, Jackson, Boott, and others with being the prime movers. But the "informing soul" of the glorious enterprise, according to Appleton, was Francis Cabot Lowell, whose primary concern was "arrangements for the moral character of the operatives employed." It is worth while to quote Appleton at length:

The introduction of the cotton manufacture in this country, on a large scale, was a new idea. What would be its effect on the character of our population was a matter of deep interest. The operatives in the manufacturing cities of Europe, were notoriously of the lowest character, for intelligence and morals. The question therefore arose, and was deeply considered, whether this degradation was the result of the peculiar occupation, or of other and distinct causes. We could not perceive why this peculiar description of labor should vary in its effects upon character from all other occupation.

There was little demand for female labor, as household manufacture was superseded by the improvements in machinery. Here was in New England a fund of labor, well educated and virtuous. It was not perceived how a profitable employment has any tendency to deteriorate the character. The most efficient guards were adopted in establishing boarding houses, at the cost of the Company, under the charge of respectable women, with every provision for religious worship. Under these circumstances, the daughters of respectable farmers were readily induced to come into these mills for a temporary period.

The contrast in the character of our manufacturing population compared with that of Europe, has been the admiration of the most intelligent strangers who have visited us. The effect has been to more than double the wages of that description of labor from what they were before the introduction of this manufacture. . . .[36]

---

[35] Jackson wrote the [Friends of Domestic Industry], *Report*, p. 14; Kirk Boott's letter in White, *op. cit.*, p. 255; for Matthew Carey and Slater's biographer, *ibid.*, pp. 15, 57, 168. The Napoleon image competed with Franklin's for the manufacturers' admiration. Samuel Slater was praised, however, for not following the *bad* example of Franklin in breaking his apprenticeship. Franklin was honored for confessing this *erratum*. For the adaptation of the Franklin image to American ideas of progress see Louis B. Wright, "Franklin's Legacy to the Gilded Age," *Virginia Quarterly Review*, XXII (1946), 268-279.

[36] Nathan Appleton, *Introduction of the Power Loom and Origin of Lowell* (Lowell, 1858), pp. 15-16. But see also Nathan Appleton, *Correspondence Between Nathan Appleton and John A. Lowell in Relation to the Early History of the City of Lowell* (Boston, 1848), pp. 18-19.

Such pronouncements largely succeeded in their deliberate design to set off and distinguish the coming of the industrial revolution to America from the supposed invasion of a morally antiseptic America by a decadent Europe.

The mission to persuade an agricultural people, North and South, to embark upon manufacturing not only gave a moral tone to American industry, but may also have contributed to practical measures different from those in Europe, not the least of which, incidentally, and perhaps the most lasting, was a higher ratio of machinery to human labor.[37] For all these reasons and perhaps for a material consideration, Davy Crockett, who, in the role of the American Adam, usually scorned the refinements of artificial civilization, was easily prevailed upon to give his blessing to American enterprise. After a visit to Lowell, he could not help "reflecting on the difference of conditions between these females, thus employed, and those of other populous countries, where the female character is degraded to abject slavery. . . ." [38] He also hailed the prospect of future comfort and respectability for the millions. The ageless dream of a rich material abundance, without carnal taint, that is, was served even better by industry than by agriculture. The factory also produced a garden of plenty. Other dreamers of an Edenic destiny added their voices to Crockett's. Both Walt Whitman and Ralph Waldo Emerson were able, at times, though in the language of ambivalence, to hymn the praises of the captains of industry; both sometimes regarded the railroad, the telegraph, the steamboat as standard bearers of Christian democracy to the shores of the Pacific. The influence of science changed the basic terms of the myth outwardly very little. The Garden, protected by the two oceans, merely turned into "the great *laboratory* of the world" in which to perfect in peace and isolation "a grand, noble *experiment*." The multiplication of inventions in this period gave rise to the widespread feeling that the nation was entering upon a new era of humane progress. A suggestive title published in 1842 was *The Paradise Within the Reach of All Men . . . By Powers of Nature and Machinery.*

---

[37] The dearth of labor, of course, partially accounted for a greater substitution of machinery at this time, but there was much discussion of the use of machines to make manual labor lighter and less degrading for women and children.

[38] From *Colonel Crockett's Tour* in Willard Thorp *et al., op. cit.,* I, 409.

Because material prosperity was conceived in a drama of good and evil, which opposed it to the degrading poverty of Europe, the self-assertive, phallic, forward thrust of "modern progress" has gained an ascendancy over the majority of Americans, who, for the most part, seem unable to understand the nature of its indictment by the "spoiled priests" in their midst. Correspondingly, American society has attached considerable moral odium to the failure to rise in life. This odium, together with the frustrating of grandiose expectations induced in every area of experience by the national mythology, as in the cult of romantic love, has undoubtedly been a major source of unhappiness. The social tragedy of failure in American life has, in any event, been an important theme of modern American writers, whose art since the turn of the last century has transmuted the Garden into the master metaphor of Wasteland. Gertrude Stein used to explain to European lecture audiences that, by comparison with Americans, Europeans did not really know anything about disillusionment; they had early learned not to expect too much of life.

But the guilt of failure is matched by the guilt of success; worldly success, as a monopoly of the few, suggested to many Americans the kind of self-aggrandizement imputed to European privilege. The pioneer industrialists studied here tried to merge their self-interest with the supposed interest of the nation. The supposed interest of the nation was defined by the myth of a moral America as a second Eden, "the last, best hope of earth." A result of this "psychic factor" of moral sanction was the concentration of energy, initiative, and intelligence in the pursuit of the profit incentive without a crippling inner guilt. It also served the more immediate end of attracting women and children to work in factories.

The objectives of a benevolent paternalism, initiated in part to alleviate guilt, became cynically perverted much later in Pullman and Hershey, but the original moralizing impulse survived in the shouts of progress, in the many incantatory protestations of innocence that regularly accompanied the scramble for wealth, in the industrial utopianism of Edward Bellamy and Edward Filene, in the lavish philanthropies of the Ford, Rockefeller, and Carnegie foundations, in various profit-sharing schemes, in the concern for good personnel relations, in the institutions of the coffee break, the cafeteria, the locker room, shower, and plant bowling team. A pietistic paternalism, complete with employee lectures on foreign policy, has continued to characterize such industrial "families" as the United States Steel Company and International Business Machines. "The real secret of American productivity," a visiting productivity team from England concluded in 1953, "is that American society is imbued through and through with the desirability, the rightness, the morality of production. Men serve God in America, in all seriousness and sincerity, through striving for economic efficiency." [39]

[39] Graham Hutton in the London *Economist;* reprinted in the *New York Herald Tribune,* July 20, 1953.

10

The Hope of Reform
and the Promise
of American Life

Millions of immigrants during the nineteenth century looked to
America as the land of promise. But so also had many generations of native Americans whose ancestors had been immigrants. The first settlers were constantly reminded of the covenant under which God's promise to Abraham was renewed and
extended to Abraham's posterity. Thus John Cotton told those
who set sail for Massachusetts that they were the heirs of God's
promise to appoint a land of Canaan for His chosen people. "And
therefore the land of Canaan is called a land of promise." He
defined a land of promise as one "where they have provisions
for soule as well as for body. . . . When God wrappes us in his
Ordinances, and warmes us with the life and power of them as
with wings, there is the land of promise." [1] As a result of the
covenant promise, Americans collectively have taken for granted
a rich inheritance of inward and outward life and have grown
accustomed to making extravagant demands upon a radiant future. This Edenic promise has made them inveterate reformers,
instruments of optimistic fatalism as well as victims of their
own impatience and frustration.

The moralistic, agrarian conception of American fulfillment

---

[1] John Cotton, *Gods Promise to His Plantations* (London, 1630), in *Old
South Leaflets,* no. 53, p. 7.

177

THE HOPE OF REFORM

did not at once accommodate itself to urban industrialism, but rather tended to identify it with the encroachment of corrupt old Europe on the vulnerable eastern seaboard, where some of the class patterns of European society had already become entrenched. For this reason Ralph Waldo Emerson wrote in the 1830's, echoing Benjamin Franklin and Thomas Jefferson before him, that Europe extended to the Alleghanies; America lay beyond.[2] The disaffection of such former ruling élites as the farmer, the planter, the clergyman, and the legislator—caused by economic and social shifts in the Northeast—not only enlisted them in criticism of the new industrial order, but helped to relocate the promises of American life farther west. It also intensified predispositions to overvalue the future in relation to the present and the European past. But attitudes toward the West compounded elements of regression with what we have come to call progress. To some Americans, the West was a place to be saved from sin by the civilizing influence of agriculture; to others, an unsullied refuge from civilization. In either case, Americans celebrated the westward trek away from Europe in their letters and literature as the archetypal rebirth out of trial. The American, "this new man," was conceived in the Adamic image to stand for America's rejection of the devilish European, and American individualism developed out of the American Adam's inner necessity to assert himself against cramping restrictions of any kind, especially those associated with an authoritarian, older civilization, in order to revert, on a more abundant level of life, to attitudes of acceptance.[3]

Thus the West became a focal center for all American idealisms. Though early nineteenth-century America vibrated in sympathy with the European Zeitgeist, its modes of expression were

----

[2] Compare Thoreau's statement, "I must walk toward Oregon, and not toward Europe."

[3] Cf. Charles L. Sanford, "The Garden of America," Modern Review, Calcutta, India, XCII, No. 1 (July, 1952), 23-32; Henry Nash Smith, Virgin Land (Cambridge: Harvard University Press, 1950); R. W. B. Lewis, The American Adam (Chicago: University of Chicago Press, 1955); Henry Bamford Parkes, "Metamorphoses of Leatherstocking," Modern Writing, No. 3 (New York: Berkley Publishing Corp., 1956), pp. 74-91. The resolution of progressive-regressive tendencies, the one rising out of the other and discharging back into it, is, of course, my own interpretation, defended throughout this book. It assumes a dynamic psychology which seems to be more in accord with the facts than a simple dichotomy would be.

its own. The many reform movements, the utopian experiments, the revivals, the sectarian ferment, the repeated removals from coastal civilization and back-to-nature cultural stirrings shared an underlying patriotic theme: that something hoped for in American life, whether the material paradise or holy commonwealth, was not being realized, but that, in conjunction with the promise of the future and the West, America might yet be rescued from some all-embracing evil. In an important sense Bronson Alcott, a latter-day Puritan, spoke for all the reformers when he said, "Our freer, but yet far from freed, land is the asylum, if asylum there be, for the hope of man; and there, if anywhere, is the second Eden to be planted in which the divine seed is to bruise the head of Evil and restore Man to his rightful communion with God in the Paradise of Good." [4] With the threat of the extension of slavery and a semifeudal social order into this holy region, all reforms were swept up by the great cause of Abolition. Fear of sabotage of the American mission by a conspiratorial devil was summed up in the northern indictment of the slaveholder. "He was, in the first place, the arch-aristocrat. . . . In the second place, he was a flagrant sinner." Avery Craven, a leader of the Revisionist school of American history, claims that the planter did scapegoat duty "for all the aristocrats and all sinners. To him were transferred resentments and fears born out of local conditions" related to the coming of the industrial revolution.[5]

Reform may be defined broadly as the effort to improve existing conditions. In this sense, American reforming zeal is not confined to spasmodic social protest movements or eccentric experiments, but is characteristic of the American people generally, whatever their class or sectional interests. For some three centuries they have been enlisted in a "permanent revolution" dedicated to progress, to social and individual betterment, variously interpreted. At the same time, after the pattern of the Puritan jeremiad, they have held it an obligation of citizenship

---

[4] Quoted in Alice Felt Tyler, *Freedom's Ferment* (Minneapolis: University of Minnesota Press, 1949), p. 172.

[5] Avery Craven, *The Coming of the Civil War* (New York: Charles Scribner's Sons, 1942), pp. 130-131, 149-150. My interpretation of reform in this period has been greatly influenced by this work, although I do not consider myself, in any sense, a Revisionist.

to search their social conscience. Thus, the conservative James
Fenimore Cooper believed that it was "the duty of the citizen
to reform and improve the character of his country." Mark Twain
once wrote that "the citizen who thinks he sees that the commonwealth's political clothes are worn out, and yet holds his peace
and does not agitate for a new suit, is disloyal; he is a traitor." [6]
If Americans have not always welcomed reformers and social
criticism, it is only that they have felt themselves already well
along the path to the good society. But while established authority and the weight of public opinion supported the view that
material progress was the reward for virtue in a now scientific
paradise, reforming critics confounded authority with the opposite view that material progress was evidence of corruption in
a society fast going the way of Europe. Whether the permanent
revolution led by industrial capitalism was delivering Americans
to heaven or hell is the central issue confronted by the reform
works examined below.

One of the most obvious facts about Thoreau's *Walden* is its
antiauthoritarian nature. Thoreau was, as Bronson Alcott said,
"the independent of independents, the sole signer of the Declaration, and a Revolution in himself," who preferred jail to supporting slavery and who, on Independence Day, 1845, marched off
to Walden Pond to conduct a social experiment in "plain living
and high thinking." [7] Thoreau's attitude toward government
("That government is best which governs not at all") merely
reflected in more extreme form the traditional American distrust
of government by an artistocratic ruling élite, evident not only
in the early demise of Federalism, but also in much opposition
to the New Deal, which paradoxically tried to restore a greater
measure of economic independence to the common (once "natural") man. If it be said that Thoreau's solution is too individualistic and therefore impractical, Thoreau would answer
that the reformation of society must begin in the hearts of individual men. It should be recalled that Walt Whitman, one of
America's greatest champions of fraternal, mass society, hoped

---

[6] James Fenimore Cooper, *Homeward Bound* (New York, 1856), p. 445;
Mark Twain, *A Connecticut Yankee in King Arthur's Court* (New York:
Harper & Bros., 1917), p. 107. Ironically, the loyalty test advocated by Mark
Twain has sometimes become a conservative weapon against liberal reform.
[7] Alcott's words are quoted in F. O. Matthiessen, *American Renaissance*
(New York: Oxford University Press, 1941), p. 79n.

that the democratic brotherhood would be realized without re-
course to the powers and authority of government.[8]

Thoreau is a type of reformer whose private solution of the
ills of society is intimately connected with an agrarian economy
(hoeing beanfields, for instance) and the invigorating influence
of nature. Our inventions, he writes, are "but improved means
to an unimproved end." [9] His own conception of ends, in the
tradition of the Puritan fathers, is millennial and progressive
in the extreme. Significantly, he makes the same metaphorical
use of clothing to garb the spiritual man as does the Puritan
Nathaniel Ward. In this one feels that he is closer to the *Simple
Cobbler* than to Carlyle's *Sartor Resartus*. Like Ward, he regards simplicity in clothing and shelter as the outward manifestation of inward grace. Indeed, he explicitly commends to the
reader the plain dress and simple architecture of the early settlers. His book as a whole urges us to simplify, simplify, simplify.
He goes beyond Ward, however, beyond mere metaphor and
symbol, in his insistence upon an organic harmony of inner and
outer nature.

Although the main tension in his work comes from the opposition between solitude and society, these poles are paralleled
by the opposition of unspoiled nature and industrial, mechanical
civilization. He prefers the solitude of nature to the society of
men, to which he must nevertheless return. Even in solitude,
however, he discovers the friendly society of nature, speaking
a variety of languages. The society of nature becomes, through
personification, almost human, while the society of man is frequently rendered by uncomplimentary animistic imagery somewhat less than human. In one finely satirical passage, for instance, he likens the village gossips idling before their stoops
to prairie dogs before their burrows. He would let owls do the
"idiotic and maniacal hooting" of men. The whistle of the locomotive penetrates disturbingly into his forest sanctuary "like the
scream of a hawk sailing over some farmer's yard." [10] The loco-

---

[8] Cf. Walt Whitman, *Specimen Days, Democratic Vistas, and Other Prose*,
ed. Louise Pound (Garden City: Doubleday & Co., Inc., 1935), pp. 279-291,
passim.

[9] Henry David Thoreau, *Walden*, Rinehart ed. (New York: Rinehart & Co.,
Inc., 1953), p. 42.

[10] *Ibid.*, p. 95; also the chapter on "Sounds" and the chapter on "The
Village." Although all Thoreau's senses were remarkably keen, his auditory

motive, chief symbol of moral and material progress for the majority of his countrymen, for him represents indeed a praiseworthy spirit of enterprise, but more importantly the degrading authority of steel over men's lives. The hawk aptly suggests the mean, acquisitive spirit of trade and commerce. The two poles of nature and civilization control the organization of *Walden* into alternating, contrapuntal chapters, the spiritual existence of "What I Lived For" being opposed to the more practical demands of "Economy" and the nature chapters of "Sounds," "The Ponds," "Brute Neighbors," and "Solitude" alternating with such acidulous glimpses of civilization as "The Village," "Visitors," and "Baker Farm." A similar tension is felt within the chapters.

Thoreau's grand objective is to redeem man out of sinful society. His hope for a regeneration is contained in such purification rituals as his immersion in the pure waters of Walden Pond, which he fancifully imagines to have existed for Adam and Eve in Eden, and in the rebirth archetype which he associates with the growing things of nature. He is most explicit in his chapter on "The Bean-field," in which he declares that he is sowing the seeds of sincerity, truth, simplicity, faith, innocence, and the like: "Why concern ourselves so much about our beans for seed, and not be concerned at all about a new generation of men?" [11] Symbolically, his book ends with the spring season.

Now, although he seems to suggest that the natural man could be restored to the primal innocence of Adam and Eve if only he could be freed from the corrupting institutions of advanced civilization, he by no means advocates literally a back-to-nature movement. Rather, he seeks an integrating midpoint, holding up the mirror of wild nature as an instrument of self-discovery. The end of self-discovery would be an integrating midpoint of the kind symbolized by Walden, an existence moored midway between the wild and the civilized, preserving the best in each

---

sense, as Sherman Paul and other critics have indicated, was most expressive of the quality of his communion with nature. The sounds which he recorded imputed to nature both sentience and intelligence. Articulation between them gave him a symbolic language; their union in a single "melodious hum" gave him an auditory image of merger corresponding to the "sky-water" of the ponds as a visual image of merger. Thoreau tried to achieve a delicate balance between the extremes of individuation and the complete submission of self.

[11] *Ibid.,* p. 136.

mode of life—simplicity without brutishness, refinement without affectation, learning without depravity. Thoreau's exploration of the depths of Walden Pond is a journey of self-discovery, recalling another voyage which led to the discovery of America, and he urges the reader to be the Columbus of America's true mission, discovering this within himself rather than in commercial enterprise. His solution is the classic one, "Know Thyself," which, in his hands, comes to mean, "Learn the difference between your deeper, truer self and the fixations and drives which your money-oriented culture has engrafted upon you." Although Thoreau's conception of the "deeper, truer self" would unite a discerning intellect to intuitive wisdom and would favor the autumnally ripe man over a crude woodchopper like Alek Therien, it must be admitted that in the all-important matter of regeneration Thoreau gave primacy to intuitive wisdom.

Thoreau's idea of progress implies a break with the past, but it does so by regressing to instinct and intuition. He felt that intelligence was commonly used by unregenerate man to rationalize ignoble ends. He had little sympathy for conventional do-gooders and reformers because most of them had not learned to know themselves, that is, to distinguish within themselves truly virtuous motives from selfish ambition. They were likely to become authoritarian moral monsters on the one hand or, on the other, to deliver themselves blindly, with the best of intentions, over to such false gods as material progress, conceived in the light of the covenant (now social compact) as a community ideal. In a nation as moralistic as America, Thoreau would want to distinguish carefully between *being* good and *doing* good.[12]

Such an understanding of the dangers to which a reform-minded public was liable was one of the chief fruits of Nathaniel Hawthorne's short-lived experience as a reformer in the utopian community at Brook Farm, an experience which he embodied in his novel, *The Blithedale Romance*.[13] Hawthorne partly shared Thoreau's conviction that scientific, industrial progress was blighting the American paradise. By locating his Garden of Eden on a farm west of Boston in the company of

---

[12] For this paragraph, *ibid.*, pp. 59-65.

[13] Nathaniel Hawthorne, *The Blithedale Romance*, in *The Complete Novels and Selected Tales*, Modern Library ed. (New York: Random House, 1939).

like-minded men, his character Miles Coverdale proposed, not unlike Thoreau, to "show mankind the example of a life governed by other than the false and cruel principles on which human society has all along been based." [14] Coverdale, too, invoked the image of the American Adam restored to paradise; he expressed the desire—without irony in this context—to lead a life "true, strong, natural, and sweet . . . something that shall have the notes of wild birds twittering through it." [15] More sceptical than Thoreau of the regenerating power of nature, Hawthorne was at least willing to give it a try. Brook Farm, like Walden Pond, constituted the experimental midpoint.

Like Thoreau, Hawthorne tentatively located the opposite poles of good and evil in solitude and society, nature and civilization, country and city. Although he attached an ambivalent love-hate value to both poles, his dominant pattern is clear. He personifies the evils of urban civilization in the pseudo-scientist Westervelt, whom he casts in the image of the devil, an image at the same time suggestive of the suave, but unprincipled European artistocrat popular in American fiction. Westervelt's smile is "metallic," characteristic of the harsh, mechanical civilization to which Thoreau's locomotive belongs. The reformer Hollingsworth, with his callous inflexibility of purpose and his heart made icy by intellect, is also given the moral attributes of a civilization founded on iron and steel. He is depicted, for instance, as a former blacksmith and described at one point as a "steel engine." The trouble with these two people, from Hawthorne's viewpoint, is that they use their fellow human beings for their own selfish ends. Thus, Hollingsworth destroys the exotic Zenobia, who brings to mind Eve in her "earliest garment" and who stands, in part, for the creative principle of love. The reward for virtue, as with Thoreau, finally goes to the child of nature, the fair, spontaneous "flower," Priscilla. But the experiment itself is a failure.

It is commonly held that Hawthorne attributes its failure to the evil in human nature. If the story is read in the context of his other works, however, I believe that it will be found that Hawthorne is not so much indicting universal human nature as rebelling against an American moralism which mistakes its

---

[14] *Ibid.*, p. 449.
[15] *Ibid.*, pp. 446-447.

own ego for an angel of God, in the name of philanthropy, progress, or manifest destiny. Especially guilty of the unpardonable sin of spiritual pride, according to Hawthorne, is the scientific-business mentality, represented in such archvillains as Westervelt, Dr. Aylmer, Dr. Chillingworth, Dr. Rappacini, Ethan Brand, Judge Pyncheon—many of whom, incidentally, have mysterious ties with the dark Old World. Like Thoreau, Hawthorne transfers the arena of reform from external institutions to the human heart. The main difference is that Hawthorne's vision is much more social and that he cannot altogether subscribe to the presumption of innocence in nature and the natural instincts. For that reason the pasteboard virtue of Priscilla in *The Blithedale Romance* is much less convincing and less viable than the full-bodied compassion of Hester Pryne in *The Scarlet Letter*, won through suffering and through sinning against the tribal laws. For Hawthorne the regeneration of Adam (or Eve) is not brought about by the instantaneous, miraculous infusion of God's spirit in nature, but through the slow, tortuous path of sin, soul-suffering, and redemption. Thus, although Hawthorne in *The Marble Faun* invokes the traditional American stereotype of Europe as Hell, Europe functions in that work much as Dante's remedial descent into the Inferno, bringing about the redemption of Miriam.[16] Without losing its symbolic associations with Hell, Europe has become "the school of worldly experience"—so central in the works of Henry James and later writers—by which Americans are saved from spiritual pride and innocence.

Although Hawthorne is often considered a "conservative," he was no less dedicated to the American mission of regeneration than Thoreau and other American reformers. Actually, he had great faith in the human capacity for love, once his fellow men discovered and accepted the "sinful brotherhood of mankind," and sin, shorn of its theological apparatus, was for him a great democratizing force. Politically, he belonged to the party of Jackson against the party of privilege. All his life he maintained a "smiling interest" in institutional reforms. He was wistful about the failure of the Brook Farm experiment, thinking that it might have succeeded if it had remained faithful to its own

---

[16] Cf. Lewis, *op. cit.*, pp. 121-122.

"higher spirit" and not lapsed into Fourierism.[17] He was sympathetic with the reformer Holgrave in *The House of the Seven Gables,* who "had better never been born than not to have" the inward prophecy of reform; and he wrote, "The world owes all its onward impulses to men ill at ease." [18] On the whole, he favored reforms which were advanced in a spirit of love and humility.

Thirty-five years after publication of *The Blithedale Romance,* American writers faced a *fait accompli.* Industrial capitalism was triumphant. Yet widespread industrial unrest, the growth of labor unions, agrarian discontent, and the rise of reform movements with large popular followings testified again to the belief that something hoped for in American life was not being realized. Against this background appeared Edward Bellamy's *Looking Backward,* a novel concerned with industrial reform. Bellamy reached into the consciences of literally millions of Americans not so much by describing poverty and social injustice, as did Henry Demarest Lloyd, Henry George, and other reformers, as by dramatizing the European specter of Inequality. His famous analogy of the coach, on which the rich leisure class rode free at the expense of the toiling masses who pulled it, clinched the identification of Inequality with a European aristocracy. As opposed to this, Bellamy held before Americans a realistic vision of a middle-class paradise based on the concept of Equality, to be fully realized by the year 2000 A.D.

The polar contrast in his book is between a past state of social and economic inequality centering in the city of Boston of 1887, and a future state of social and economic equality in the same city some one hundred years later. The imagery characterizing the old city of Boston as a hellish inferno (not unlike the New York of Dos Passo's *Manhattan Transfer* or of Scott Fitzgerald's *This Side of Paradise*) provides a subconscious link with the European past. Bellamy assigns to the city of the future, the American future, the same paradisiac qualities formerly associated with pristine nature by Thoreau and to some extent by Hawthorne. The new-model "City on the Hill" is a scientific

----

[17] Hawthorne, *op. cit.,* p. 584. But see also Lawrence Sargent Hall, *Hawthorne, Critic of Society* (New Haven: Yale University Press, 1944), pp. 26-31.

[18] *The House of the Seven Gables,* pp. 350, 428.

paradise, but a scientific paradise modified and naturalized by beautiful parks and gardens. It is described as the "new heaven on earth." Some people in the new city hold that they have "entered upon the millennium" and in the pattern of the rebirth archetype feel wholly rejuvenated upon retiring from the industrial army at the age of forty-five.[19]

Although Bellamy finds his solution to social problems entirely within the framework of an industrial society, the concept of nature and natural law is never far from his mind. Thus, in answer to the charge that the compulsory features of his industrial army are an abridgment to freedom, he argues that people in the new society are freer in all respects, except for the fundamental law of work, which is a "codification of the law of nature —the Edict of Eden."[20] Government is minimized, since the machinery of production and distribution is so "logical in its principles and direct and simple in its workings, that it all but runs itself."[21] Most important for Bellamy, the natural man is good. Without the old institution of property (Thoreau also made this point), men are not tempted to lie and cheat and steal. Bellamy discards social Darwinism in favor of reform Darwinism and the older, sentimental view of nature. That Bellamy's thinking is still conditioned by the original terms of the American mission is revealed in the garden imagery by which he states his purpose, to realize the idea of the nation "not as an association of men for certain merely political functions affecting their happiness only remotely and superficially, but as a family, a vital union, a common life, a mighty heaven-touching tree whose leaves are its people, fed from its veins, and feeding it in turn." Such an achievement would seem "nothing less than paradise." "So it came about," he writes elsewhere, "that the rosebush of humanity" was "set in sweet, warm, dry earth, where the sun bathed it, the stars wooed it, and the south wind caressed it." Its fragrance "filled the world."[22] In this garden Bellamy's hero and heroine discover the rebirth of an old love.

Bellamy's proposal is a middle-class paradise. He accepts the

----

[19] Edward Bellamy, *Looking Backward, 2000-1887*, University Classics (Chicago: Packard & Co., 1946), pp. 57, 135, 141.

[20] *Ibid.*, p. 79.

[21] *Ibid.*, p. 125.

[22] *Ibid.*, pp. 175-176, 200-201.

dream of material abundance and shows that it need not be incompatible with the dream of innocence. He is against breaking the large nationalized industries down into smaller, competitive units, because in practice it would arrest material progress. At the same time, he revitalizes the middle-class success story by holding out real economic opportunity for everybody. It is important, he says, "that not only the good but also the indifferent and poor workmen should be able to cherish the ambition of rising." [23] He is insistent that economic democracy, or nationalization, retain and extend the libertarian features of the old society. But he is opposed to freedom for the few to exploit the many. Trusting in man's essential goodness of heart, he has the middle-class faith in reason to put things right. He embraces the middle-class philosophy of gradualism. His is a peaceful transformation led by the middle class. In assuming that the middle class will co-operate with the direction of industrial evolution toward larger and larger units, he rejects completely the Marxist class analysis and formula for revolution. It is no wonder that his program gained so many ardent supporters and was regarded not as utopian, but as a blue print for reality.

The publication of Bellamy's book was followed the next year by Mark Twain's *A Connecticut Yankee in King Arthur's Court*, which represented a middle-class utopia already realized in the actual achievements of nineteenth-century American civilization, but projected back into sixth-century, feudal England. The resulting sharp contrast between American material achievement and the backwardness of feudal England unwittingly exposed the psychological basis for the conservative American businessman's often-heard claim to being "progressive," to being already enlisted in the cause of a "permanent revolution." The measure of social progress was not the inherent conditions or contradictions of American society, but the reverse image of Europe.

Mark Twain was essentially an innocent who grew up to great expectations in the rural Midwest, who succumbed to bonanza fever in Nevada gold mines, and who came to accept material progress as a great good. But emotional frustrations, crushing business disasters in the East, the loss of loved ones, and a growing sense of guilt for having surrendered to material success

----

[23] *Ibid.*, p. 87.

tended to embitter him. His *Connecticut Yankee* was written in that period of soul-searching and doubt which preceded the bleak pessimism of his old age. In this period he combined a nostalgia for the halcyon days of youthful innocence in pre-industrial Hannibal with savage criticism of the social order and the materialistic morality upon which it was founded. Against this background the *Connecticut Yankee* may be regarded, I think, as a symbolic attempt to persuade himself that all was right in the American garden after all.[24]

In this book his missionary zeal finds an outlet in the traditional polarity of Europe and America, past and future, abundance and poverty, freedom and authority, democracy and aristocracy. It is significant that he does not attempt the conversion of modern England, which has led the world in scientific, industrial progress as well as in democratic, humanitarian reforms and which set an example for America in ending slavery. Rather, he is concerned, as he was on the whole during his travels abroad, with the intensely Protestant American stereotype of Europe as a priest-ridden, backward land, dominated by the same wicked nobility which the colonists had left behind and whose example helped to reinforce in the American South the psychology of a master race. His book, therefore, symbolically re-enacts both the American Revolution and the Civil War. His hero, Hank Morgan, the superintendent in a Bridgeport Colt factory, is suddenly transported into sixth-century Camelot by a blow on the head. There his knowledge enables him to work miracles greater than those of Merlin, the king's magician, and he becomes Sir Boss of all England. The rest of the story concerns his attempt to bring the abject, bigoted masses to accept the blessings of American industrial progress some thirteen centuries before the industrial revolution. He hopes at the same time and by the same means to root out human slavery. The inhumanity of the ruling hierarchies of feudal England is symbolized by the metallic qualities of armor suits, about which Mark Twain writes some of his funniest passages. But his divided state of mind involves him in metaphorical inconsistency. He

---

[24] This statement takes into account both those critics who interpret *Connecticut Yankee* as a veiled attack upon American business practices and those who take his praise of modern times at face value. Cf. Kenneth Andrews, *Nook Farm* . . . (Cambridge: Harvard University Press, 1950), p. 187.

calls his hero's factories "iron and steel *missionaries* of future civilization." [25] He has not altogether succeeded in reconciling the American garden with the scientific paradise.

Hank Morgan, the composite, archetypal American (Yankee) of the machine age, combines the qualities of Benjamin Franklin and Leatherstocking. Although he is an industrial type, he was raised on a farm and has learned to use the lariat and revolver in western fashion. Mark Twain styles him a "Unique," as if he came from a race newly sprung from God. His typically American missionary zeal to reform society, it is hinted, derives from his early proximity to American soil. While these features of Hank's character draw upon American nature as the source of divinity and moral superiority, the standard of nature is also implied in Hank's faith in the youth of England as a means of accomplishing his mission. Hank's assumptions, it must be said, are basically those of Edward Bellamy: that man is at heart good and that a peaceful revolution can be achieved through education and the ballot. The Hobbesian concept of the state of nature is also present in this book, but in general it is reserved for the degenerate state of the English people, inhabiting the Garden after the Fall, from which only the youths of England are exempt.

But Hank Morgan early encounters a problem which Bellamy ignores. Hank's system of education trains the minds of these people for industrial techniques; but their hearts are not moved. He finds it almost impossible, except with youths, to train out the cruel loyalties and inherited prejudices which support the *ancien régime*. In this, he is reminded of the poor whites in the American South. Though the poor whites were always despised and frequently insulted by the slaveholders around them, though they owed their lowly condition solely to the presence of slavery in their midst, they "were yet pusillanimously ready to side with the slave-lords in all political moves for the upholding and perpetuating of slavery." He concludes that all successful revolutions must begin in blood: "What this folk needed . . . was a Reign of Terror." [26] Whereupon he sets himself up as a dictator and willfully slaughters 30,000 of the elite of English knighthood, thereby

---

[25] Mark Twain, *A Connecticut Yankee in King Arthur's Court* (New York: Harper & Bros., 1917), p. 76. Italics are mine. This contradiction again reveals the existence of "covert culture."

[26] *Ibid.*, pp. 171, 298.

becoming the kind of moral monster so often portrayed by Hawthorne. Hank and material progress are finally bested by Merlin,
representing the Church.

Now this conclusion may indeed have been dictated by the
need to get Hank Morgan back to Bridgeport and to prevent
the industrial revolution from humming thirteen centuries too
soon, but it is certainly inconsistent with the story's underlying
assumption of an identity between material and moral progress.
If Mark Twain does not directly question the supposed blessings
of material progress, he at least suggests that the industrial order
lacks captivating symbols and that the new American may have
lost the sense of heart which characterized the simpler, agrarian
past. He calls Hank Morgan at the end the "champion of hard,
unsentimental common sense." [27]

Mark Twain's tentative identification of material prosperity
with democratic progress, an identity underlying both Andrew
Carnegie's "Gospel of Wealth" and the Horatio Alger success
story, has in the twentieth century become the basic premise of
the two major political parties, making a choice between them
often difficult and defections from one party to the other a
rather easy matter. Twain's theory of revolution, on the other
hand, was meaningful only in those countries, as in feudal England, where an *ancien régime* was firmly entrenched. Professor
Louis Hartz has shown that it was almost unthinkable in the
United States, where the *ancien régime* had never had a foot-
hold, except as fictions in the mind, where the major parties
largely agreed in principle, and where any kind of social progress
was thought of as part of a continuing revolution.[28] The pervasive
American "liberal" mentality of big and little Whiggism described
by Hartz has commonly looked upon socialistic and revolutionary
ideologies as foreign importations and attempts of the devil
to sabotage the communal mission. Such ideologies were there-

---

[27] *Ibid.*, p. 386.
[28] Louis Hartz, *The Liberal Tradition in America* (New York: Harcourt,
Brace & Co., 1955), pp. 70-74, 99-100, 207-209. But Hartz, whose work
shows the influence of Tocqueville, does not adequately stress the importance of symbol transference as a source of real tensions in American
political life. The supposed invasion of America by Europe has helped to
set city against country, eastern seaboard against grassroots West, class
against class, individuals against government and authority in general.
Success in fastening the devil label upon the southern planter was undoubtedly a major factor in the Civil War.

fore acceptable only to those Americans whose chief devil image was the rebirth of European privilege in the American business élite.

One of the few native reformers to consider revolutionary doctrine in the twentieth century was Lincoln Steffens. His well-publicized exposés of crime and graft found a people ready for "progressive" reforms of a limited, pragmatic nature, but not for revolution, which finally became abhorrent even to himself. Although the logic of his muckraking *Autobiography* demanded revolution, the book ended as a primer on the dangers of innocence, or false moralism, and like Bellamy's novel prophesied that the good society would come about through the natural course of industrial evolution.

Steffens prided himself upon being a scientific reformer rather than a moralist; yet the structure of his *Autobiography* depends fundamentally upon the archetypal patterns of the American myth of Eden. It follows the initiation ritual, marking Steffens' progress from innocence to a knowledge of the fruit of good and evil (Steffens first acquires a sense of guilt in adolescent sexual experience). As regards society, it builds upon the traditional polarities of America and Europe, East and West, country and city as being roughly equivalent, symbolically, to the moral conditions of Paradise and Hell. Steffens' spiritual journey takes him from the American West, which infuses him with instinctive moral character and visions of the promised land, to the corrupt eastern seaboard and thus to Europe, which becomes for him, finally, a school of worldly experience. He is as much concerned with the "sins upon the land" as the Puritan covenanter, Michael Wigglesworth, and his muckraking contributions constitute one prolonged jeremiad as he traces, in his words, "the trail of the serpent" from city to state to nation, from West to East to Europe.

His imagination kindled by a boyhood on horseback, he elevates the standard of nature, advocating an almost Emersonian self-reliance and honest self-expression. Like Mark Twain before him, for instance, he advises American tourists to the art galleries of Europe to place greater trust in their own instinctive reactions to art than in the standards of sophisticates.[29] His emphasis on

----

[29] Lincoln Steffens, *Autobiography* (New York: Harcourt, Brace & Co., 1931), I, 130.

pioneer self-reliance frequently delivers him to an admiration of strong men like Mussolini or gang bosses, whom he prefers to regard as natural leaders. Although he insists throughout his book upon the need of intelligence before conventional "goodness" if men are to recognize their own greater good and that of their society, he puts before intelligence the need for a regenerating vision akin to Emerson's of the holy commonwealth on earth.[30] He shares the garden enthusiast's suspicion of urban centers, where he begins his supposedly "empirical" investigation of corruption and which he invariably describes in the imagery of a festering inferno. Thus, Pittsburg is "Hell with the lid lifted." [31] But his "scientific" method of reasoning from effects back to causes brings him to the discovery that the eastern cities and the old American stock are more corrupt than the new western states. He therefore considers the "hypothesis" that the process of corruption which is blighting "God's country" is an evolutionary process in which the time factor corresponds with the westward development of the country—or, alternately, that it is the result of an evolutionary change from an agrarian to an industrial order bent on exploiting natural resources of which America is the end product. If he but knew it, he was merely reiterating, in spite of his borrowing of such "scientific" concepts as evolution, what Americans had long believed, that the evils in the land came from the encroachment of Europe upon the eastern seaboard and were spreading westward. This belief is related also to the favorite American oversimplification which locates good in the country and evil in urban areas.

It was almost inevitable that Steffens should trace the process of corruption back to the European past—not only inevitable, but, in the framework of the mythology, appropriate, since he finally decided that the devil in the American garden was the "organization of economic privilege" and the ancestral home of all privilege was Europe. At first he reacts to Europe according to the convenient American Protestant stereotype, which, as Henry Seidel Canby has said of Mark Twain, is no more absorptive of the Old World than a clam of a grain of sand. Venice is "a beastly collection of one-time palaces, now slummy tenements

---

[30] See, for instance, *ibid.*, II, 449, 525-526, 613-614, 670, 700-701, 821.
[31] *Ibid.*, I, 399-401.

set down upon a network of stinking sewers navigated by intelligent rats who lived well upon the garbage dumped into the tideless, motionless drainage of a community of dirty thieves." Everywhere he finds "the fruits of evil done in the interest of the leisure class" and a "throne" awaiting in every European state for a bold leader.[32] But part of the lure of Europe for Americans is that, excepting possibly England, it provides a release from the repressions of an intensely moral climate of opinion in America and a wider range of exciting—even "devilish"—opportunities for self-enrichment. As Steffens says, "Tourism is a moral rest."[33] He luxuriates in the sexual freedom of Paris. He likes the French because they have preserved the integrity of their minds; although they are thoroughly corrupt, unlike the English and Americans, they know it and admit it to themselves. The very moral code of the Anglo-Saxons, according to Steffens, often blinds them to their faults. Most important, Steffens learns, as had Hawthorne and Henry James before him, that Europe has a tragic lesson for Americans: "How could one make a young, vigorous, optimistic people on a virgin, rich part of the earth's surface look ahead to those old peoples on old ground and see that the road we were on would lead up over the hill and down to Rome, Egypt, or China? . . . We shall come through it as the English have; Alaska will become like Pennsylvania; Pennsylvania will become like New England, which is now getting to be more and more like old England; and England may go on into the condition of France or Italy."[34] It is a lesson in humility and can only be learned in the school of worldly experience.

Steffen asks his countrymen to review their image of themselves. He concludes that the strange combination in the American character of unworldliness and corruption is the result of a false moralism which confuses material success with moral and spiritual progress. Thus, the midwestern Progressive reforms were a test of the "so-called New England ideals which came over from England to us with the Puritan, Pilgrim, and other fathers when they had moved west in search of land and liberty,"

---

[32] *Ibid.*, I, 143; II, 702, 816.
[33] *Ibid.*, II, 702.
[34] *Ibid.*, II, 710, 706.

194

and they failed.[35] Only Tom Johnson, the reform mayor of
Cleveland who tried, in Steffens' words, to re-establish "The City
on the Hill," seemed to realize that the shame of the cities was
not the fault of a few "bad" men, or even of big business, but of
all the supposedly "good" men, of the whole system of special
privilege, sanctioned the country over by the gospel of wealth
and its attendant "virtues" of freedom, opportunity, industry,
thrift, etc. The self-righteous reformers, infected with these false
principles themselves, were going all wrong through trying to go
all right. Steffens recognizes that he himself in his early reforming
has been guilty of this same mistaken righteousness. When he
comes to Boston, the queen of the American infernos, therefore,
he muckrakes its "virtues" instead of its bad conduct, with the
result that he cannot get his book published. At the end of his
career he wishes that he had spent his passion for reform on
muckraking the muckrakers. His final position is very close to
that of Hawthorne and Thoreau, as he convicts his countrymen
of the unpardonable sin of pride. But he retains his faith in his
countrymen's capacity to arrive at self-knowledge: "there is
enough good will in all men of imagination and power to do any
good, hard job, even if it is not obviously in their own selfish
interest. They are not often asked to do any such thing." [36]

The testament of Progressive reform, published in 1909, was
Herbert Croly's *The Promise of American Life*. Written in the
same spirit of realistic self-examination in the attempt to explain
where and how American reform had gone astray, it was more
analytical, more penetrating than Steffens' work and went farther
than any previous work in the direction of emancipating the intellect from a voluntary bondage to a simple native tradition. In
it Croly called for a declaration of intellectual independence
which would not be merely negative, not merely a protest against
"feudalism," against "social classification, social and individual
discipline, approved technical methods, or any of those social
forms and intellectual standards which so many Americans
vaguely believed to be exclusively European." He sharply
criticized a national paranoia which would cross the Atlantic
to look for the enemies of American national fulfillment, when

[35] *Ibid.*, II, 473.
[36] *Ibid.*, II, 683.

our real enemies were ourselves. We needed to be liberated "not from Europe, but from the evasions, the incoherence, the impatience, and the easy-going conformity" of our own intellectual and moral traditions.[37] Our own intellectual vices were responsible for such national sins as industrial and commercial chicanery, unjust monopoly, legislation for special interests, public corruption, vulgar boasting and chauvinism, and an apparent preference for the material over the spiritual. In a number of historical chapters, he traced our flabby mental habits back to what he believed was the original, self-damning postulate: the false antithesis between democratic theory and practice on the one hand and on the other European theory and practice, so widely proclaimed and believed since Jefferson's time. Croly was almost wholly, Steffens only partially, emancipated from the Edenic simulacrum.

The theory of American democracy and its practice assumed, according to Croly, that the natural goodness of human nature— so long constrained and denied by the privileged rulers of Europe, whose interest demanded the perpetuation of unjust institutions—would automatically assert itself under the conditions of political liberty and economic opportunity which prevailed in this favored land. Provided that no individuals were allowed to have special privileges, individual and public interest would, on the whole, coincide. Croly did not accept this dogma. His chief symbol of American intellectual superficiality was Thomas Jefferson, who sought equalitarian, socialistic results by means of individualistic machinery. The Jeffersonian tradition brought a wide divergence between democratic theory and practice. In practice as opposed to theory, the European nations were moving in the direction of greater democracy. In practice, the easy fulfillment of the promise was no longer guaranteed either by the existence of the virgin wilderness, which had largely disappeared, or by the Atlantic Ocean, which had shrunk to a channel. In practice, the new industrial order, following Jefferson's policy of drift, which had worked moderately well for a society of farmers, had permitted the rise of special interest groups and a concentration of wealth which murdered equality in the name of liberty. Many reformers, on

---

[37] Herbert Croly, *The Promise of American Life* (New York: The Macmillan Co., 1910), p. 426; but see also pp. 12-13.

the other hand, would murder liberty in the name of equality. In both theory and practice, Americans from the beginning had been following contradictory principles. If the promise of American life were to be realized in the future, thought Croly, the naïve faith in an inevitable American destiny would have to give way to a conscious national purpose which reconciled the contradictions inherited, in name at least, from Jefferson.

Of the founding fathers of the American democracy, only Hamilton, according to Croly, had a clear conception of national purpose, for he would use the powers of the central government not merely to maintain the Constitution, but, by active interference with the natural course of American political and economic life, to promote the national interest. Here we find in Croly, as in Edward Bellamy, a repudiation of the American Adam's almost instinctive distrust of government and centralized authority, a distrust which had caused William Jennings Bryan and a number of other reformers to spend their energy abortively and negativistically on such superficial remedies as currency reform, civil service reform, the referendum and recall. But Hamilton's policies were unfortunately tainted by his identification of the national interest with the interest of the well-to-do. Although Hamilton had a sound, constructive mind, he lacked Jefferson's sincere faith in the American people. Croly therefore proposed to unite the chief virtues of each in a new reform program for all. He proposed what was then, in 1909, a novel idea, but which now seems commonplace: to seek Jeffersonian ends by Hamiltonian means. He did not stop there, however, as some political scientists would have us believe. He was still concerned with the inconsistency between liberty and equality, twin objectives whose desirability he did not question, however much they might owe their native origin and persistent popular appeal to stereotyped images of European society. He concluded that the two contradictory principles could only be reconciled in a third, the principle of *fraternity*.

This conclusion implied a utopian vision of democracy such as found in Whitman, Bellamy, and others. As Croly put it, "Such a democracy would not be dedicated either to liberty or to equality in their abstract expressions, but to liberty and and equality, in so far as they made for human brotherhood." [38]

_____

[38] *Ibid.*, p. 207.

Although Croly clearly saw and honestly faced the possibility that all human relations are corroded and all dreams tainted by self-interest, he could not finally relinquish the American Edenic faith in human nature. He was quite explicit in his affirmations. He admitted the implications in his work that human nature could be raised to a higher level by an improvement in institutions and laws. He revived Montesquieu's statement that the principle of democracy was *virtue*. "Democracy must stand or fall," he wrote, "on a platform of possible human perfectibility." He felt that his faith was pragmatically justified in that the better American has, in fact, "continually been seeking to 'uplift' himself, his neighbors, and his compatriots." Failure was due not to wrong-hearted motives, but to wrong-headed ideas. Democratic dogmas of the past led one to choose the wrong means for the present. One was taught wrongly that " 'uplifting' must be a matter of individual, or of unofficial associated effort" and that the only means are "words and subsidies." In a sense then, Croly, like Steffens, was engaged in muckraking the individualistic assumptions which the great majority of Americans uncritically accepted as virtues. Both Steffens and Croly located their ultimate hopes for the regeneration of American society in the re-education of minds already well disposed, already well intentioned if not always receptive. Re-education, Croly hoped, would inspire a faith which would remain "innocent and absolute without being inexperienced and credulous." [39]

The Great Depression of the 1930's again inflicted a heartbreaking string of broken promises on Edenic expectations, and a noticeable gap again appeared temporarily between the major political parties, although both were more committed to the material paradise than to the holy commonwealth. Neither Herbert Hoover nor Henry Wallace could forget the call of the frontier and the sense of mission connected with it. As Wallace put it in 1934, "To enter the kingdom of heaven brought to earth and expressed in terms of rich material life, it will be necessary to have a reformation even greater than that of Luther and Calvin." [40] His *New Frontiers*, embodying the New Deal

---

[39] *Ibid.*, pp. 399-403, *passim*, p. 454.

[40] Cited in Ralph Henry Gabriel, *The Course of American Democratic Thought* (New York: The Ronald Press Co., 1940), p. 306; see also Henry A. Wallace, *New Frontiers* (New York: Reynal & Co., 1934), pp. 9-10.

198

THE QUEST FOR PARADISE

philosophy, in effect borrowed Croly's blueprint of reconstructed Republicanism for the Democratic party. Individualists like Hoover, though forced by necessity to extend the functions of government activity into the area of human welfare, were still too busy erecting intellectual stop-look-and-listen signs against varieties of European socialism to heed Croly's message. The Democratic party consequently undertook to apply in practice the first major reorientation of American political thought in 150 years. Its often blundering attempts to achieve Jeffersonian ends by Hamiltonian means have inevitably exposed it to charges of socialism and, more recently, of communist infiltration. It is small wonder that advocates of a "regulated capitalism" in the twentieth century have characteristicaly defended big government as the protector of the freedom of the little man and hence as the embodiment of modern individualism.

If one were to judge the public's understanding of these new developments on the basis of the most popular reform work of the New Deal period, John Steinbeck's *Grapes of Wrath,* he would be forced to conclude that the process of re-education begun by Steffens and Croly has not been very successful. This proletarian novel is fundamentally the story of the dispossession of a chosen people and of their westward trek toward the long-heralded promised land which had been denied them in Oklahoma. Their peculiar virtues do not conform to the rigid public standard of morality but flow from a sense of heart, from the creative principle of love, to be found, according to Steinbeck, in unaffected nature. The regeneration of the profane Preacher Casey symbolically realizes, as had the emergence of the savior Lincoln from the prairie sod, the millennial hope of the American Puritans of Christ's Second Coming to the blessed new land. Casey is a second Christ resurrected from the American soil. His spiritual rebirth into the magnetic chain of humanity is brought about according to the formula of Thoreau and many other American saints. "I ain't saying I'm like Jesus," the preacher explains, "But I got tired like Him, an' I got mixed up like Him, an' I went into the wilderness like Him, without no campin' stuff. Nighttime I'd lay, on my back an' look up at the stars; morning I'd set an' watch the sun come up; midday I'd look out from a hill at the rollin' dry country; evenin' I'd foller the sun down. . . . There was the hills, an' there was me, an' we wasn't separate no more. We was one thing. An' that one thing was holy." [41] This merger of the American individual and deific American nature, sometimes called pantheism, is but another expression of that impulse which in the United States has set city against country, East against West, America against Europe, democratic freedom against authority.

A central theme running through Steinbeck's book is that of Hart Crane, that "iron deals cleavage." Against the values of the heart are set those of an intellectually callous, authoritarian, industrial order, which, beginning on the eastern seaboard, has gradually despoiled the whole land and whose chief symbols are iron and steel (one is reminded of Henry Adams' Dynamo). The devil in the garden is an iron monster astride a tractor and set in motion by an impersonal Bank, representing the privileged interests of industrial capitalism. "The man sitting in the iron seat did not look like a man; gloved, goggled, rubber dust mask over nose and mouth, he was a part of the monster, a robot in the seat. . . . He loved the land no more than the bank loved the land. . . . The land bore under iron, and under iron gradually died." [42] The farms are becoming mechanized and the surviving farmers more "petit bourgeois" than ever. Better rank animal behavior than this sterility! The Joads and their friends behave with all the license and freedom of Adam and Eve in the original paradise, their behavior translated in animistic imagery. Steinbeck treats the creative life principles of love, compassion, sacrifice, embodied in these people, in the unabashed sexual terms of a Whitman. And Rosasharn, tendering her bared breast to a starving man, is another Eve, another Hester Prynne—if you will, another Zenobia or Pocahontas.

What is Steinbeck's solution to the imagined problem of concentrated economic power? He is perhaps more aware of the group character of modern society than earlier reformers, but not more aware of the indivisibilty of humanity, properly understood. In part, he stands for an almost mystical vision of a material yet holy paradise. He assumes that given moderately decent living and working conditions, as in the government work camps, men can live in harmony and love. In this he looks back

----

[41] John Steinbeck, *The Grapes of Wrath* (New York: The Viking Press, Inc., 1939), p. 110.

[42] *Ibid.*, pp. 48-49.

to a simpler, earlier time when the country was new. Distrustful of industrial progress, he is not altogether willing to suggest a solution which would exploit science and technology for purely human ends. His is a Marxian, class analysis which yet favors character transformation over revolution. Like Bellamy, he dodges the problem of human nature by deifying it, or at least that part of it which has access to the inspiration of American nature. On the other hand, and on occasion in this book, he is a crusading moralist whose precepts and sharp lines between good and evil, if practiced extensively, would result in holy wars of mutual extermination such as we are bordering on today on an international scale. Thus, he says in one of his interlarded, philosophical chapters:

This you may say of man—when theories change and crash, when schools, philosophies, when narrow dark alleys of thought, national, religious, economic, grow and disintegrate, man reaches, stumbles forward, painfully, mistakenly sometimes. Having stepped forward, he may slip back, but only half a step, never the full step back. This you may say and know and know it. This you may know when the bombs plummet out of the black planes on the market place, when prisoners are stuck like pigs, when the crushed bodies drain filthily in the dust. . . . If the step were not being taken, if the stumbling-forward ache were not alive, the bombs would not fall, the throats would not be cut. Fear the time when the bombs stop falling. . . .[43]

This is the language of Mark Twain's Hank Morgan, quintessential Yankee; this is the moral imperative against which Hawthorne and Steffens warn us.

One of the most instructive lessons of American reform literature is that the important desiderata in reform are not so much the conditions of the real world as the pictures of the world which men carry in their minds. Although these pictures may be shaped by such human "drives" as the economic, the sexual, and power-craving impulse in contact with problem situations in the real world, they are not *one* with the real world and adapt themselves to changes in the real world with almost glacial slowness. On the basis of this study one finds much truth in Lincoln Steffens' observation that against the headwaters of the main stream of corruption American reformers were trying to "swim back—back to Jeffersonian democracy." [44] In this respect, except for Herbert Croly, the industrial reformers repre-

---

[43] *Ibid.*, pp. 204-205.
[44] Steffens, *op. cit.*, II, 495.

sented here do not greatly differ from the agrarian reformers. The reform literature as a whole points up the main strength and weaknesses of the American mind at work, but especially the dangerous incongruity of great vitality, good intentions, and warm hearts divorced from intellect. Only Croly perceived clearly the hypnosis of American reformers by reiterated suggestions of a new American world. Only Croly saw the fundamental fallacy in basing criticism of the industrial order upon a myth of newness.

American reformers of all types have been so obsessed through long cultural inheritance with the hobgoblin of a satanic conspiracy originating in Europe to subvert the American paradise that one mistrusts the accuracy of their judgments. Has industrial capitalism truly released diabolical forces? Are we truly victims of a "power élite?" Is bigness—big corporations, big labor unions, big government, big cities—truly a sin? We are hardly beginning to confront such questions realistically. Working out of a background of Protestant dissent, American reformers have tended to be moralists rather than social analysts, unconsciously putting the religion of Americanism before human betterment. Such preconceptions incline them, too, to place too great confidence in a popular stereotype of the American as Adam which they then let stand for unshackled human nature. Even Croly evaded the issue of human nature when he refused to inquire whether the choice of wrong-headed ideas by otherwise well-intentioned Americans did not have something to do with the rationalization of self-interest. Of the writers studied, only Hawthorne and to some extent Lincoln Steffens responded maturely to the story of the Fall of man.

The sense of moral outrage which breathes through American reform reflects the dogged refusal to accept anything short of perfection. It results from the wrench given to optimistic fatalism when the land of promise turns out to be, by contrast with the ideal, a land of broken promises. Yet the *idée fixe* has prevented the kind of conscious social experimentation in the main arena of reform which would bring about the readjustment of dream to reality. America has not really been, as Daniel Boorstin argues in a recent work, a "disproving ground" for ideals— or not, at least, until relatively lately. The Colonial quest for a perfection of desire, including a final victory over sin, was never abandoned, but merely diverted into more secular paths. Chief of these was the path of material abundance, to which both agriculture and industry gave access. The question then arose whether the greater material plenty of industry as opposed to agriculture was not too costly in terms of certain democratic virtues and of the nation's moral, spiritual, and intellectual life. In answering to the contrary, that the factory was indeed the laboratory of human betterment, conservative reformers, represented by Mark Twain, Andrew Carnegie, and the pioneer industrialists, not only prevailed with a majority of their countrymen, but also influenced many liberal reformers, who were persuaded to believe also in the supposed benefits to be derived from wealth, differing mainly in wanting to see the wealth distributed more equally. Consequently, in times of relative prosperity and expanding opportunity for all classes of people, liberal reformers have too often found themselves in the ridiculous fencing position of Don Quixote. Having individualistic assumptions and functioning meaningfully only from crisis to crisis, their leadership has lacked continuity of effort and a coherent, constructive social philosophy.

Such literary reformers as Thoreau and Hawthorne, who refused to accept an identity between material progress and moral and spiritual improvement, and who with justice attacked intellectual insincerity, self-righteous pride, moral materialism, complacency, and conformism, vices which they vaguely associated with the new industrial ethos, were themselves too deeply imbued with the geographical protestantism of New-Worldliness to see that the real enemy of reform was what Herbert Croly called a canting Americanism of national irresponsibility and indiscriminate individualism. Calling for a change of heart rather than a change of mind, they did little to encourage the kind of tough intellectual discipline necessary to combat the pervasive superficiality of thought. Thoreau's whole bias, indeed, was anti-intellectual. And placing the whole responsibility for salvation upon the individual, they perforce overlooked and ignored social and political means to the same end. Perhaps their greatest contribution to an intellectual awakening was a dramatic demonstration of the extensive spiritual poverty which existed side by side with rich material abundance. Reformers might do well in the future to address themselves more to this problem and less to the problem of "progress and poverty."

11

Henry James
and the American
Rush of Experience

Up to this point I have presented a picture of Americans as a nation of energetic, moralizing reformers, passionately and actively engaged, dizzily, exhaustingly involved, in the serious business of realizing the delights of heaven on earth. This picture conflicts with one frequently encountered in the literature of the social sciences which depicts a national scene of political indifference and apathy, evasive compromise, smug complacency, and stifling conformity. Yet the two pictures are not as dissimilar as they might at first appear. Conformity is a matter of the voluntary association of free persons united under the banner of the same individualistic goals. Free individuals are likely to be politically indifferent and apathetic, for they distrust the machinery of government and the semblance of authority. They prefer compromise to so-called "bureaucratic planning," feeling at the same time that political action of any kind, especially where there is no real difference between the two major parties, has very little to do with the fulfillment of the promise of American life, whose chief instrumentality is individual effort.[1] Optimistic fatalism, born of the illusion of being a favored people, has been chiefly responsible for complacency.

---

[1] Cf. Morris Rosenberg, "Some Determinants of Political Apathy," *Public Opinion Quarterly*, XVII (Winter, 1954-1955), 349-366.

But in the areas of individual effort and aspiration, Americans have hardly been indifferent; they have cared mightily and heroically about such things as prosperity, success, personal freedom, happiness, and would not consciously compromise these for all the international good will in the world. Where an American is indifferent about some things, one can be certain that he is seeking a heavenly beatitude in another respect. Unfortunately no matter what path of self-fulfillment he follows (and, as will be seen, the number of rewarding choices is not nearly as great as may be imagined), he is doomed like a spoiled child by the very enormity of his expectations to varying degrees of frustration or disillusionment. He anticipates a perfection of fulfilled desire in a world which must remain forever imperfect, suspended forever in a specious present between past and future.

His pursuit of the Promise to the edge of the Pacific, where some of the more hysterical, not to say exotic, forms of American idealism now flourish, has produced, as I have pointed out, a significant tension in American life between the western parts of the country and the older eastern settlements. The domestic cleavage of West and East, which exists even today in the long-time rift within the Republican party, originally described relationships of power and status. The economic dependence of a debtor West upon a creditor East combined the same attitudes of servility and rebellion which earlier defined Colonial dependence upon Europe. The proud boast of the Kentucky orator that the West "defies and transcends criticism" often concealed —if the writings of Andy Adams, Hamlin Garland, and Joseph Kirkland are to be believed—a private experience of loneliness, dirt poverty, hardship, and cultural drabness hardly in accord with dreams of romantic plenitude. The self-sufficient, superior westerner, professedly contemptuous of eastern refinement, was forced to seek out the paths to power and dominance in the East. The unsatisfied yearning after perfection in an imperfect world might find even hell an improvement over what was once fancied paradise. So was born a tragic tension which has caused some Americans to look backward and eastward, with a heightened sense of the urgency of time and lost opportunities, toward the hellish Old World.

As the westward pole of experience became exhausted of

value, long before the end of the physical frontier, the historical pilgrimage to the West began to be replaced by a smaller, though no less significant, reverse migration of Americans to the eastern seaboard and the Old World. Something of the trepidation, the anguish, and the embarrassment of the westerner's initial assault upon refined eastern society is contained in the career of Mark Twain. His humiliation at the famous Whittier birthday dinner helped to make the formal dinner party a major literary symbol of American inexperience in the ways of the world.[2] The provincial American, whose smug superiority hides a deep sense of cultural inferiority and whose Edenic expectations thrill to the promise of a spectacular material success, has also been fatally attracted to the city. Its incandescent spires and towers have exerted the romantic fascination of another Camelot transplanted to America. A favorite theme of American novelists, a theme closely related to studies of failure in our society, has been the contrast of country and city—the innocent boy or girl from the country destroyed physically, morally, and spiritually by the temptations of city life.[3] This is the story of Scott Fitzgerald's Jay Gatsby, for instance, whose descent into hell parallels his pilgrimage from West to East.

But the chief chronicler of the reverse migration has been Henry James, whose concern with the "rush of experience" has been less the corruption of innocence than the possibility for a richer self-fulfillment.[4] The main issue which his international novels pose is the possibility of cultivating, broadening, refining the sensibility without a corresponding loss in moral and spiritual qualities. One learns in Europe the meaning of the fall from paradise as the condition of a greater humanity, and James effects a symbolic marriage of morals and manners, of American and European civilization, not solely on American terms. At the

---

[2] Silas Lapham's entrance into Boston society at the unfortunate Corey dinner party, for instance, parallels Christopher Newman's reception at the party of the Bellegardes in France. The perils of the dinner party as the main vehicle of social initiation also figure largely in Lewis' *Babbitt*.

[3] Blanche Housman Gelfant, *The American City Novel* (Norman: University of Oklahoma Press, 1954).

[4] Robert Ornstein, on the other hand, does not feel that the reverse migration had the special significance for James that it had for Fitzgerald as a "profound displacement of the American Dream." Cf. Robert Ornstein, "Scott Fitzgerald's Fable of East and West," *College English*, XVIII (December, 1956), 139-143.

same time, his work is a continuation of the traditional American quest for experience.

James was brought up in the lap of the same polite society which administered a public spanking to Mark Twain and which, from Colonial days, had prided itself upon its ties with Europe in opposition to the prevalent New-Worldliness of outlook. Its representatives liked to forget that they were themselves essentially backtrailers to the more sophisticated overseas society. More specifically, James was a spokesman for the relatively small group of Americans with aesthetic and intellectual interests who, as Herbert Croly noted, discovered that the first step in achieving standards of individual excellence was to go abroad. If they were scholars like Edward Everett, Channing, Longfellow, Charles Eliot, and William James, they were likely to be attracted to one of the German universities, where they could study under some eminent specialist. If they were writers, painters, sculptors, architects like Hawthorne, William Wetmore Story, Horatio Greenough, and Thomas Cole, they would flock to Paris and Rome for tutelage.

In their pursuit of ripening experience, they were the more restrained forerunners of Lost Generation intellectuals of the 1920's who, as Ford Maddox Ford has said, "from the limitless prairies leapt, released, on Paris." [5] They were reacting to the felt limitations of their own cultural environment as well as to the possibilities abroad. But James was even more concerned in his writing with the invasion of Europe after the Civil War by a class of new rich—the sons, daughters, and wives of industrial tycoons, for whom Europe provided pleasing toys, diversions, examples of prestige spending, and élite social behavior. If these people were to constitute the new American ruling class, as James supposed, he was concerned that they learn to aspire more worthily, and he tried to uncover the layers of experience upon which true culture is based.

James was, and remained, as much an individualist as any patriot, but he believed that the truest and highest development of the individual was a function of culture. As a passionately dedicated and gifted writer whose art was his sole bulwark against chaos and who, except for the brief flurry of excitement
_____
[5] In his "Introduction" to Ernest Hemingway, *A Farewell to Arms* (New York: Random House, 1932), p. xii.

created by *Daisy Miller,* was singularly unappreciated in his
own country, James had the right to ask and attempt to answer
the question, what in American experience stifled the growth of
true individualism? His answer, though often embodied intui-
tively in metaphor and dramatic situation, was as searching as
that propounded by Herbert Croly, based on his knowledge of
comparative cultures. In this connection, too much—far too much
—has been made of the "terrible denudation"of American life
found in James' early study of Hawthorne. James' lament for
the absence in America of courts, sovereigns, palaces, castles,
manors, thatched cottages, ivied ruins, an aristocracy, and a
priesthood expressed, as with Hawthorne, a deeper want, a want
closely related to the character of American individualism as
well as to the plight of that much-written-about, but little-
understood figure, "the alienated artist." The alienated artist—
and in what society is he not alienated in some sense?—is but
a special case of the failure of individualism in a country which
boasts above all of its libertarian tradition of individualism. It
is this irony which makes the situation of the artist in America
often seem desperately unique.

James' poetic formulation is valuable and significant precisely
because it applies not only to aesthetic self-fulfillment, but to
every aspect of individual fulfillment, understood and judged
in the light of a whole culture. James' answer to the problem
of American individualism was that the nation's value system—
the whole body of laws, rules, habits, traditions, customs—acting with an imperious force binding upon the whole community,
forced the main currents of American life down a rather few
large tributaries. Brave individuals who chose to swim elsewhere chose to swim alone and apart at the risk of being left to
drown. James was, in other words, essentially at odds with a
Puritan tradition that made individual responsibility a matter
of collective mission rigidly and narrowly defined.

It was not simply that American businessmen had a way of
becoming fundamentally alike, however different from one another in temperament, circumstance, and habit, since the ultimate measure of the value of their work was much the same
in the appraisal of its results by its cash or philanthropic value.
James objected more to the moralizing odor of sanctity which
surrounded all such approved activity. The moralizing impulse

tried to confine the organic, temperamental needs of complicated individuals within a simple set of abstractions or utilitarian principles. James clearly saw and understood the dangerous social consequences—so widely felt today—of emotional starvation in the midst of industrial plenty when the normal human craving for power, love, and prestige can be satisfied in rather few ways. We still face a situation where, in theory, the individual has a bewilderingly broad latitude of choice, but where, in practice, his choices are most often made for him by the culture or subculture from which he springs.

Because moralistic preconceptions screened out a vast range of enrichening experiences, James opposed to the rationalized public code a private, intuitive code which passionately embraced the novelty, even the danger, of difference and in which, in his case, the social, aesthetic, and moral goods of life lay very close together. James nevertheless owed the force of his energy, aspiring after a nonutilitarian beatitude of refined human relationships, to the American dream of Eden; he could rebel against it, he could give it a new twist, but he could not altogether deny it.[6] It was most natural, therefore, according to the mythology, that Europe should for him, as for Hawthorne, Steffens, and others, best symbolize the novelty and danger of difference. To the extent that his personal salvation lay in wanting to complicate life by retiring to Europe, the ancestral home of artifice and ritual, his biographer, Frederick Dupee, is surely right in observing that he opposed the great tradition of American saints such as Thoreau or certain of the pioneers, who wanted to simplify life. But he did not essentially challenge the myth of the West, and, indeed, in his later works especially, vigorously reaffirmed it. He learned, even, to appreciate Walt Whitman, whom in an earlier review he had considered a childish barbarian.

James was led to his great theme of the initiation of innocent Americans into the European "school of worldly experience" largely by his own passion for experience, from which he was barred by the moral predilections of his society. In an important

---

[6] The fruitfulness of this approach to Henry James has been pointed out before. Cf. R. W. B. Lewis, *The American Adam* (Chicago: University of Chicago Press, 1955), p. 153; Charles L. Sanford, "The Garden of America," *Modern Review*, Calcutta, India, XCII, No. 1 (July, 1952), pp. 29-30.

sense, however, he never departed from this theme, for the central consciousness of his purely European stories was usually that of some loyal, innocent, generous spirit, like Fleda Vetch of the *Spoils of Poynton* or Nanda of *The Awkward Age* or Hyacinth Robinson of *The Princess Casamassima,* who is exposed for the first time to the complexities and intrigues of *mondaine* society. In both his international and European novels one finds rather similarly endowed heroes and heroines salvaging, finally, some kind of personal triumph out of otherwise crushing defeat at the hands of a hard, shrewd set whose exquisite taste and manners blind the intended victim to cool, calculating treachery in a world which pretends to be supremely civilized. If, as an expatriate, James depicted the limitations of American experience, as an American he pronounced a judgment upon European civilization. It is almost a truism by now to say that he wanted the best of both worlds: an affirmation of life even at the cost of life, high intellect grafted to fine, intuitive insight, and great sensitivity to textures coupled with complete moral integrity. "Yet from youth to age," Austin Warren writes of James, "he gives unpleasant pictures of the merely intelligent and cultivated. . . . High exalted above the bright and cultivated are the *good*." [7] James' accent everywhere in his work upon a nontraditional, nonutilitarian, transcendental "goodness" is the familiar mark of the American intuitionist, or primitive, rebelling against a rationalized public code.

A friend of James' English countryhouse set, Mrs. W. K. Clifford, once said of him: "How thoroughly English Henry believed himself to be, and yet, poor dear, he was always *so* American." [8] The English critic, V. S. Pritchett, to whom James also seemed aloof from the English imagination, located his essential Americanism in a quality of innocence or moralism which prejudged experience. Indeed, James' whole career was rooted in the attempt to break through the complex of scruples which hedged about his little corner of the American world so that he might assert himself in the greater world. The struggle between his Faustian and un-Faustian self was resolved, if at all, only through

---

[7] Austin Warren, "Myth and Dialectic in the Later Novels," *Kenyon Review,* V (1943), 567 (italics are mine).

[8] Quoted in Henry Seidel Canby, *Turn West, Turn East* (Boston: Houghton Mifflin Co., 1951), p. 213.

THE QUEST FOR PARADISE

his art as an image of power. Characteristically, he expressed his sense of the fact of his American bondage, as opposed to the American promise of an ineffable bounty, in terms of his art. Thus, with a feeling for the irony of the situation, he wrote: "'Art,' in our Protestant communities, where so many things have got so strangely twisted about, is supposed in certain circles to have some vague injurious effect upon those who make it an important consideration. . . ." Conversely, he felt drawn to Turgenev because Turgenev did not have in his mind "a grain of prejudice as large as the point of a needle. . . . Our Anglo-Saxon, Protestant, moralistic, conventional standards were far away from him, and he judged things with a freedom and spontaneity in which I found a perpetual refreshment." [9] Nevertheless, James spent the rest of his life revising downward his early, supposedly "emancipated" impressions of European writers and artists on grounds of vulgarity (meaning often aesthetic grossness and disorder as well as immorality). He correspondingly thought better of his own country. The American heroes and heroines of the later novels are more finely motivated than are Daisy Miller and Christopher Newman of the early novels.

James' lover's quarrel with his country was not limited to a defense of art against prurient Philistia. His sense of being trapped within the bright, bare little box of American conventionality came out in many other ways. He understood, for instance, that there was very little that was unconventional or radical about American reforming zeal, and he tired of the "overwhelming questions" pushed at him so earnestly by his reforming father and circle of family friends. His father was a Swedenborgian, who, with each new social enthusiasm such as Fourierism or the abolition of slavery, heralded the coming of the new heaven and new earth, differing from other reformers of his day mainly in that his vision of the New Jerusalem was founded on a concept of personal freedom which would be consistent with a knowledge of human perversity. The younger James inherited the difference.[10] He embodied his dislike for American

[9] Henry James, *Partial Portraits* (London, 1888), pp. 296-297, 381.

[10] For a full discussion of the influence of the father's religious and philosophical ideas on Henry James, see Quentin Anderson, "Henry James and the New Jerusalem," *Kenyon Review*, VIII (1946), 515-566; also his book, *The American Henry James* (New Brunswick: Rutgers University Press, 1957). This attempts (rather too literally) to read the father's cosmic analogies into the texture of James' writing.

institutional reform in *The Bostonians*, which satirized the feminist movement, best represented perhaps by Miss Birdseye, with her "faint odor of sanctity." He not only questioned the motives of such reformers, but exposed their life-denying contempt for true individualism in placing abstract principle before the sentiment and distinctions of sex. His wholesale condemnation of social revolutionary movements in *The Princess Casamassima* was based upon a vision of a finer, freer society than either that envisaged by the reformers or the existing one presided over by the decaying European aristocracy.

James had called *The Bostonians* "a very *American* tale, a tale very characteristic of our social conditions." Boston, for James, was the hub from which radiated Protestant American moral culture. He once wrote to his brother's wife in Cambridge warning her against the predominance of the moral and spiritual in her daughter Margaret's education. "*We* (father's children)," he said, "were sacrificed to that too exclusive preoccupation: & you see in Wm and me, & above all in Bob, the *funeste* consequences! . . . With her so definite Puritan heritage Peggy could easily afford to be raised on almost solely *cultivated* 'social' & aesthetic lines." [11] One of the *funeste* consequences of this moral education was undoubtedly James' portrayal in *The Turn of the Screw* of a well-intentioned governess whose narrow upbringing in a Hampshire vicarage did more to destroy the childhood Eden at Bly than all the blandishments of the devilish Peter Quint and his partner Miss Jessel.[12] The governess' success in imposing her pre-formed conviction of sin upon little Miles, far from saving him, drove him to his death.

This story of inadequacy in Eden and of the perils of growing up suggests the life-denying qualities of New England moral culture. James' favorite adjectives for New England were "little," "old," "dusky," "wintery." The image which summed up his final impression of Hawthorne, toward whom he was otherwise sympathetic, was the Keatsian "cold pastoral." He leaned especially heavily on the season of winter for such literary place names as

---

[11] Quoted in Frederick W. Dupee, *Henry James* (New York: William Sloane Associates, Inc., 1951), p. 219.

[12] Cf. Robert B. Heilman, "The Turn of the Screw as Poem," *University of Kansas City Review*, XIV (1948), 272-289; Joseph Firebaugh, "Inadequacy in Eden: Knowledge and 'The Turn of the Screw,'" *Modern Fiction Studies*, III (1957), 57-63.

212

Winterhaven, Woollet, and *Grimwinter* to suggest the frozen
emotional lives of New England communities. Winterbourne, the
expatriate in *Daisy Miller* who had found the Calvinism of
Geneva congenial, came originally from Boston. Though his
long stay in Europe had caused him to lose "the right sense for
the young American tone" of Daisy Miller, a Schenectady girl,
his origins were betrayed by a certain stiffness of mental set
and bearing.

The New England origin of such characters as Benjamin Babcock, Jim Pocock, Caspar Goodwood, Susan Shephard Stringham,
and Henrietta Stackpole was not only suggested by their names,
but also by their physical angularity, their briskness, their simplicity of judgment, and sometimes their dour, finicky natures.
But their chief deficiency was the institutionalized manner which
for Americans from the grassroots, if not for James, marked
the invasion of America by European culture. From this deficiency James excused certain New Englanders either because, like
Ralph Touchett, they had received their early education elsewhere, or because, like Lambert Strethers, they succeeded somehow in transcending their provincial limitations, or because,
like Susan Stringham, they came from the hinterland of Vermont,
where James supposed a certain natural spontaneity still existed.

James' most unpleasant Americans, as well as most comic and
pathetic, came from New England. In general, one of two
things happened to them in Europe: they took their moral sense
to Europe to condemn or ignore what lay beyond their compre-
hension—and that was almost everything—or they took it to
be befuddled and corrupted. The former was the fate of the
many "passionless pilgrims" of James' stories, the latter of such
apostate American characters as Winterbourne, Roderick Hudson, Gilbert Osmond, and Chad Newsome. Almost as unsuccessful as a group on both counts were James' metropolitan New
Yorkers, who took with them chiefly the morality (and the vulgarity) of the pecuniary incentive. But these were not the
people who best represented to James America's latent capacity
for building a higher civilization.

His archetypal American heroes and heroines, true heirs of
the promise, who combined a zest for life with a moral spontaneity and freshness of outlook quite unknown to the rationalized public code, usually acquired grace somewhere west of

the Hudson.[13] Christopher Newman of *The American* had sat around western campfires. Of him, James wrote that a more completely healthy mortal had "never trod the elastic soil of the West." One of Whitman's athletic race of reborn men and women, Newman was named "Christopher" after the discoverer of the Western world, "Newman" after the new Adam who was to inhabit it. Christopher Newman, Isabel Archer, Milly Theale, Adam and Maggie Verver, even Daisy Miller, had she lived— these were the innocents who could profit most from the deepening and broadening experience of Europe, who had the courage to brave, to enter into, the dangers of difference and had also the straight-grained, though pliant, firmness of character to preserve an essential goodness beneath their accretions. These were the people in whom James lived out most fully, if only symbolically, his inmost desires for himself and his country.

Nursing an American Adamic conviction of inexperience, James' impulse to plunge into experience, as Philip Rahv and others have noted, was matched only by the contrary impulse to withdraw from it. In his social life the self-assertive ego suffered at the hands of the tribal censor raised up in him by "that too exclusive preoccupation." [14] In his literary life, however, his American heroes and heroines learned to assert the "rights of personality." They more than compensated for his sense of personal failure, which was best illustrated in the symbolic autobiography of such stories as "The Jolly Corner" and "The Beast in the Jungle." "The Beast in the Jungle" invites comparison with Melville's *Moby Dick*. Both stories portray human pride and vanity as the major ingredients of idealizing self-delusion; both utilize the imagery of land and water to parallel callow inexperience and passional involvement; both employ the journey pattern

---

[13] James himself was a native New Yorker, but his American heroes and heroines are in important ways related to his feeling for his cousin Minny Temple of Albany, who died early of tuberculosis and whom he regarded as "a symbol of all kinds of beautiful lost things . . . a plant of pure American growth." Cf. Dupee, *op. cit.*, pp. 45-46. James may also have had in mind his friend William Dean Howells from Ohio.

[14] My emphasis here, as elsewhere, is cultural rather than psychoanalytic. Two classic Freudian interpretations which have been hotly debated are Saul Rozenweig, "The Ghost of Henry James: A Study in Thematic Apperception," *Partisan Review*, XI (1944), 436-455; Edmund Wilson, "The Ambiguity of Henry James," *The Question of Henry James*, ed. Frederick W. Dupee (New York: Henry Holt & Co., Inc., 1945), pp. 160-190.

to register movement between the poles of submissiveness and assertiveness; in both the perils of existence are represented by a lurking monster of nature. But where Captain Ahab is Faustian man, John Marcher is, in the words of Clifton Fadiman, the un-Faustian coward of James' own unlived life. Ahab is willing to launch his ill-fated ship into the deeper, shark-infested waters of life; Marcher's boat ride begins and ends at Sorrento, leaving him metaphorically abandoned, looking at May Bartram "across some gulf or from some island of rest." The fate of both Ahab and Marcher is nevertheless much the same, though spelled out at the opposite poles of experience: that is, a tragic failure of communication with their fellowmen—Marcher by withdrawing into the privacy of his illusions, Ahab by trying to impose his illusions upon his crew. Their idealizing passion prevents them from recognizing the sin of pride in their own natures.

There is, of course, a vast difference in artistic conception. James' intention requires that nothing actually happens. There is no exciting chase or adventure as in *Moby Dick*. Melville's whale has an independent existence, while James' beast does not exist independently of the mind of Marcher. Marcher's immense loneliness and spiritual emptiness are communicated in a language of abstraction floating in an airless, timeless, unpeopled, almost unfurnished medium relieved only by a few splashes of color associated with May and the boat ride. May is the Eve of Marcher's silent vigil, "a rare flower," the full meaning of whose loss comes to him in the image of scarred passion on the face of a stranger whom he meets at May's tomb. He has loved May not for herself, as he supposed with his delicate, small tributes and his scrupulous concern to let her live her own life, but rather for her interest in him and the precious secret which separated him—them—from the commonality.

Marcher's fall from paradise, bringing a tragic self-knowledge which Captain Ahab never learns, is developed thematically through an ironic juxtaposition and echoing of the seasons of the year. The story opens prophetically, ominously, during autumn at Weatherend, where Marcher and May reminisce about their boat ride at Sorrento in the spring of their youth ten years before. Their intimate community of hushed conversation begun here continues for many years, culminating in an

April visit which reverses the conventional symbolic meaning of the Easter month. May's heroic last effort to bring about a fulfillment of the promise of their first meeting fails. She sits without a fire. The faded green of her scarf is all that remains of the early greenery of Sorrento. The waxy whiteness of her face, the pallor of approaching death, holds up only an artificial lily to Marcher. The last scene is enacted in autumn, when, filled with a horror of waking knowledge, Marcher flings himself, face down, on May's tomb.

An ironic tension is maintained throughout the story between Marcher's meticulous recording of the passage of time and his failure to heed its urgency. He keeps a calendar of his regular visits to May and almost religiously observes dates, birthdays, anniversaries, but hardly notices the slow erosion of the years until May is suddenly old. His failure at first to remember the one important event of his life, his first meeting with May, contrasts incongruously not only with his mental habit of noting dates, but with the many metaphors of uneventful time which fill the story: "Year after year, he brought his inevitable topic . . . the very carpets were worn with his fitful walk. . . . The generations of his nervous moods had been at work there, and the place was the written history of his whole middle life." [15] The final futility of Marcher, whose fate was to be "the man of his time, *the* man, to whom nothing on earth was to have happened," illustrated one of James' favorite morals, "Live, live while you can," where to *live* meant not to live alone, but to live in the hearts of beautiful, refined men and women who have experienced the fruits of the knowledge of good and evil. The one unpardonable sin in James, as in Hawthorne, is to exploit people for selfish ends, as Marcher unconsciously does May. May suffers the fate of pure self-sacrificial goodness in an evil world, and the names of May and Marcher together suggest the seasonal extremes of the life-giving force of regenerative sympathy and the life-denying force of cold egotism.

From early to late, James' central characters are dominated by the desire to surrender themselves to the rush of experience before it is too late. Lambert Strether's pronouncement in Glori-

---

[15] Henry James, "The Beast in the Jungle," *The Novels and Tales of Henry James,* New York ed., 26 vols. (New York: Charles Scribner's Sons, 1907-1917), XVII, 86.

ani's garden in 1903 is merely a more impassioned version of
Christopher Newman's statement in 1877 that he wants "to
live for the first time." But the surrender to experience is an
engagement with time, bringing loss as well as gain. Everywhere
in James' stories the passage of time is keyed to the theme of
the fall from paradise. Metaphors of light and shadow trace the
progression from innocence to painful experience. Many of the
great climactic scenes, scenes both of spiritual stress and temptation and of ripe fulfillment, take place in a garden. Like Henry
Adams, Mark Twain, and other late nineteenth-century American
writers, James expressed a distinct nostalgia for the undefiled
Eden of his youth in preindustrial, pre–Civil War America. In
his later years, according to Edith Wharton, he considered "summer afternoon" the two most beautiful words in the English
language. He drew his nature-molded American heroes and
heroines from parts of the country relatively untouched by the
passage of time. Many of his stories concern the ravaging effects
of modernism.

In "The Jolly Corner," a product of his visit to America in
1904, the contrast of innocence and corruption is related to the
contrast between an ideal past and sordid present. Spencer
Brydon returns to his native New York after a long sojourn in
Europe, afraid that he might have missed something good, that
his "selfish frivolous scandalous life" as an aesthete in Europe
might have spoiled him for his childhood sweetheart, Alice
Staverton. He finds that the earlier, simpler, more natural society has been supplanted by a rude industrial society devoid of
humanity and spirituality, represented by the maimed phantom
of his other self. Except for his dismayed discovery in himself
of a latent capacity for business and rental values, he feels utterly
foreign to this new world. His sense of being dispossessed as
well as his need to conquer the phantom of his acquisitive
instinct almost blinds him to the fact that some comforting reminders of his boyhood past survive in the present. The bare
rooms of the Jolly Corner are furnished with memories which
have values other than the "beastly rental values," and Alice
Staverton has been unspoiled by modernism.

Alice Staverton, as an intuitive life force—like May Bartram
another Eve figure—and the architecture of the Jolly Corner
with its interesting multiplication of doors in contrast to the

"hardfaced" modern houses, are symbols of the past. James
introduces Alice Staverton in the metaphor of a "pale pressed
flower" who keeps a garden oasis in the "vast wilderness of the
wholesale," among the "dreadful multiplied numberings which
. . . [reduced] the whole place to some vast ledger-page, over-
grown, fantastic, of ruled and crisscrossed lines and figures."
She stood off the "awful modern crush" to accept the challenge
to the spirit "of *their* common, their quite far-away and ante-
diluvian social period and order." [16] It is she who restores
Spencer to spiritual life and human society, though she first
has to compete successfully with the furniture of his childhood
memories and overcome in him the cowardly egotism of Dis-
cretion. He passes through the door of sexual love held open to
him, as Marcher does not. He, too, like his *alter ego*, has had a
ravaging experience which confers upon him the "interest of
difference," but, unlike the black stranger he might have been,
he has not fallen from grace. Or if he *has*, he has succeeded in
regaining paradise on a higher level of awareness, has achieved
through the death of the stranger a rebirth. After his fall to the
floor at the conclusion of his ghostly bout, he tells Alice Staverton, "I can only have died. You brought me literally to life." [17]

"The Jolly Corner" should be read in conjunction with James'
poetic record of his 1904 visit to America, *The American Scene*,
which also concerns the ravages of time. The image of the
black stranger in the story obviously relates to James' mental
impressions of New York City as "the black over-scoring of a
white page by science." The crisscross lines which surround the
garden oasis of Alice Staverton, suggesting the multiplicity and
confusion of the modern city, symbolize in *The American Scene*
the organization of society by the bank book. The great material
power of the new America, unharnessed to worthy ends, is
summed up for James in the perpendicular thrust of the city skyscrapers with their awesome defiance of natural laws. Turning
from the bristling pincushion of the perpendicular, James looks
for the organizing lines of a simpler, earlier age and finds them
in the restful horizontal lines of Trinity Church, one of the few
remaining symbols of permanence. Others are Central Park and
Independence Hall in Philadelphia. Philadelphia has somehow

[16] James, "The Jolly Corner," *Novels and Tales*, XVII, 439-440.
[17] *Ibid.*, p. 480.

managed to preserve more of the quiet charm of its past than
has New York. But, in the main, James' theme in *The American
Scene* is the corruption of a land of great natural beauty by the
instrumentalities of technology and business enterprise. This
theme appears in "The Jolly Corner" in the corruption metaphor
of the "small tight bud" of Spencer Brydon's youthful *alter ego,*
blossomed into a monstrous growth, blighted and spoiled.

The theme of the corruption of a once Edenic land in *The
American Scene* fixes upon the contrast of past and present. I
have already mentioned the contrast of Central Park and the
city skyscrapers. As James traveled northward, he was appalled
at the brazen, commercial effrontery of the two railroads along
the banks of the majestic Hudson. In Boston he juxtaposed the
new Harvard football stadium and Longfellow House and remarked upon the barbarization of the European immigrant. In
Newport he complained that the resort of his youth had become
"all house and no garden." James' indictment of the "modern
crush," largely a product of his early upbringing, appears almost
everywhere in his stories, European as well as American. The
organization of society by the bankbook is the main source of
treachery and intrigue involving the victimizing of innocents,
whether European or American. The major difference between
the scheming American Moreens in "The Pupil" and the scheming
European Maude Lowder of *The Wings of the Dove* is one of
refinement and sophistication. And in those stories where rich,
depraved Americans do *not* try to buy impoverished European
princes and princesses as trophies to take back home, the impoverished, but elegantly turned-out princes and princesses are
likely, as in *The Golden Bowl,* to try to catch an American
millionaire. James is not concerned that the exchange be to
the mutual advantage of both parties unless there is some kind
of spiritual regeneration, and the means of regeneration is almost always an American who, possessing money, is at bottom
untouched by the commercial ethic.

Two other important aspects of modernism which James deals
with at length are the commercialization of art and the scientific
mentality. The scientific mentality is displayed most thoroughly
in the character of Dr. Sloper in *Washington Square.* Dr. Sloper
is another Chillingworth: in this case, a conscientious father with
a great deal of justice on his side in wanting to prevent his

daughter Catherine's marriage to a fortune-hunter but who nevertheless takes such a cruel pleasure in being "in the right" and in inspiring a "salutary terror" that he is transformed into a fiend. Like Hawthorne's Chillingworth, his interest in human beings is clinical and speculative, and he runs to an excess of head over heart.

Mrs. Penniman, the matchmaking widowed aunt who would sacrifice Catherine to her own romantic fascination for the young man, tells the doctor, quite truthfully, "You have no sympathy." He confesses to being "amused with the whole situation." At first he is "very curious to see whether Catherine might really be loved for her moral worth." He rather wishes that Catherine would, "for the sake of a little more entertainment," put up a stronger resistance to him. Under the guise of being a *physician* to her in her time of distress and confinement, he practices an exquisite torture. Indeed, his cultured, gentlemanly masquerade casts him in the classic American image of the devil. When Mrs. Penniman tells Morris Townsend, Catherine's "lover," that the worst they have to face is "my brother's hard, intellectual nature," Morris answers, "Oh, the devil!" The full revelation of the father's iniquity comes to Catherine in the fallen garden of Europe as the two are walking in a beautiful Alpine valley and she senses "the neat, fine, supple hand of a distinguished physician"—at her throat.[18]

The ethical implications of Dr. Sloper's role as a scientist have something to do with place and time and social behavior. Dr. Sloper has followed the tide of fashion to Washington Square, a genteel backwater amidst the shrill murmur of trade, a trade which has built his fortune. The relative quiet and peace of this place provides a link with the past. But the contrast of past and present is paralleled by a polarity of morals and manners. Catherine is all goodness without airs or arts. Dr. Sloper has all the art without goodness, save for a deceptive air of righteousness. Morris Townsend's "grace of expression" is in sharp contrast to his "hollowness of tone." Dr. Sloper regards Morris, characteristically, as a "specimen," but he also says of Morris, "He has the assurance of the devil himself." This is not only the doctor's point of view. Throughout the story it is strongly hinted that

---

[18] Henry James, *Washington Square* (New York: Albert & Charles Boni, 1926), pp. 53, 98, 113, 143, 178.

Morris' cleverness and hardness have come from his living or traveling abroad. Arthur Townsend agrees with Catherine that "He's more like a foreigner." [19] Catherine, an old-fashioned American girl, is surrounded by "devils" whose treachery has a distinctly international flavor. Modernism, in James' thinking, would seem to be associated through metaphor and symbol with an inverted form of his international ideal, with both the Americanization of Europe and the Europeanization of America.

For James the role of the artist, like that of innocent young girls, is to test society: to test the extent to which it permits and encourages the development of the fullest potentialities of human personality. James' artist must not succumb to cowardly evasions in order to be popular and make money. He must maintain the integrity of his insight even at the risk of obscurity. Therefore, the state of the serious artist is also a state of goodness, even of innocence, except that the artist is already possessed of the fruit of the knowledge of good and evil. James treats the subject of the commercialization of art in such stories as "The Aspern Papers," "The Death of the Lion," and "The Lesson of the Master." In "The Death of the Lion" the artist Neil Paraday is literally lionized to death by Mrs. Weeks Wimbush, a patron of art, "the wife of the boundless brewer and proprietess of the universal menagerie."

The ravaging effect of modernism upon art is treated most unsparingly, however, in "The Aspern Papers." Here the spirit of the past personified by Juliana Bordereau, the aged mistress of a famous long-dead poet, exacts a poetic and ironic revenge on a prying American editor, who says half-jokingly that he would stoop to any baseness to gain access to Jeffrey Aspern's private papers. His final predicament is "the just punishment of that most fatal of human follies, our not knowing where to stop" trifling with human affections and the sanctity of private life. The scene of the editor's downfall is Venice, a city of multivalent meanings: the ancestral "Venice all of evil" representing the "immense collective apartment" of the greater European metropolis, but also a city containing within it the mystery and romance of a glorious past.

The magnificent Juliana is surrounded with the aura of the

[19] *Ibid.*, pp. 38, 55, 119.

"visitable past." Her very name breathes a "perfume of impenitent passion." The green shade over her "extraordinary eyes" renders her inaccessible to an age of photography that would annihilate surprise. The walls of her dilapidated old palazzo shelter a garden giving off "just such an air as must have trembled with Romeo's vows when he stood among the thick flowers and raised his arms to his mistress's balcony." (Gardens are rare in Venice.) She belongs to a society "less awake than the coteries of today—in its ignorance of the wonderful chances, the opportunities of the early bird. . . ."[20] But she has more than ample resources to deal with the present shallow opportunism, the "vision of pecuniary profit," the lack of poetry and feeling. She pays the editor back in kind, using the bribe of the Aspern papers to obtain special favors: an exorbitantly high rent, tributes of flowers, gondola rides for her spinster niece Tina, and even a proposal of marriage for Tina, the one baseness to which the editor, whether from fitful remorse or from Tina's middle-aged dinginess, cannot stoop. The great scene of renunciation is enacted on a golden autumnal morning in the Bordereau garden after Juliana's death. But the editor's "experiment," as he calls it, has placed him beyond the redemption held out in the "look of forgiveness, of absolution" on Tina's face. His last thought after he learns that Tina has burned the papers is, "I can scarcely bear my loss—I mean of the precious papers."[21]

James both recoiled from and passionately embraced the ravages of time. His approach to painful experience from the tiny, chaste enclosure of Edenic innocence which he associated with the past and a largely countrified America left a strong imprint upon his literary style and themes. In the first place, it accounted for the prevalence in his work, as in that of so many American writers since the Civil War, of the theme of initiation and fall from paradise. In *The Ambassadors* James developed the initiation theme primarily through the image of the current, the stream of life, which immersed Strether ever deeper in worldly experience. Strether's first actual glimpse of the "sinister," confirming an earlier suspicion which he had discarded as unjust and bigoted, came when he saw Madame de

[20] James, "The Aspern Papers," *Novels and Tales*, XII, 48-49, 52.
[21] *Ibid.*, p. 143.

Vionnet and Chad approaching their lovers' rendezvous in a rowboat, waterborne partners in sin, both, as it were, "in the same boat." Strether's own gradual involvement in their fate required a constant revising, reversing, or suspending of judgment. The metaphor of the current and the sea also appeared in such works as *The Wings of the Dove*. Merton Densher and Milly Theale found themselves "afloat" together in a "sea" of intrigue. For Milly, the portrait at Matcham was a "sign of her consciously rounding her protective promontory, quitting the blue gulf of comparative ignorance and reaching her view of the troubled sea." [22]

The view of the troubled sea, in whatever concrete form it took, usually came to James' central characters from the protective shelter of their inexperience, as reflected in the many "peep-hole" images. Catherine Sloper's knowledge of Morris Townsend's true nature thus takes her out of the narrow embrasure of her fears to a window which stands open to a balcony. "She had had a great shock." [23] Lambert Strether surveys the "performance of Europe" from the shelter of Chad Newsome's balcony. Christopher Newman in *The American* has his first view of fashionable European society from the box seat of a theater. Merton Densher senses the threat which Lord Mark poses for himself and Milly Theale when he sights Lord Mark in Venice through the plate-glass window of a café and later sees him in London through the window of Mrs. Lowder's carriage. Milly first comes face to face with her tragic destiny in the portrait of the Bronzino. The portrait of the dead princess hangs deep within the countryhouse at Matcham, where "the prospect, through opened doors," stretching "before her into other rooms, down the vista," unveils layer upon layer of meaning and possibility, of romance and menace.

Open doorways and arches in particular provide the frame for sudden shocking experience. Stalking the empty rooms of the Jolly Corner, alone, at night, Spencer Brydon expects to meet the apparition at the turn of one of the dim corridors or at the opening of a door, a possibility so horrifying that he finds himself at moments "stepping back into shelter or shade, effacing

---

[22] James, *The Wings of the Dove*, in *Novels and Tales*, XX, 144.
[23] James, *Washington Square*, pp. 255-256.

himself behind a door or in an embrasure, as he had sought of old the vantage of rock and tree." [24] He discovers one night an open door that should have been closed. He finally comes upon the apparition framed in the archway made by the silvery nimbus of early dawn. In much the same manner, though quite unprepared for the revelation, Isabel Archer, heroine of *The Portrait of a Lady*, stops just beyond the threshold of a drawing room which opens upon a scene of intimacy between Madame Merle and Gilbert Osmond. From this point on, her world "seemed to open out, all round her, to take the form of a mighty sea, where she floated in fathomless waters." Fleda Vetch, heroine of *The Spoils of Poynton*, also pauses at open doors: "one day, at the turn of a corridor, she found her hostess standing very still, with the hanging hands of despair and yet with the active eyes of adventure." [25] But Fleda is still unprepared for the shock which greets her later at the threshold of the apartment at Ricks when she discovers herself an accomplice to the transfer of the most precious art objects and museum pieces of Poynton to this melancholy place.

James' doors are charged with social meaning involving complex human relationships. They open into parlors and drawing rooms, James' dens of intrigue and schoolhouse for innocents. James' master metaphor for Europe and urbane society is the drawing room. Thus, Milly Theale's Piazza in Venice, after she has rejected Merton Densher, is likened to "a great drawing-room, the drawing-room of Europe, profaned and bewildered by some reverse of fortune." Thus, too, the great house at Poynton "was the record of a life." Its chambers held "all France and Italy, with their ages composed to rest." [26] The drawing room also suggests the "abyss" of experience which draws Milly Theale down from the lonely heights of her hungry inexperience, first from the Alpine precipice from which she launched her flight and then, once, from the elevation high in the "divine, dustless air" of her Palazzo, to passional involvement with humanity, ending in sacrificial, transfiguring death.

James' theme of the fall from grace frequently juxtaposes the

----

[24] "The Jolly Corner," XVII, 457.

[25] James, *The Portrait of a Lady*, in *Novels and Tales*, IV, 164, 435; *The Spoils of Poynton*, in *Novels and Tales*, X, 56-57.

[26] *The Wings of the Dove*, II, 261; *The Spoils of Poynton*, X, 22.

garden and the drawing room. In *The Wings of the Dove*, Milly
Theale is first found in the spring of the year enjoying Alpine
scenery, "the taste of honey and the luxury of milk, the sound
of cattle-bells and the rush of streams, the fragrance of trodden
balms and the dizziness of deep gorges." The story draws toward
an end during an autumnal storm in the drawing room of Venice.
It is a Miltonic storm such as accompanied the expulsion from
Eden—or as James writes, "a Venice all of evil that had broken
out . . . a Venice of cold, lashing rain from a low black sky, of
wicked wind raging through narrow passes" of the abyss.[27] Rain,
of course, is a conventional symbol for death and resurrection.
The resurrection takes place on Christmas Eve when Merton
Densher renounces both the money and Kate Croy, his partner
in crime. Milly's compassion and forgiveness, her interest in
him, has been Densher's "crucifixion."

James' development of the initiation theme, whereby the
import of events is joyously and agonizingly inward, leads directly to the use of the restricted point of view and the technique of gradual revelation. The initiation theme is one with
the theme of the fall from grace. James' innocents are plunged
into a world of shifting values which must be made out, a world
of increasing complexity which must be understood. Milly
Theale has to confront not only the different connotations which
Kate Croy and Lord Mark affix to such deceivingly simple words
as "beautiful" and "good," but also misleading information, lies,
conspiracies of silence, and above all the concealment of ugly
motive by refined behavior. As Joseph Warren Beach has remarked, James' novels should be read like detective stories in
which clues are dropped, something is "blurted out," every fifty
pages or so. But the technique of gradual revelation, adapted
to the process of knowing, of slowly developing awareness, is
also embodied in James' sentence structure. R. W. Short, in a
very able analysis, has shown that James' long, complex sentences
with their many qualifying words and interpolations order their
word sequence in such a way as to emphasize connectives and
prepositions of relationship.[28] They help to locate James' characters in a changing relationship to one another and to the social

---

[27] *The Wings of the Dove*, I, 119-120; II, 259.
[28] R. W. Short, "The Sentence Structure of Henry James," *American Literature*, XVIII (1946), 71-88.

situation. A point needing greater emphasis, however, is that they tend to be *periodic* sentences, contributing to the suspense of discovery by withholding important information or key words and phrases until the end of the sentence, when final meaning for both reader and central character is released.

In *The Spoils of Poynton,* for instance, early in the story, Fleda and Mrs. Gereth are discussing the likely disposition of the treasure within Poynton. This treasure belongs legally, with the house, to the son Owen Gereth, but is most deeply appreciated for its intrinsic value by Mrs. Gereth, from whom it has been expropriated by "cruel English custom." Mrs. Gereth is speaking of Owen's rather vulgar fiancée, Mona Brigstock. The passage as a whole releases its meaning gradually:

"And day after day, in the face of every argument, of every consideration of generosity, she would repeat, without winking, in that voice like the squeeze of a doll's stomach: 'It goes *with the house—It goes with the house.'* In that attitude they'll [Mona and Owen] *shut themselves up."*

Fleda was struck, was even a little startled by the way Mrs. Gereth had turned this over—had faced, if indeed only to recognize its futility, the *notion of a battle with her only son.* These words led her to take a sounding she had not thought it discreet to take before; she brought out the idea of the possibility, after all, of her friend's *continuing to live at Poynton.*[29]

Discussions like the above, passages of systematic exploration and cross-examination by confederates, belong, according to Austin Warren, to a dialectical act of intelligence. Insofar as James himself shrank from the ravaging experience for which he yearned, he was committed to ways of knowing that did not demand emotional involvement or active participation. He approached life at a distance through the eye and ear, through the overheard conversation, through the scenes which greeted his eye as he strode through the streets, the drawing rooms, the museums of Europe. Beneath his urbane exterior he was still essentially the American innocent, trying to open intercourse with the world through tiny peepholes. His ear and eye corresponded to his two principal ways of gaining worldly knowledge, the dialectical and the intuitive. As intuitionist, he was primarily the "seer," a spectator at a performance of many acts with a fatal attraction for the theater and a special fondness for paint-

---

[29] *The Spoils of Poynton,* X, 17-18 (italics are mine).

ings. In his writing one finds him perpetually raising curtains, unveiling pictures, grouping scenes around central situations, alternating dialogue and picture, suggesting hidden depths of character and meaning in strong visual images.[30]

The central images by which he grouped toward revelation, however, clustered around the garden and the drawing room, the polar terms of his apocalyptic theme, man's fall from grace and resurrection. The images of the garden and the drawing room counterpoised his American and European experience, attaching ambiguous values to each: especially a concept of intuitive goodness without the interest or maturity of worldly knowledge, and ripe worldly knowledge without goodness. As a traditionalist, James made a compact with the past, uniting in the ancient story of man's Fall the best traditions of America and Europe that survived the blight of modernism. For James, Europe continued to function, on the whole, as the convenient Protestant American stereotype of hell, a "damned, blood-soaked soil," a metropolis whose drawing rooms are inhabited for the most part by devils masquerading as aristocrats like Urbain de Bellegarde or as suave, bogus counts like Giovanelli and Osmond, but it also served the remedial function of initiating lonely Americans into the human community. James' American heroes and heroines learned abroad not merely a new sensitivity to aesthetic textures, which alone was not enough to complete James' vision of the New Jerusalem, but, more importantly, a new sensitivity to the plight of their fellowmen born of suffering. In them the self-assertive pride of national superiority gave way to self-sacrificial love and compassion.

One would like to add that James thus succeeded in transcending parent-child patterns of dominance and submission on the higher level of tragedy. But James' heirs of the promise come off more like Christian saints and martyrs than like fallible human beings who sin by trying to exceed their measure. They love virtue more than life and finally renounce life for virtue, sacrificing themselves in vicarious atonement for the sins of

---

[30] For the bulk of this paragraph, see Austin Warren, *loc. cit.*, pp. 551-568; Francis Ferguson, "James's Idea of Dramatic Form," *Kenyon Review*, V (1943), 551-568; Edwin T. Bowden, *Themes of Henry James: A System of Observation Through the Visual Arts* (New Haven: Yale University Press, 1957), *passim*.

others. The symbolic gesture is essentially religious, not secular; apocalyptic, not tragic. The wound of "generous suffering" inflicted upon the American Adam and Eve is Christ's wound, not the world's. Surely, it is presumption in these days to continue to suppose that Americans can count in their midst a "saving remnant" whose mission is to bring about the redemption of a fallen Europe. One can only conclude that James leaves the myth of the West virtually intact.

At the same time, paradoxically, he was not a chauvinist: he had too profound a respect for what was admirable in European culture and an acute firsthand knowledge of the isolation of the American individual from a truly satisfying emotional and communal life. He had considerably more insight into the problem of lonely individualism, for instance, than the most recent literary exponent of the American cult of experience, Jack Kerouac. Also realizing the lateness of the hour, the heroes of *On the Road* act out of compulsive necessity the reflexes of an earlier day, roaring wildly back and forth across the continent in borrowed cars, seeking to recover from the lost ancestral groves a holy moment, mad for a completely physical realization of life-bliss, blindly feeling at the portals of the soft feminine source to return to their origins.

James understood that the rebellious apotheosis of sensate experience within a provincial culture merely aggravated the problem of lonely individualism, and he tried to find a solution within the more mature traditions of a world community. Converting animal heat into intellectual intensity, he almost succeeded in discovering a universal human condition. He comes nearer than any other American writer to sustaining a tragic vision of life.

12

Diplomacy in Eden,
1900-1950

Henry James' literary internationalism received little response from a people whose chief interests were still national. The pioneer energies which had but recently carved an empire out of the wilderness were now engaged in carving it up. In a relatively few short years, however, the rapid economic and industrial development would bring Americans not only unparalleled material rewards, but with them responsibilities of world power for which they had not asked and were not prepared. Once drawn into world affairs, they would vacillate between the same extremes of passional involvement and fearful withdrawal, self-assertiveness and self-denial, idealism and disillusionment, superiority and inferiority which had marked the initiation of James' heroes and heroines. Henry James was the literary prophet of America's painful appointment with destiny at Versailles and Yalta.

James shared one important thing in common with isolationist America: that was the mission of salvation, a theme central both to America's westward progress and to its industrial development. According to the American fable, we are "saved" from corrupt city institutions by removal to such rural Edens as George Ripley's Brook Farm, Thoreau's Walden Pond, and Silas Lapham's Vermont farm. On an international level, Henry James' suave, drawing-room Europeans are ultimately "saved"—if these urbanites can be—by the sacrificial idealism of American "country" boys and girls like Daisy Miller or Christopher New-

man, whose very names breathe the requisite qualities of innocence, freshness, and spontaneity. Such benevolent innocence
assumed a world mission of regeneration which has been the
great underlying postulate of American foreign policy. Indeed,
the American sense of an Edenic mission supplied the necessary
bridge from isolationist attitudes to a predominantly international
outlook.[1]

Thomas Jefferson set forth the traditional policy of neutrality and isolation in his first inaugural address, which contained the famous stricture against "entangling alliances," but
he nevertheless expected the moral force of America's example to
spread the passion for liberty and democratic institutions throughout the rest of the world. One hundred and fifteen years later
Woodrow Wilson reluctantly crusaded by force of arms to "make
the world safe for democracy." The objective was practically
identical. Although Wilson explicitly repudiated the policy of
isolation which for so long had united principle with the nation's
best interests, he nevertheless envisaged a league of nations
which would make the world over in the image of a universal
Monroe-ism. "I am proposing, as it were," he anounced to the
Senate in January, 1917, "that the nations should with one accord
adopt the doctrine of President Monroe as the doctrine of the
world. . . ." [2] He hoped that with the help of American leadership the carnivora of Europe would, in a single, unprecedented
act of magnanimity and self-denial, transform themselves into a
gentle, herbivorous folk not greatly unlike Americans.

The Wilsonian world view belonged essentially to that earlier
Edenic image of the world which held that Americans were an
innocent people in an evil world that needed saving, or, conversely, an innocent people in a fundamentally innocent world
in which virtuous foreign peoples needed to be saved from their
wicked rulers. Isolationism would save the world by presenting
it a messianic example of the paradise regained in America;
the new internationalism by messianic intervention in world

---

[1] Cf. Edward McNall Burns, *The American Idea of Mission: Concepts of
National Purpose and Destiny* (New Brunswick: Rutgers University Press,
1957), pp. vii, 161, 259-286. Professor Burns is not concerned with the
Edenic myth as the overarching framework for the idea of mission.

[2] In *The Record of American Diplomacy*, ed. Ruhl J. Bartlett (New York:
Alfred A. Knopf, Inc., 1947), p. 454.

affairs. The Monroe Doctrine was an instrument of messianic example, assuming a radical incompatibility between the virtuous democratic political system of the Americas and the wicked monarchical system of Europe. The extension of the Monroe Doctrine by Theodore Roosevelt and Woodrow Wilson took the form of messianic intervention, with a similarly self-righteous role. Thus, Theodore Roosevelt defended United States intervention in the internal affairs of Latin American countries quite sincerely, if mistakenly, as the justifiable exercise of an international police power against "flagrant cases of . . . wrongdoing." [3]

The policy of messianic intervention, which has come to characterize much of American diplomacy in the twentieth century, was launched in 1898. Whatever the motives of the influential naval clique surrounding President McKinley, it is extremely doubtful that the American people would have been so enthusiastic about going into Cuba and the Philippines if they had not been persuaded of their mission to save a virtuous native people from their wicked Spanish overlords. Once the force of self-assertive idealism had spent itself, however, they reverted temporarily to the self-denying postulates of the messianic example as they debated the agonizing question of annexation of the Philippines. On both sides the question was interpreted primarily as a moral issue involving Edenic conceptions of national virtue, and both sides employed a similar rhetoric. Senator Beveridge argued for annexation: "We will not renounce our part in the mission of our race, trustee, under God, of the civilization of the world. . . . God . . . has marked us as His chosen people, henceforth to lead in the regeneration of the world." To opponents this language seemed so much moral cant to disguise the fact of America's sinful involvement in the European "game" of imperialism. William Jennings Bryan, whose leadership had been influential in the support of war, but who repudiated the fruits of war, answered that the republic which had already shaken thrones and dissolved aristocracies could become the supreme moral factor in the world, "hastening the coming of a universal brotherhood" and giving "light and inspiration to those

---

[3] Dexter Perkins, *Hands Off: A History of the Monroe Doctrine* (Boston: Little, Brown & Co., 1941), chs. I-II, p. 240.

who sit in darkness," *only "by its silent example."* [4] Exponents of both the messianic example and messianic intervention borrowed heavily upon the imagery of light and darkness long familiar to worshippers of a millennial sun.

Mark Twain's satirical essay "To the Person Sitting in Darkness" set the tone for the period of disillusionment and self-abnegation which followed the first international crusade:

Our traditions required that Dewey should now set up his warning sign and go away. But the Master of the Game happened to think of another plan— the European plan. . . . This was to send out an army—ostensibly to help the native patriots put the finishing touch upon their long and plucky struggle for independence, but really to take their land away from them and keep it. That is, in the interest of Progress and Civilization. . . . To [the Filipinos] it looked un-American, uncharacteristic, foreign to our established traditions. And this was natural, too, for we were only playing the American Game in public—in private it was the European.[5]

The issue posed here was similar to that which greeted the coming of the industrial revolution: did America's performance as a world power come up to the standard of a paradise of righteousness, or did it betoken a power-hungry society gone the way of Europe? While the mission of civilization was an important factor in the decision to retain the Philippines, an equally important reason, as given by Henry Cabot Lodge and others, was to prevent the Philippines, in their present weak state, from falling into the despotic hands of powerful nations like Germany or Japan. Business leaders, who had opposed the war with Spain, indeed saw vistas of trade in the acquisition of the Philippines, but also saw the strategic value of the Philippines in sustaining China and all Asia against the aggressions of Europe.[6] America's interest in preserving the territorial and po-

---

[4] *The Record of American Diplomacy*, p. 385; Robert Endicott Osgood, *Ideals and Self-Interest in America's Foreign Relations* (Chicago: University of Chicago Press, 1953), p. 87.

[5] Mark Twain, "To the Person Sitting in Darkness," in Bernard DeVoto, ed., *The Portable Mark Twain* (New York: The Viking Press, Inc., 1946), pp. 607-608.

[6] Cf. Lodge's Senate speech, March 7, 1900, *The Congressional Record*, Vol. 33, Part 3 (60th Cong., 1st Sess.), pp. 2618-2630; A. Whitney Griswold, *The Far Eastern Policy of the United States* (New York: Harcourt, Brace & Co., 1938), p. 17; Samuel F. Bemis, *A Diplomatic History of the United States*, 3d ed. (New York: Henry Holt & Co., 1950), pp. 463-475; Tyler Dennett, *Americans in Eastern Asia* . . . (New York: The Macmillan Co., 1922), pp. 615-632.

litical integrity of China stemmed less from commercial self-interest itself than from the same traditional fear and distrust of the colonial powers of Europe which had given birth to the Monroe Doctrine.

It is significant in this respect that American Far Eastern policy has been distinguished by a sentimental partiality for China over Japan, even though the commercial value of Japan's trade far exceeded that of China. Japan supposedly had developed into an aggressive industrial nation after the European model, following a European brand of *Realpolitik*, while China remained a great agricultural preserve of simple peasant people dedicated to peace and therefore more receptive to American missionary activity. Henry Stimson, Secretary of State under Herbert Hoover, while noting Japan's "imperious economic problem," nevertheless condemned Japan's occupation of Manchuria and added in China's behalf: "For several centuries Eastern Asia has owed its character mainly to the peaceful tradition of this great agricultural nation." At the same time, according to Stimson, American prestige was bound up in the effort of many years to educate and develop China "toward the ideals of modern Christian civilization." China had been the object of the "greatest private missionary effort which had ever been made by the people of one country towards those of another," an effort whose breadth and influence "have not always been adequately appreciated by historians." [7]

That America's permanent involvement in world affairs should begin in the Far East was a result both of a missionary effort to save Asia from corrupting European influences and a natural outlet for the traditional hatred of Europe which had followed the frontier westward. As a continuation of the westering impulse, America's leap across the Pacific represented on a mythic level a culmination of Western man's long geographical journey toward a new Eden. Walt Whitman thus celebrated the "Passage to India" as

> . . . the voyage of his mind's return,
> To reason's early paradise,
> Back, back to wisdom's birth, to innocent intuitions,
> Again with fair creation.

---

[7] Henry L. Stimson, *The Far Eastern Crisis: Recollections and Observations* (New York: Harper & Bros., 1936), pp. 14, 34-35, 90-91, 153.

The architects of messianic intervention were not insensitive to this appeal. Henry Cabot Lodge, for instance, uncovered this deeply buried, but profoundly moving, vision which so many Americans shared when, in his speech before the Senate urging retention of the Philippines, he traced the "mighty movement westward" back to the very edge of the cradle of the race, "whence our far distant ancestors started on the march which has since girdled the world." [8] The course of empire had come full circle.

Completion of the cycle meant to American internationalists, for the most part, the end of the old world order and the beginning of a new world order under American hegemony. Destiny had singled out America to encircle the earth and unite the future and the past, the most advanced nations and the most primitive, the East and the West, in bonds of universal brotherhood, everlasting peace, plenty, and liberty. But such a mission could be brought to fulfillment only by innocent or disinterested action. America must play her messianic role in the world without motives of self-interest and without gaining material or strategic advantage; to act out of self-interest and in a spirit of jealous rivalry would be to play the European game under the old dispensation. Thus messianic intervention from the beginning displayed impulses both regressive and self-assertive. America would assert herself in world affairs only to deny herself in behalf of a restoration throughout the earth of an Adamic condition of innocence and bliss. She would give to the world the blessings of advanced industrial civilization without the taint of advanced civilization.

It is no wonder that Americans have been so often blind to their self-interest in the conduct of foreign affairs, so easily deceived by their own rationalizations, so hesitant to employ military or economic sanctions to enforce their principles and policies, so quick to preach pious doctrine without regard to immediate practical consequences, and so susceptible to moods of cynicism and despair when their high expectations and noble

---

[8] Lodge, *op. cit.*, p. 2630. For the background of the ideas in this paragraph, see Henry Nash Smith, "Passage to India: Thomas Hart Benton and Asa Whitney," in his book, *Virgin Land; the American West As Symbol and Myth* (Cambridge: Harvard University Press, 1950), pp. 19-34.

intentions collapse in the wreckage of ignoble results.[9] For the influence which America exercised in world affairs must, above all, be a moral influence. Thus, the Philippines once taken by force of arms, American statesmen began at once to consider how best to withdraw. This vexing question was finally solved to the satisfaction of the American conscience by the promise of independence in the Jones Act of 1916. The signpost of destiny which pointed from the Philippines to China also required the exercise of virtuous self-denial in that region. The Open Door policy was represented again and again as a barrier to "the selfish attempts of the European powers to carve out spheres of self-interest at the expense of China." [10] The territorial and political integrity of China, at first viewed as a means to equality of commercial opportunity, very quickly became the *sine qua non* of American policy. American influence helped to make it a basic principle of the covenants of the League of Nations and of the so-called Nine-Power Treaty.

Yet Japan's willful disregard of this principle in 1931 brought from the United States government only the rebuke of a righteous schoolmaster. Secretary of State Stimson, it is true, wanted to invoke economic sanctions, but was overruled by President Hoover in favor of a policy of moral condemnation and non-recognition. The national claim to innocency precluded a frank exercise of material power as a weapon of diplomacy, and a pacifistic public temper was not willing to run the risk of war. American statesmen and diplomats had to content themselves

---

[9] I am aware, of course, that this interpretation comes very close to a body of criticism stemming from the work of Reinhold Niebuhr, Walter Lippmann, George Kennan, and Hans Morgenthau, but I am more interested in understanding than condemning. Both the critics and supporters of American foreign policy have agreed in finding a high moral and ideological content in it, but differ in their evaluation of this content. For a favorable evaluation see Frank Tannenbaum, *The American Tradition in Foreign Policy* (Norman: University of Oklahoma Press, 1955), pp. 114-124, *passim;* Dexter Perkins, *Foreign Policy and the American Spirit* (Ithaca: Cornell University Press, 1957), pp. 9-15, 37-52, 91-106. In the course of this debate, nobody to my knowledge has analyzed the connection between the conduct of American foreign relations and the American Edenic myth. The fine semantic distinctions in Robert Osgood, *Ideals and Self-Interest in America's Foreign Relations,* are more often confusing than helpful.

[10] Stimson, *op. cit.,* p. 13; Griswold, *op. cit.,* pp. 6-7; *The Record of American Diplomacy,* pp. 409, 420, 594-595; Osgood, *op. cit.,* pp. 74-75, 278-279.

with the satisfaction of firing a broadside of high principles at Japanese evil-doing. In Japan, on the other hand, Ambassador Grew was not sure that moral ostracism was either effective or justifiable. In comparing the Manchurian crisis with the Cuban situation of 1898, he even had to assure himself that the Cuban situation was different—"for our action was basically humanitarian while Japan's action was expediency pure and simple." When Hugh Wilson, representing the United States, watched the Japanese delegation to walk out of the League, he "began to have a conception of the rancor and resentment that public condemnation could bring upon a proud and powerful people" and to question the nonrecognition policy. "Condemnation," he wrote, "creates a community of the damned who are forced outside the pale, who have nothing to lose by the violation of all laws of order and international faith." [11] The Japanese Exclusion Act of 1924 further defined the community of the damned. In 1945, Henry L. Stimson, for thirty years a high priest of international law and morality, authorized the dropping of atomic bombs upon Japanese cities.

Dedicated to the moral reformation of the world, but unwilling to assume the responsibilities and consequences of moral commitment unless these were clearly joined to a national self-interest which yet scruple hesitated to ackowledge, the United States from 1900 to World War I tried to adhere to a policy of messianic intervention without guilt. It did so by playing the part of the great neutral arbiter of the world's disputes. President Theodore Roosevelt helped to negotiate a peaceful settlement of the Russo-Japanese War, presided over the arbitration at Algeciras, and was instrumental in calling the second Hague peace conference. It is ironical that the militant rough-rider of 1898 should receive a Nobel Peace Prize in 1906. His successor William Howard Taft made efforts to obtain arbitration agreements of a more general nature. Both Roosevelt and Taft tried to exert a beneficent influence in the affairs of Latin America. It is ironical that the Roosevelt Corollary of 1904, invoked

---

[11] For this paragraph see William S. Myers, *The Foreign Policies of Herbert Hoover, 1929-1933* (New York: Charles Scribner's Sons, 1940), pp. 157-159; Stimson, *op. cit.*, pp. 61, 95-97; Joseph C. Grew, *Ten Years in Japan* (New York: Simon & Schuster, Inc., 1944), pp. 78-79; Hugh R. Wilson, *A Diplomat Between Wars* (New York: Longmans, Green & Co., 1941), pp. 280-281.

ostensibly to sanction the disinterested exercise of a police power in Latin America, should under Taft become the instrument of what has subsequently been called "dollar diplomacy."

Throughout World War I and the peace negotiations which followed, the United States played the part of the grievously wronged, innocent neutral nation. President Wilson in 1914 thus noted a parallel between himself and James Madison at the outset of the War of 1812: both were peace-loving Princetonians defending the sacred cause of neutral rights.[12] He might have added that both, assuming without warrant a world rule of law which had universal sanction, made their entrance into war contingent not upon the nation's self-interest but upon abstract conceptions of honor, justice, and legality. Madison, encouraged by western and southern jingoism, interpreted the impressment of American sailors as an issue of national honor and international morality. Wilson, with his southern Presbyterian background, similarly interpreted the submarining of neutral ships and attendant loss of American lives as an issue of national honor and international morality. He sincerely believed and widely publicized the view—to the consternation of many of America's allies in the war—that the United States was best equipped to take the lead in formulating a just and lasting peace because the United States was the only nation at war whose motives were wholly disinterested. Only the example of disinterested initiative could bring the nations of the earth to discard their petty jealousies and rivalries and embrace a new world order.

Once embarked upon war, releasing the pent-up energies of self-assertion, Americans again waved high the banner of a militant world crusade. Wilson dreamed that all the world would turn to the American standard for moral inspiration, "that America will come into the full light of the day when all shall know that she puts human rights above all other rights and that her flag is the flag not only of America, but of humanity." [13] That the source of Wilson's millennial vision lay in the old Edenic

[12] Edward M. House, *The Intimate Papers of Colonel House*, ed. Charles Seymour, 4 vols. (Boston: Houghton Mifflin Co., 1926-1928), I, 303-304.

[13] Woodrow Wilson, *The Public Papers of Woodrow Wilson*, ed. Ray Stannard Baker and William E. Dodd, 6 vols. (New York: Harper & Bros., 1925-1927), III, 147.

conception of American destiny is clear, not only in the character of his imagery, but in the over-all structure of his thinking. As early as 1894, in a *Forum* article, he linked this destiny with the task, "at once material and ideal, of subduing a wilderness and covering all the wide stretches of a vast continent with a single free and stable policy." He considered Abraham Lincoln the exemplar of the American spirit at work, because Lincoln was a provincial who came to behold and comprehend great affairs, yet held always "the express image of the ungainly frontiers- man," "kept always the shrewd and seeing eye of the woodsman and the hunter, and the flavor of the wild life. . . ." [14] This spirit, according to Wilson, was something unique and different from the old Anglo-Saxon spirit and yet was capable of assimilating to itself and renewing the consciousness of mankind.

To Wilson, the United States still possessed a quality of Edenic newness. Through the assimilation of foreign immigrants, for instance, it was constantly being renewed from generation to generation by the same process which had created it. "This is the only country in the world," he said at a naturalization cere- mony in Philadelphia, "which experiences this constant and re- peated rebirth." [15] It was also being renewed by the ceaseless rededication and return to the principles of the founding fathers, which for Wilson meant the Jeffersonian tradition. The series of Wilsonian reforms which began with his presidency at Princeton thus belonged to the pattern of the millennial rebirth: out of the sad declension in the present state of affairs Wilson would bring forth a better future state. As the savior and prophet of a new order, he nevertheless asserted himself in behalf of the restoration of our simpler, earlier condition. He tried to solve the problems of industrial capitalism by the reassertion of Jeffer- sonian principles, defying time and change with eternal truths, hoping to preserve for the nation a timeless youth.

His regressive reforms began with his attack upon the con- centration of privilege in the eating clubs of Princeton. He regarded his fight against privilege, however, not as a fight for the development, "but as a fight for the restoration of Prince- ton." He represented his plan to reorganize Princeton along

---

[14] Woodrow Wilson, "A Calendar of Great Americans," *The Forum*, XVI (1893-1894), 721, 724-725.

[15] Wilson, *Public Papers*, III, 318.

egalitarian lines as "a scheme of salvation." Although he lost this fight, it brought him to prominence and made him a candidate of the Democratic party for the governorship of New Jersey. As governor he again became the messiah of a new order, reactivating the great principles of America's heroic age; his "thoughtful reconstruction" of New Jersey, he announced in his acceptance speech, would make peoples' thoughts "hark back to the great age in which democracy was set up in America. With the new age we shall show a new spirit." He carried this new spirit into the White House. But his "New Freedom," he claimed, was "only the old revived and clothed in the unconquerable strength of modern Ameirca." He intended to restore politics and the national life "to their full spiritual vigor again," to a former "pristine strength and freedom." Looking forward at the same time that he looked back, as at Princeton, he addressed himself, as at Princeton, specifically to the youth of the nation. He would make the Democratic party the party of young men.[16]

The story of Wilson's reforms during his administration of the presidency of the United States has been told elsewhere. The important point to note here is that they were conceived essentially within a Jeffersonian ideological framework of democracy against aristocracy. Wilson proposed to break down the authority of privilege and aggregated capital by returning the country to the control of the "less concentrated, more dispersed, smaller, and more individual economic forces." From Herbert Croly's point of view, this was the same old self-defeating, self-contradictory reform program of seeking Jeffersonian ends by an obsolete libertarian machinery. It assumed a harmonious moral order in nature. Wilson's own words tend to confirm such an interpretation. Answering the question of what Jefferson would do in his place, Wilson argued that Jefferson would restore the freedom of smaller competitive units, eliminating the "rank weeds" of concealed monopolistic power "which were sure to choke out all wholesome life in the fair garden of affairs." "The utility, the vitality, the fruitage of life," he wrote in *The New Freedom*, "does not come from the top to the bottom; it comes,

---

[16] For this paragraph see Ray Stannard Baker, *Woodrow Wilson: Life and Letters*, 8 vols. (Garden City: Doubleday, Page & Co., 1927-1939), II, 213-260; Donald Day, *Woodrow Wilson's Own Story* (Boston: Little, Brown & Co., 1952), pp. 85, 103, 120-121; Wilson, *Public Papers*, II, 305.

like . . . a great tree, from the soil up." [17] When economic power was once again dispersed among the people, he expected that the tree of life in his garden of desire would find its true rootage in "intimate affection."

The language in which Wilson described his new freedom borrowed heavily from the myth of Eden. He compared his ideal society to a rosebush as well as to a tree. "Everything that blooms in beauty in the air of heaven draws its fairness, its vigor, from its roots." He would restore this paradisiac condition: "And now we are going into this garden and weed it. . . . We are going in there to see to it that the fertilization of intelligence, of invention, of origination, is once more applied to a set of industries now threatening to be stagnant, because threatening to be too much concentrated." Looking for a devil in this garden, he, in effect, revived John Cotton's conspiratorial theory of history. One sensed that he was fighting not merely flesh and blood, but "principalities and powers." He professed to find an existing democratic soil for his reforms sooner in the country than in the city. The last chapter of his book recalled the voyage of Columbus which first launched the New World enterprise to restore man to a second Eden.[18]

Wilson projected this Edenic image upon the rest of the world. He thus read World War I as the outcome of an international plot of a few sovereign lords—masters of "governments clothed with the strange trappings and the primitive authority of an age that is altogether alien and hostile to our own"—to tyrannize and further subjugate the helpless people of the earth. "The plot is written plain upon every scene and every act of the supreme tragedy." In this respect, it was an extension of his battles at home against entrenched autocracy. He told Oscar T. Crosby, for instance, that "Europe is still governed by the same reactionary forces which controlled this country until a few years ago." Reluctantly he accepted the role of a New World savior leading not merely America, but the nations of the earth into the sunlight of a millennial rebirth. Out of the sad declension of world affairs, out of the apocalyptic holocaust of World

---

[17] Wilson, *Public Papers*, II, 426; *The New Freedom* (Garden City: Doubleday, Page & Co., 1913), p. 79.
[18] Wilson, *The New Freedom*, pp. 88, 100-104, 157-158.

War I, would come, hopefully, a new world order not greatly
different from the New Freedom. "I say to you," he wrote in the
Saturday Evening Post in May, 1914, "that the old order is
dead. It is my part . . . to aid in composing those differences . . .
that the new order, which shall have its foundation on human
liberty and human rights, shall prevail." His task at the Paris
peace conference, he remarked on his way to Europe, was "to
set up a new international psychology, to have a new atmosphere." [19] His insistence upon a new order uniting the moral
forces of the world against the forces of selfish ambition required on his part a firm rejection of what he called "a body of
European settlements" along the old lines of the balance of
power in favor of a world federation of states modeled after
the New World example and principle of mutual co-operation.

The fate of Wilson at Versailles and afterwards raises grave
questions not only about the basis of American diplomacy in
the twentieth century, but more importantly, about the capacity,
within the major value orientations of the national character as
outlined in this book, of the great majority of Americans to
respond sensitively, maturely, and realistically to important human and world problems. American foreign policy, though a
product of complicated political processes and decisions, ultimately reflects a consensus of public opinion which more sharply
defines national character than the multitude of voices heard in
debate of more purely domestic issues. Was Wilson at Versailles
like a character out of one of James' international novels—the
great American innocent, a naïve, doctrinaire idealist baffled and
humiliated by the wily diplomats of the wicked Old World who
yet did not realize what a poor instrument he brought back to
the United States Senate for ratification? Or should one compare
him to a tragic hero, the victim of an impersonal world fate
compounded of an inevitable complexity of human motives,
traditions, and historical circumstances which brought all his
messianic pride, like Creon's, to a thought of dust? Finally,
should one defend him as a pragmatic idealist whose acceptance
of the necessity for compromise in an imperfect world laid the

---

[19] For this paragraph see Woodrow Wilson, *The Messages and Papers of
Woodrow Wilson*, ed. Albert Shaw, 2 vols. (New York: The Review of
Reviews Corp., 1924), I, 499; Baker, *op. cit.*, VIII, 253; Wilson, *Public
Papers*, III, 112; Day, *op. cit.*, pp. 312, 316.

foundation for the imperfect, but improvable structure of the United Nations? [20]

As Walter Lippmann has pointed out, Wilson's league was attacked in the Senate both as a concealed alliance in the realm of European *Realpolitik* and as a utopian soap bubble. But the view which dominated American policy in the period between two world wars was the view inspired by Lord Keynes' unsparing portrait of Wilson as a blind and deaf Don Quixote or Nonconformist minister impaled upon the "swift and glittering" blade of the more tough-minded Old World adversary. This was a viewpoint congenial to the nativistic mental stereotypes held both by Wilson's "isolationist" critics and by disillusioned "internationalists" whose high hopes had followed Wilson to Europe. The reaction which set in was one of "realistic" debunking as public sentiment swung from self-assertive idealism to self-flagellation, disillusionment, and withdrawal. Thus Hoover's foreign policy was defended by followers of the old messianic example as being more "realistic" than that of Wilson, who, no matter how high his ideals, had allowed himself to be enmeshed "in the tangled net of European diplomacy." Former followers of messianic intervention were also converted to "realism," repenting their sins in the sudden discovery of the role of power and self-interest in human relations. One of their spokesmen was Walter Lippmann, who, looking back upon the series of diplomatic failures since Versailles, observed: "We have brought along with us from our age of innocence, from the 19th century when we were isolated from the rivalries of states and empires, an ideological picture of the world that is imaginary and false. It holds that the struggle for existence, and the rivalry and strife and conflict among nations for advantages are wrong, abnormal and transitory." [21] In a series of books and articles he recommended that we, too, recognizing a common human involvement in guilt, should seek through enlightened self-interest to establish our own spheres of influence and balance of power.

---

[20] These and similar related questions are raised in Amherst Problems in American Civilization, *Wilson at Versailles*, ed. with an introduction by Theodore P. Greene (Boston, D. C. Heath & Co., 1957).

[21] Walter Lippmann, "The Rivalry of Nations," *Reader's Digest*, April, 1948, p. 16. The preceding quotation is from Myers, *op. cit.*, p. 3. But see also Walter Lippmann, *U.S. Foreign Policy: Shield of the Republic* (Boston: Little, Brown & Co., 1943), pp. 47-77; Osgood, *op. cit.*, pp. 309-332.

But American idealism during the twenties and thirties did not altogether abandon its world mission. Rather, it returned, on the whole, to its prewar role of the great disinterested nation and neutral arbiter of the world's problems, salving its conscience by seeking peace through the paper legalities of self-denying disarmament pacts, pacts outlawing war, pacts embodying the principles of the Open Door and the territorial and political integrity of China, pacts establishing a "good neighbor" policy in Latin America, pacts setting up a world court at the Hague, the doctrine of nonrecognition, and finally the Neutrality Acts of 1935 and 1937. One of the main defects of such conscience-saving diplomacy was voiced by Senator Carter Glass of Virginia, who, in voting for the Kellogg-Briand pact on the ground that its defeat would be psychologically bad, said nevertheless that it would "confuse the minds of many good and pious people who think that peace may be secured by polite professions of neighborly and brotherly love." [22]

The role of the "big brother," of course, assumed a division of the world into a few wicked rulers and a basically innocent people who shared American aspirations. The role of the moral policeman with a big stick on the other hand assumed an innocent American nation in a largely evil world. American diplomacy oscillated between both views. A consequence of the first has been much open, personal, people-to-people diplomacy; of the second, policies which, in effect, damned a whole people. Wilson's call for a general European peace conference in 1916, with the strongly implied suggestion that the United States would be morally justified in entering the war against those nations which did not comply, was addressed to friendly populations over the heads of their rulers. So too was Colonel House's proposal to stage an open debate on war aims between the *New York World* and an influential German newspaper. Private citizens of the United States often felt a similar responsibility and sometimes meddled in world affairs in unorthodox, unofficial ways embarrassing to their government, as when Henry Ford dispatched Jane Addams and a group of pacifists to Europe on his peace ship under the illusion that this would end the war. When Wilson could not get his way over the question of Fiume in the official

---

[22] *The Record of American Diplomacy*, p. 525.

diplomatic negotiations at Versailles, he appealed from the Italian government to the Italian people and seemed unable to accept the fact that the Italian people were not of his mind. From the moment that the United States entered the war, as Charles Seymour tells us, Wilson adopted the principle of "undying hostility to the imperial régime and of friendship to the German people." [23]

President Franklin D. Roosevelt, whom Harry Hopkins looked upon as a Wilsonian idealist, also displayed a marked tendency to communicate directly with the heads of governments or with peoples rather than go through the usual diplomatic channels of foreign offices. In World War I, World War II, and even during the so-called Cold War, the American leadership constantly hammered upon the note that the United States objective was to liberate innocent peoples from their wicked masters. Secretary of State Dulles' frequent appeals to captive peoples behind the Iron Curtain in recent years attempted to drive a wedge between the people and their rulers, hoping to hasten the collapse of communism. But American diplomacy frequently pursued a contradictory view. Under the public pressures of war madness, for instance, Wilson found it increasingly difficult to adhere to his distinction between friendship to the German people and undying hostility toward their autocratic masters. He was forced as much by the nearly unanimous sentiment in his own country as by French demands to accept the clause in the Versailles Treaty which branded the German people with war guilt. The big brother became the moral policeman.

The principle of unconditional surrender, first invoked by Americans during World War I, under which Germany had to submit to the charge of war guilt, became the principle of World War II out of which grew the Morgenthau plan for a prostrate Germany. The Morgenthau plan would have stripped Germany of all her heavy industry and reduced the country permanently to the condition of a helpless, defenseless agricultural nation like early America. The plan also called for the immediate military execution of the Nazi "arch-criminals." Although President Roosevelt favored the plan because it made the German people as a whole and not merely a few Nazi leaders responsible

---

[23] House, *op. cit.*, III, 127.

for what had happened, the experience of several years of occupation in Germany, together with the realization of the inter-
connectedness of the German and European economy, forced the
British and American governments ultimately to move away
from the vengeful Morgenthau philosophy.[24] The American
moral will as a retributive force after World War II expressed
itself chiefly in the Nuremberg trials, which were represented
not as *ex post facto* law imposed upon a defeated enemy with
no other sanction than the armed might of the victor, but as
the enforcement of an existing standard of justice to which the
world could repair.[25]

By this time, American public sentiment was beginning to favor
the German people over both the Nazi leaders and America's
former Russian ally. The longer American occupation troops
remained in Europe, for instance, the better they liked the Germans and the less they liked the French and Italians. They indicated that the Germans most resembled themselves in their
general cleanliness, friendliness, industry, and enterprise.[26] In
the face of the growing need to play Germany off against Russia
and of the rapid fluctuation and reversal of American public
attitudes, the sins of the German people were largely forgotten.
Ideological warfare, on the other hand, intensified dangerously
by becoming polarized around the two great monolithic powers
which rose out of the ruins of Europe, the United States and
Russia. The American imagination, long conditioned to vigilante
justice and the drama of cowboys and Indians, was once again
encouraged to read world history as a gigantic conspiracy of
satanic forces arrayed against the children of God.

The American moral imagination as a whole has tended to be
out of touch with the realities of the twentieth-century world.
The story of Yalta is essentially the story of Versailles all over
again, both in the kind of sentimental, moralistic considerations
which influenced American decisions at Yalta and in the later
impact of Yalta on the American public mind. Even Stimson

[24] Cordell Hull, *Memoirs,* 2 vols. (New York: The Macmillan Co., 1948),
II, 1603, 1622.
[25] Cf. Henry L. Stimson and McGeorge Bundy, *On Active Service in Peace
and War* (New York: Harper & Bros., 1948), p. 589.
[26] Hadley Cantril, ed. *Public Opinion, 1935-1946* (Princeton: Princeton
University Press, 1951), pp. 948, 953-956, 962-963.

admitted that Yalta dealt "a good deal in altruism and idealism." Secretary of State Hull, who derived his fundamental propositions of what should govern relations among nations from Thomas Jefferson, wrote that both President Roosevelt and himself "felt we could work with Russia. . . . It might be said that the President and I were taken in by Russia's promises and written pledges," pledges and promises seemingly backed up, Hull thought, by Russia's honorable record and excellent progress since 1917.[27] The American delegation, according to Chester Wilmot, was indeed more suspicious of England than of Russia at Yalta.

This assessment of American motives is well founded. At Yalta, as during the wartime alliance, Americans were inclined frequently to revert to traditional stereotypes of England as the haughty imperial power and to see in the Russians an honest, courageous peasant people who were traveling by different paths toward the same goal of economic justice and individual well-being as Americans under the New Deal. Harry Hopkins thus hoped that these two great peoples would ultimately meet at the Jeffersonian intersection of liberty and equality. The traditional American principle of the self-determination of free and independent peoples expressed in the Monroe Doctrine and reaffirmed in the Open Door policy, the Nine Power treaty, and Wilson's Fourteen Points, on the other hand, presented a sizable obstacle to British-American wartime understanding. As President Roosevelt told Churchill during the Atlantic Charter conference, "I can't believe that we can fight a war against fascist slavery, and at the same time not work to free people all over the world from a backward colonial policy." [28] America's profound prejudice against "colonialism" was embodied in article three of the Atlantic Charter, which Roosevelt and Hull interpreted to apply to all people, including British India, but which Churchill meant to apply only to the European nations under Nazi occupation.

Another related source of Anglo-American friction early in the war was the condition which Hull attached to the Lend-Lease arrangement, striking at British imperial preference and

---

[27] Stimson and Bundy, *op. cit.*, pp. 610-611; Hull, *op. cit.*, I, 173-174; II, 1467-1468.

[28] Quoted in Chester Wilmot, *The Struggle for Europe* (New York: Harper & Bros., 1952), p. 633.

246

trade barriers. The British cabinet quite rightfully regarded this as an attempt to infringe upon British imperial sovereignty, as it did Roosevelt's and Hull's plan to put former colonies under an international trusteeship. "Our prime difficulty," Hull said,

was to induce the colonial Powers—principally Britain, France, and the Netherlands—to adopt our ideas with regard to dependent peoples. Britain had refused to go along with us on the idea of eventual independence for her colonies, believing instead that they should in time achieve self-government within the Empire. . . . It might be said that the future of that Empire was no business of ours; but we felt that unless dependent peoples were assisted toward ultimate self-government . . . they would provide kernels of conflict.[29]

What irked the British most, perhaps, about these differences was American self-righteousness in giving the United States policy in the Philippines and the federation of the thirteen original American colonies as examples for the liquidation of the British empire.

Roosevelt was already thinking of a world organization of united nations when he proposed an international trusteeship for the colonies, while Churchill was pressing for a settlement which would establish regional spheres of influence and balance of power. To Roosevelt, therefore, Churchill seemed a reactionary of the old school. His impression of Churchill was strengthened when English military forces in Greece and Italy backed what seemed to him the more conservative elements in these countries against the liberals or leftists who had been most active in resisting the Germans and Fascists.[30] Following the Greek crisis, as Robert Sherwood notes, relations between the White House and Downing Street were more strained than ever before. Yet this discord came on the eve of the Yalta conference. It is small wonder that at Yalta Roosevelt privately told Stalin that British Hong Kong ought to be given back to China or internationalized, or that after Yalta Churchill suspected Roosevelt of planning to stop off at Egypt on his way home in order to hatch "some deep laid plot to undermine the British Empire in these areas."[31] Chester Wilmot, a vigorous defender of the British point of view, suggests that Roosevelt's eagerness to bribe

---

[29] Hull, op. cit., II, 1477-1478, 1599.
[30] Robert E. Sherwood, Roosevelt and Hopkins, an Intimate History, Rev. enlarged ed. (New York: Harper & Bros., 1950), p. 837.
[31] Ibid., pp. 866, 871.

Stalin to aid in the war against Japan was actuated in part by the hope that Russia's intervention would compel Japan's surrender before the British, French, or Dutch could regain possession of their colonies.

Nevertheless, President Roosevelt did not make concessions at Yalta which it was in his power to withhold in the light of the knowledge which he then had. The testimony of Admiral Zacharias, Charles Bohlen, and others shows indisputably that Russia was brought into the war against Japan in the expectation that the Japanese homeland would have to be invaded at great cost to American lives. The atomic bomb had not yet been successfully tested. Chiang Kai-shek and the Chinese government, moreover, were consulted about the Far Eastern agreement and approved the disposition of Chinese territories, especially since it brought recognition by Russia of the sovereignty of the Chinese Nationalist government over Manchuria. The most serious criticism against Roosevelt at Yalta is that he was more visionary than Churchill about Russian promises to hold free elections in Poland. Yet Russian troops were already in occupation of Poland and gave Stalin the same advantage in bargaining power with respect to Central Europe that he enjoyed from a similar power situation in the Far East.

The American disillusionment with Yalta had as its psychological basis much in common with the disenchantment over Versailles. President Roosevelt and Yalta became the scapegoat for all the frustrations of the Cold War when high expectations for a new world order encountered only the expanding menace of communism and the possibility of a new Armageddon. The Roosevelt administration, to be sure, was partly to blame for creating a fool's paradise of impossible expectations, though the instrument of illusion was not Yalta, but the various pronouncements of high principle and faith which saturated Yalta in a sea of sentimentality. Thus, Roosevelt, in giving to the world his Four Freedoms, not unlike Wilson in delivering his Fourteen Points to an awaiting world, assured Americans and all mankind that his was "no vision of a distant millennium. It is a definite basis for a kind of world attainable in our own time and generation." [32] A similar fanfare of faith accompanied the issu-

----

[32] *The Record of American Diplomacy*, p. 610.

ance of the Atlantic Charter. This faith in a future world order based on mutual trust and co-operation was transferred in turn to a faith in the co-operation of the Russians after the war which was tragically not forthcoming.

Roosevelt and his chief aides, for reasons already apparent, tended to see the Russians in the American Edenic image of a courageous, anticolonial people who had fought side by side in the same noble cause with the Americans. One of the best expositions of this idea appeared in a memorandum which Harry Hopkins wrote six months after Yalta: "We find the Russians as individuals easy to deal with. The Russians undoubtedly like the American people. They like the United States. They trust the United States more than they trust any other power in the world . . . above all, they want to maintain friendly relations with us. . . . They are a tenacious, determined people who think and act just like you and I do." [33] Hopkins did not think, in spite of fundamental ideological differences, that there need be between the United States and Russia any conflict of interests in the sphere of foreign affairs which would lead to future war. General Eisenhower, whose *Crusade in Europe* became a best-seller, endorsed this view, noting that the ordinary Russian seemed to him "to bear a marked similarity to what we call an 'average American.'" He felt that "in the past relations of America and Russia there was no cause to regard the future with pessimism." The two countries had, he said, "maintained an unbroken friendship that dated back to the birth of the United States as an independent republic," and "both were free from the stigma of colonial empire building by force."

The disenchantment with this roseate picture focused, unfortunately, upon Yalta and Roosevelt rather than upon the real problem, which was the self-deceiving character of traditional messianic American idealism. Criticism of Roosevelt at Yalta, partaking of the same conspiratorial theory of history which provided the intellectual framework for the messianic impulse, duplicated the twofold criticism of Wilson at Versailles: Roosevelt was pictured both as the naïve dupe of a satanic Stalin and a Machiavellian student of *Realpolitik*. At the congressional hearings on the Yalta agreement, Representative O'Konski,

---

[33] The quotations in this paragraph are cited by Wilmot, *op. cit.*, p. 640.

speaking for his Polish-American constituency, charged Roosevelt with "the Crime of Crimea" which delivered 100,000,000 human beings into slavery. He also charged, inconsistently, that Roosevelt, holding four aces, let himself be bluffed by a pair of deuces.[34] John T. Flynn, in his book *While You Slept*, on the other hand, conjured up a vast conspiracy of two world-devils wherein Roosevelt swapped his Grand Design for becoming president of the world for Stalin's Grand Design to absorb eastern Europe and Asia.[35] General Patrick J. Hurley rested his case for conspiracy before Congress on the obvious fact of secret diplomacy. Indeed, the devil theory of Yalta developed by these and other critics of Roosevelt relied heavily upon the argument of secret diplomacy as judged by the traditional American standard of open diplomacy, and Roosevelt's chief aide, Harry Hopkins, was viewed in the same suspicious light as Wilson's Colonel Edward M. House.

The most reasonable guess would be that the Russians were neither as good nor as bad as they were made out to be—nor the United States the only morally responsible nation concerned with world affairs. American public opinion, by a sizable majority, seemed to adhere to this sane view when it blamed the impasse over international control of atomic energy in 1946 equally upon the United States and Russia. But unable to appreciate the practical implications of this general sportsman-like viewpoint, only 41 per cent of those interviewed believed that the United States should make any concessions; the majority, indeed, believed that the United States should stand firm.[36] Throughout the postwar period, in fact, there was a noticeable lack of connection between generally endorsed principles and their application in specific instances. In principle, the United States endorsed the United Nations, but took unilateral action in Greece and Turkey and went about, ostensibly within the framework of the United Nations charter, building a system of regional alliances, calling them "collective security pacts" out of tradi-

---

[34] Cf. *Congressional Record*, 79th Cong., 1st Sess., Vol. 91, Part I (1945), pp. 1069-1072.

[35] John T. Flynn, *While You Slept; Our Tragedy in Asia and Who Made It* (New York: The Devin-Adair Co., 1951), pp. 25-29, 54-56, 145-150, 166-172.

[36] Cantril, *op. cit.*, p. 964.

tional prejudices against entangling alliances. It defended the principle of collective security, but actively sought to establish a balance of power by which to contain communism, at the same time condemning the Soviet Union for similar tactics. It branded the Soviet Union a wicked nation for employing fifth column activities and the threat of military intervention to create spheres of influence, but self-righteously employed economic and political pressures to the same end. After his death James V. Forrestal, one-time Secretary of Defense, was proclaimed a national hero for spending $150,000 of his own money to influence the Italian elections of 1948.

America's foreign aid programs were based upon self-interest in the fight against communism; yet we talked ideals and felt hurt when the recipients of our aid were not grateful for our generosity. We argued that foreign aid to economically disorganized or underdeveloped nations was the strongest deterrent to the spread of communism, but often attached political conditions to this aid and expended the greater proportion of it on armaments. Too many of our ambassadors of democratic humanitarianism in Europe, according to Herbert Kubly, a Fulbright scholar in Italy, preached the superiority of the American gospel of wealth and hobnobbed almost exclusively with former fascists and members of the nobility. The authors of *The Ugly American* depict our ambassadors in Asia as preaching, through interpreters, the abstract virtues of liberty to people who were starving, in the meanwhile surrounding themselves with a never-left-home, air-conditioned, bourbon-highball comfort. At home, the schoolmasters of policy debated the salutary effects of a firmer application of the birch rod. During the ERP vote on Spain, at a time when a back-to-normalcy public sentiment had brought American military might to a low ebb, congressmen indulged in military gestures and warlike talk. When the country's military defenses had once again been built up, the world was threatened with "agonizing reappraisals" and "massive retaliation"—and nothing happened.

When the United States at last decided to back principle with power, as in Korea, it did so under the illusion that it was enforcing a world mandate, but was in fact still pursuing its own negative policy of containment. It came closest to placing the United Nations squarely behind an impartial anticolonial policy when England and France invaded Egypt, but it has yet itself to resolve the problem of whether to adhere steadfastly to an anti-colonial position for both principle and long-run advantage or on occasion to sacrifice principle to expediency in the interest of short-run gains against communism. It continues to behave, in the main, as if the central issue before the world were a gigantic Communist conspiracy to subvert democratic principle and not revolutionary changes in the outlook of millions of people who for centuries before their recent awakening have been resigned to misery. As a result, it has defined rather too easily and too narrowly what it has been *against* and has been confused about what it is *for*. Hence, recent foreign policy has tended to be merely negative and retaliatory rather than positive.

The divisions and inconsistencies in American foreign policy reflect a domestic dislocation of image and reality. This connection is evident in the widespread failure to realize the impact of domestic policies upon foreign relations. Our leadership has been too content to follow and not responsible enough to lead in pointing out that an immigration policy founded upon suspicion and bigotry is not only inconsistent with our complacent picture of ourselves as the "good neighbor" of the world, but is losing us friends all over the world; that racial discrimination in any form is not only inconsistent with our loudly proclaimed ideals, but is infinitely harmful to our well-intentioned efforts to help shape the future of a world in which a majority of populations do not belong to our "race"; that the hue and cry over internal security since the McCarran-Walter Act not only stifles creative thinking at home, but engenders distrust abroad of our capacity for mature leadership; that material well-being, far from evincing a superior virtue and ability, might be taken abroad as evidence of selfish exploitation; that a "fortress" nation which cannot lower its tariff barriers cannot benefit from its foreign aid.

Jerome Bruner has suggested that a possible way of modernizing the American people's nineteenth-century notions of tariff would be, for instance, to dramatize such headlines as "Tariff Raises Grocery Bill Three Dollars a Week." [37] But any such

---

[37] Cf. Leonard S. Cottrell, Jr., and Sylvia Eberhart, *American Opinion on World Affairs in the Atomic Age* (Princeton: Princeton University Press, 1948), p. 55.

remedy, while it might have a limited pragmatic value if it could be done on a large scale, would ultimately fail because it does not strike at the root of the problem, which is a congenital habit of mind. Nor will it do to defend the dislocation of image and reality in foreign affairs as "pragmatic idealism." For one would end up with Dexter Perkins, praising the reversal of policy which led to our negotiations with General Franco after we had made every effort to indicate our displeasure with the fascist government in Spain.[38] Such apologetics, far from disproving the kind of doctrinaire inflexibility of which American policy-makers have so often been accused, merely highlight a discrepancy between democratic theory and practice while giving sanction to the congenital habit of mind. This habit of mind, if the analysis in this book is correct, has a great deal to do with the Edenic dream.

Our statesmen, having brought to their task an oversimplified world view whose application in recent years has resulted in bafflement and bewilderment, tried one makeshift after another, the only common denominator being the concept of "containment." Undoubtedly, they have felt less the masters of destiny than did the leaders of the small, backward nation which confidently confronted the world 150 years ago across 3,000 miles of sheltering ocean. At least Cordell Hull and John Foster Dulles have each bewailed the loss of a "golden age" of statecraft. Its disappearance has been lamented after the pattern of the Puritan jeremiad—almost as if Americans, by willfully sinning, had been driven out of paradise. We have been exhorted, therefore, to stop sinning, to rearm ourselves morally and spiritually with the old sense of mission, when the real problem is that our moral tradition is out of touch with a revolutionary world situation.

----

[38] Perkins, *op. cit.*, p. 42.

13

Conclusion:
East of Eden

The period of America's emergence as a world power provided the sternest possible test for the American character and its capacity to respond maturely to the traumatic experience of two world wars within a single generation, a major economic depression in which almost half of the total laboring force was at one time or another unemployed, the realistic debunking of sacred and secular lore which had once been the mainspring of optimistic faith, the reduction of human behavior by the new social sciences to deterministic drives and environmental pressures, the gradual subordination of the once proud, self-assertive individual to the larger collective units of industrial society. Yet Americans, for the most part, have hardly begun to confront tragedy. They first met it, briefly, during the Civil War. The death of Lincoln gave them a great culture hero created in the image of the sacrificial god and the crucified Christ of the Rebirth archetype. But the process of initiation was somehow never completed. Without a tragic sense of limitations, Americans have tended to dwell at opposite poles of buoyant optimism and stark despair, naïve faith and utter cynicism, arrogant pride and complete self-doubt.

All the materials for a tragic vision of life, as has been noted, have long been present in America: the classic sin of pride, the inevitable disjunction of ideal and reality, the guilt and shame of failure, the voids of disillusionment. But out of these materials Americans have been able to summon only anguish and nostalgia for a golden age, bewailing their expulsion from a paradise which existed only in their minds, unable to comprehend the kind of spiritual fortitude which enabled Lear to hurl defiance at the elements even in defeat and Oedipus, emerging from the palace with his bleeding eyeballs, to recognize that his punishment was just. As Reinhold Niebuhr has said, we, the once proud masters of destiny and prophets of a new world order, have allowed ourselves to become uncomprehendingly mystified by "the endless complexities of human motives and the varied compounds of ethnic loyalties, cultural traditions, social hopes, envies and fears which enter into the policies of nations."[1] At the same time, we did not want to be told by Dean Acheson that there was no magic key which the United States could find "to open the golden door on to the secret garden of total, perpetual, and profitable world security."[2] Many of us preferred to believe with Senator McCarthy that the cause of all our woes could be attributed to a few devils in our garden—devils like Dean Acheson, General Marshall, Owen Lattimore, and Alger Hiss.

The average American, it is safe to say, is largely oblivious to the great issues of the day, still living in a dream world of Eden, protected from the need to think troublesome thoughts by his cushions of creature comfort, by escapist fantasy on film and television, by the tranquilizers of popular art and music. That is to say that those Americans who do not despair because something expected of life has somehow been lost tend to be apathetic about world problems. Although both experience and public opinion polls suggest that since 1939 the American people have begrudgingly accepted their international responsibilities, even to the point of employing sanctions, they have not embarked upon this Atlantic and Pacific of troubles with their traditional optimism, resolution, and high faith in themselves and their mission. A recent study reveals, for instance, that a majority of Americans expect their best efforts to be unavailing in the prevention of another world war.[3]

------

[1] Reinhold Niebuhr, *The Irony of American History* (New York: Charles Scribner's Sons, 1952), p. 41.

[2] Edgar S. Furniss, Jr., and Richard C. Snyder, *An Introduction to American Foreign Policy* (New York: Rinehart & Co., Inc., 1957), p. 207.

[3] Cf. Elmo Roper, "American Attitudes on World Organization," *Public Opinion Quarterly*, XVII (1953-1954), 406.

For these reasons, the Eisenhower administration, whose entrance upon the political scene at the Republican national convention was accompanied by the singing of "Onward Christian Soldiers," was concerned to revitalize the American sense of mission. At a speech at Denver in 1952, John Foster Dulles said that something had "gone wrong" with the American environment, and he urged a rekindled "faith in freedom" to shatter "the hypnotic spell of tyranny around the world." [4] But Dulles' own faith was retrospective and nostalgic as he also bewailed the expulsion from Eden. In his book *War or Peace* he wrote that we once believed with our founding fathers

that men had their origin and destiny in God; that they were endowed by Him with inalienable rights and had duties prescribed by moral law, and that human institutions ought primarily to help men develop their God-given possibilities. We believe that if we built on that spiritual foundation we should be showing men everywhere the way to a better and more abundant life. . . . That made it easy to conduct the foreign policy of the United States. In those days influence and opportunity abroad and security at home came naturally. . . . Then, as our material power waxed, our spiritual power seemed to wane.

Secretary of State Hull had, a few years before, struck the same note, addressed to despairing or apathetic Americans "who are but a few generations removed from those who fought and conquered the wilderness." [5]

The main theme in American literature during the twentieth century has been the dispossession from paradise, America's abandonment of the security and innocence of an earlier day through some essentially sinful act, an act most frequently associated with industrialism and the commercial ethic. The core of this disillusionment has been the Middle West. The most hallowed soil in America from its long-time connection with the Edenic dream—where the self-reliant pioneer farmer, driven ever westward in quest of the New Jerusalem, had lost his momentum, become weighted down with mortgages and surrounded by skyscrapers—the Mississippi Valley, "the valley of democracy," became in the hands of America's most talented modern writers

---

[4] Quoted in the *New York Herald Tribune*, December 12, 1952.

[5] John Foster Dulles, *War or Peace* (New York: The Macmillan Co., 1950), pp. 254-255; Cordell Hull, *The Memoirs of Cordell Hull*, 2 vols. (New York: The Macmillan Co., 1948), II, 1732.

a Wasteland. Three great American writers who saw their
Garden turning into a Wasteland placed their hopes for America's
ultimate salvation in her youth. In *Huckleberry Finn,* Mark
Twain relived his own boyhood on the Mississippi. Sherwood
Anderson bequeathed the task of socializing the machine to
the "unborn Hugh McVey" of his novel *Poor White.* Sinclair
Lewis' Babbitt told his son to do what he himself had never
dared to do.

Although the major American writers of the twentieth century,
most of them midwesterners, have, almost without exception,
severely criticized their country, the myth of Eden survived in
the moral indignation which fired their bitterness. Morally outraged at the flagrant lapse from an earlier standard, they sought
to raise a new Garden out of the dust of the Wasteland. As
Hamlin Garland expressed it, the modern realistic writer aimed
to "hasten the age of beauty and peace by delineating the ugli-
ness and warfare of the present. . . . He knows [that] the unrotted
seed of loveliness and peace needs but sun and air of freedom
to rise to flower and fragrance." [6] The many ironies and the
illusion of objectivity which pervade modern American writing
hide a "heavenly hurt."

They were all heartsick, these American writers born to promises and nourished on lies. But the profound displacement of
the American dream which one finds in their books was intimately
connected with the Mississippi Valley. Ed Howe, Edgar Lee
Masters, Zona Gale, Sherwood Anderson, and Sinclair Lewis led
the revolt against the Midwest village. Sinclair Lewis, born in
Sauk Center, Minnesota, located the Main Street of bourgeois
America in the Midwest, later selected as the site of the Lynds'
sociological studies, *Middletown* and *Middletown in Transition.*
T. S. Eliot, whose poem "The Waste Land" summed up the
moral and spiritual sterility of all Western civilization in a "heap
of broken images," was born in St. Louis, Missouri. Ezra Pound,
who thought that American Christianity had become a kind of
Prussianism, was raised in Idaho and taught school for a few
months in Indiana, the birthplace of Theodore Dreiser, author

---

[6] Hamlin Garland, *Crumbling Idols; Twelve Essays on Art and Literature,*
Introduction by Robert E. Spiller (Gainesville: Scholars' Facsimiles and
Reprints, 1952), p. 52.

of *An American Tragedy*. Chicago produced James T. Farrell and John Dos Passos, who created two more American epics of disenchantment. Ernest Hemingway was born in Illinois; Ring Lardner, in Michigan. Scott Fitzgerald was first exposed to the shoddy values of café society in St. Paul, Minnesota. William Faulkner fixed his roots in Oxford, Mississippi.

The dénouement of Fitzgerald's novel *The Great Gatsby* revealed that this had been a story of the West, after all—"Tom and Gatsby, Daisy and Jordan and I, were all Westerners, and perhaps we possessed some deficiency in common which made us subtly unadaptable to Eastern life." That deficiency was innocence—and a belief, bred of Edenic expectations, in an "orgiastic future," which made them easy victims of material success and of the lateness of the hour. The central images of the novel are thus images of blighted nature. Gatsby did not know that his dream was already behind him, "somewhere back in that vast obscurity beyond the city, where the dark fields of the republic rolled on under the night." [7] Perhaps the most disillusioned of American writers, however, was Hart Crane, who came from Ohio. In his poem "The Bridge" he tried unsuccessfully to link in steel the teeming industrial reality of America with the Promise:

> O Sleepless as the river under thee,
> Vaulting the sea, the prairies' dreaming sod,
> Unto us lowliest sometime sweep, descend
> And of the curveship lend a myth to God.
>
> . . . .
>
> This was the Promised Land, and still it is
> To the persuasive suburban land agent
> In bootleg roadhouses where the gin fizz
> Bubbles in time to Hollywood's new love-nest pageant.

Hart Crane committed suicide, as did another midwesterner who began his life as an idealist in the region of hope, Vachel Lindsay. A native of Pittsburgh, educated in Europe, Robinson Jeffers followed his Western Star to the edge of the Pacific, where he developed a protective layer of stoic indifference:

[7] F. Scott Fitzgerald, *The Great Gatsby*, in *The Portable F. Scott Fitzgerald*, ed. Dorothy Parker, Introduction by John O'Hara (New York: The Viking Press, Inc., 1949), pp. 163, 168; James Westbrook, "Nature and Optics in *The Great Gatsby*," *American Literature*, XXXII (March, 1960), 78-84.

> Now I, the latest, in this solitude
> Invoke thee from the verge extreme, and shoal
> Of sand that ends the west, O long-pursued.

Archibald MacLeish of Glencoe, Illinois, who in many a poem celebrated the promise latent in the memorial grasses of Iowa, Illinois, and Indiana, at last wondered in "Land of the Free" whether

> . . . the dream of American liberty
> Was two hundred years of pine and hardwood
> And three generations of the grass
> And the generations are up: the years over. . . .

Of the major American writers from the Midwest, only Carl Sandburg has continued the hopeful tradition of Walt Whitman, celebrating with indiscriminate democratic rapture sun-soaked cornfields and grubby tenements, cornhuskers and convicts, red-wood trees and skyscrapers, little people and empire-builders, dreaming land and industrial sprawl—and even he has turned with increasing nostalgia to a heroic past.

It is possible to suggest only briefly here the extent to which America's recent Nobel prize winners in literature, Willam Faulkner and Ernest Hemingway, have written under the spell of the Edenic myth. The larger story of Yoknapatawpha County, with all its individual family chronicles, is, after all, the story of a primal curse brought upon an "indomitably virgin continent" by the sins of white men, seeking profit first by trade in human chattel, then by the shrewd manipulation of business ledgers as practiced by the Snopeses and Jason Compson. The girl who scratched her name on the pane of the Jefferson county jail in 1861 left with a battered lieutenant to begin life anew in a country "which was not even simple frontier, engaged only with wilderness and shoeless savages and the tender hand of God, but one which had been rendered into a desert . . . by the iron and fire of civilization." [8] God had discovered for the descendants of Abraham and Isaac after they had been driven forth from "the old world's corrupt and worthless twilight" a new world, a second Eden, "where a nation of people could be founded in humility and pity and sufferance and pride of one to another," and they

---

[8] William Faulkner, *Requiem for a Nun* (New York: Random House, 1950), p. 257.

spoiled that. "And let me say it," Faulkner writes: "Dispossessed of Eden. Dispossessed of Canaan." [9]

Again and again, as one critic says, "the Faulkner hero relives both his paradise and his expulsion, the first innocence and the fall, without hope and without a redeemer." [10] Occupying a central position in Faulkner's novels, the overpowering scent of flowers expresses both an unbearable yearning for life-everlasting through union with nature and the undefiled beauty of southern womanhood and an oppressive sense of guilt associated with sexual voluptuousness, promiscuity, and betrayal in a mechanical civilization which treats all things as property and objects of physical gratification. The odor of honeysuckle bears these important connotations in both *The Sound and the Fury* and *Sanctuary.* Wisteria is the odor for the morbid mood of *Absalom, Absalom!* The agonizing renunciation of *The Unvanquished* carries with it the tantalizing odor of verbena.[11] The main mission of the Faulkner hero is, by acts of self-sacrificial idealism, to attempt to lift the ancestral curse from the land. Sacrificial innocence characterizes Nancy Mannigoe in *Requiem for a Nun,* Bayard Sartoris in *The Unvanquished,* Isaac McCaslin in "The Bear," Narcissa Benbow of *Sartoris,* Charles Mallison of *Intruder in the Dust,* the groom with his passional love for a horse in *Notes on a Horsethief,* and many others. Most of them are conceived as primitives with a strong sense of heart. "If you got something outside the common run that's got to be done," Lucas Beauchamp, the condemned negro in *Intruder in the Dust,* tells the boy who saves his life, "get the womens and the children to working at it." [12]

Hemingway is less tortured by the weight of the past than Faulkner, and his style is one which, unlike the Faulknerian rhetoric, undercuts the complexities of civilization with a decep-

---

[9] From "The Bear," *The Portable Faulkner,* ed. Malcolm Cowley (New York: The Viking Press, Inc., 1949), pp. 292-293.

[10] Rabi, "Faulkner and the Exiled Generation," in Frederick J. Hoffman and Olga W. Vickery, ed., *William Faulkner: Two Decades of Criticism* (East Lansing: Michigan State College Press, 1954), p. 128.

[11] For a fuller discussion of Faulkner's flower image see Harry M. Campbell and Ruel E. Foster, *William Faulkner, a Critical Appraisal* (Norman: University of Oklahoma Press, 1951), pp. 54 and 54n.

[12] William Faulkner, *Intruder in the Dust* (New York: Random House, 1948), pp. 71-72.

tive sensory simplicity and directness. Nevertheless, the Hemingway hero is quite as disillusioned and heartsick to realize the
dream of ineffable happiness and innocence in a second Eden.
"A continent ages quickly once we come," Hemingway wrote in
The Green Hills of Africa. "The earth gets tired of being
exploited. . . . *A country was made to be as we found it.* Our
people went to America because that was the place to go then.
It had been a good country and we had made a bloody mess of
it and I would go, now, somewhere else as *we always had the
right to go somewhere else.* Let others come to America who
did not know that it was too late. . . ." [13] As against the hypoc-
risies of advanced civilization, the typical Hemingway hero
has sought the more enduring values of love, heroism, ritual form,
and sacrifice inspired by contact with nature. Like Huckleberry
Finn, he wants to "light out for the frontier." He is an uninhibited
primitive with the sensitivity of a connoisseur, an American
Adam who has yet learned the dangers of innocence and been
educated to life's hurts.

The myth of Eden continues to dominate the American imagination, especially in the compulsive writing of the so-called "beat
generation." I have already mentioned Jack Kerouac in this
connection. But no writer of this group has been more keenly
aware of what he feels to be the failure of the American dream
than Lawrence Ferlinghetti. He places the sham, the hypocrisy
and commercialism of American life, in ironic juxtaposition with
the ideality of classical myths. "I am waiting," he wrote in *A
Coney Island of the Mind,*

>   for a rebirth of wonder
>   and I am waiting for someone
>   to really discover America
>
>   . . . . . .
>
>   and I am waiting for the discovery
>   of a new symbolic frontier
>
>   . . . . . .
>
>   I am waiting for the Second Coming
>   . . . I am waiting for them to prove
>   that God is really American

---

[13] Quoted in Delmore Schwartz, "The Fiction of Ernest Hemingway,"
Perspective U.S.A., no. 13 (Autumn, 1955), p. 87.

261

I am waiting for Tom Swift to grow up
and I am waiting
for the American Boy
to take off Beauty's clothes
and get on top of her [14]

Is one waiting for a restatement, a revitalization, of the old dream—or a more mature estimate of possibilities in relation to the limitations of the human condition? On the answer to this question, it seems to this writer, hinges the future of American civilization.

At present, one sees few signs of a deepening and maturing of the popular mind; rather, one finds during this time of crisis, as evidenced by the recent resurgence of anti-intellectualism, the new popularity of the Western story, the sentimental appeal of former President Eisenhower, and other indicators of cultural trends, a search for security in the earlier symbols and traditions of nationality. The main theme in all this is again the regression to nature. The regress to nature and to the domain of the instincts as a source of divinity has sometimes transformed the common man into a demigod who came from God's country or the "Creation State," was a crack shot, killed unhuntable bears and forty-two pound turkeys, was an epidemic to bad men, rode thunderbolts, and carried sunrise in his pocket. Supposedly endowed by nature with an intuitive knowledge of right and wrong, he has become a guardian of the public conscience, appearing before the small fry in such roles as Lone Ranger, Roy Rogers, Hopalong Cassidy, or Davy Crockett, and before adults in the person of Senator Joseph McCarthy (who once acknowledged a spiritual bond with "Indian Charley"), the commander of the American Legion, the heads of Senate and House investigating committees, and J. Edgar Hoover. His rough exterior and courage have spelled doom to evil-doers, but endeared him to lovers of morality.

Indeed the great stress in our society upon athletic masculinity derives from the contrast of morals and manners, nature and civilization. While exhibitions of masculinity may compensate for doubts as to sexual virility, more importantly they offset the fancied effeminacy of an immoral, tea-drinking, hand-kissing, book-reading, panty-waisted aristocracy, give assurances

[14] Lawrence Ferlinghetti, *A Coney Island of the Mind* (Norfolk: New Directions, 1955), pp. 49-52.

of a capacity for vigorous moral action, and altogether function culturally as a supporting mark of high Americanism. The "tough-guy" postures of Mickey Spillane heroes, dead-end kids (now juvenile delinquents), and even business leaders derive from this aspect of the myth. Reinforcing the common man's emphasis upon masculinity, and in turn reinforced by all his other cultural values, is a strain of anti-intellectualism. By anti-intellectualism is meant not so much an attitude based upon a mature, intelligent understanding of the limitations of human reason, but an irrational impatience with disciplined analytical thought and contemplation and a preference for swift action following snap judgments. Such anti-intellectualism must inevitably flourish in a moralistic atmosphere which takes nature as its standard, which believes in the religion of work as opposed to the indolence of an aristocratic leisure class, and which tends to regard all cultural sophistication and learning—like refined manners—as the monopoly of a corrupt aristocracy, native or European.

Adlai Stevenson was undoubtedly to a large extent the victim of such thinking. But so also have been our intellectuals, our artists, our teachers, our scientists, and many of our professional people. The status of our scientists has risen considerably, to be sure, but only in proportion to our respect for Russia's scientists and for material progress. Insofar as we tend to erect the anti-intellectual stance into a national virtue, moreover, we make little effort to understand the culture of other lands, place little emphasis upon the study of foreign languages, and tolerate a sloppy inarticulateness in the use of our own language. In fact, the American language, to the extent that it differs from the English (and it does differ), has also been adapted to the standard of nature as a source of moral and national superiority. Far from being an indication of lower-class origins, a certain ungrammatical plainness, even uncouthness of speech, is valued for its Adamic qualities. This is an important reason why American students, particularly male students, after some fifteen years of studying the English language still do not know how to write or speak well. When some of them at last begin to *care* about cultivated self-expression, they tend to the opposite extreme of pretentiousness.

"We're a dramatic people," Perry Mason said in justification of his unorthodox methods of storybook detection. "We're not like the English. The English want dignity and order. We want the dramatic and the spectacular. It's a national craving. We're geared to a rapid rate of thought. We want to have things move in a spectacular manner." [15] H. L. Mencken's scholarly study of the American language reveals unmistakably that the two great, uniform principles underlying it have been linguistic chauvinism and the urge to simplify.[16] He notes, for instance, the general paucity of adjectives and adverbs, indicative of a desire to pass over the finer discriminations of an older civilization, the omission of so-called pansy or "lady" words as effete court Briticisms, the universal preference for simplified or phonetic spelling, and the addiction to slang. American slang, the single most distinguishing feature of the American language, is described as "a form of colloquial speech created in a spirit of defiance and aiming at freshness and novelty. . . . Its figures are consciously far-fetched and are intentionally drawn from the most ignoble sources. Closely akin to profanity in its spirit, its aim is to shock." [17] All these things, like the American Revolution, represent a revolt against unnatural bonds and restraints, convention and routine. Yet linguistic chauvinism is assertive in order to *simplify,* suggesting once more self-assertion in behalf of the restoration of a paradisaic condition.

The path from self-assertion to attitudes of submissiveness without defeat has been difficult, indeed, for most Americans. The build-up of unreleased nervous energy in the never-never land between abstraction and substance, between theory and practice, between dream and reality would seem to have something to do with the definition of the woman's role by the Edenic myth.[18] The woman in America, in her inherited role of an un-

---

[15] Erle Stanley Gardner, *The Case of the Howling Dog* (New York: Pocket Books, Inc., 1954), p. 177.

[16] Mencken does not himself draw this conclusion, but his book contains enough documentary evidence to warrant such a conclusion. Cf. H. L. Mencken, *The American Language,* 4th ed. (New York: Alfred A. Knopf, Inc., 1949), pp. 90-93, 125; Book IV; Book V, chs. 4-8; Book VIII; Book IX, chs. 4-6, pp. 502, 518, 556-567. It is possible, of course, that Mencken's work itself reflects a chauvinism.

[17] *Ibid.,* p. 556.

[18] An interesting thesis which yet does not connect the influence of women in America with the Edenic myth is Eric John Dingwall, *The American Woman, an Historical Study* (New York: Rinehart & Co., Inc., 1957).

defiled Eve, has exercised a dominion over the male spirit which leaves the flesh in continual torment. In a society such as ours in which money, righteously employed, has been the primary measure and fulcrum of power and status, the chief underlying causative factor of historical change and ideology is likely to appear superficially to be the economic. But the real culprit, if the present analysis is valid, is probably an unsatisfactory relationship to authority which is most frequently expressed in economic behavior and is largely acerbated by myth pictures in the mind. The relationship to authority, however, begins in the home and the school, where the woman holds forth. Following a moralism based on a code of works and sanctified by the mythology, for instance, the woman not only "mothers" the child with her own unfulfilled aspirations, but withholds affection when the child is "naughty" and lavishes affection upon him when he is "good." As a result, the child may ever afterwards try to win respect and affection by a life-long campaign of utilitarian achievement sometimes called "success-striving." His future behavior in this respect is reinforced by the culture. It is doubtful that an intelligent person would seriously argue that such endlessly competitive striving would put one in a more secure relationship with his fellow man and with authority than unconditioned love freely bestowed and received.

At the very time that status-seeking has become intensified in this country, class lines would seem to be somewhat more stratified, opportunities for fulfillment in traditional ways more restricted. Something has got to give, and at the present moment the institution which exhibits the most strain is the family, as the male members of the family seek masculine dominance by creating a sexual paradise outside the home. When more than anything else we need a tragic vision of life in order to confront our problems more realistically, all we seem to be getting is a "romantic agony," which is, after all, but a parody of the tragic view. One cannot transcend his human condition. On the basis of the analysis in this book, it would seem that the impulses to self-assertion and submission, with their visions of Paradise and Hades, are basic to human nature and not only to Americans. The best that we can humanly do is to substitute for the overly simple Paradise-Hades dichotomy studied here a more mature vision which holds the two poles together in a state of tragic tension. The rise of such a tragic sense of life in this country has been marked historically by the Rebirth archetype in connection with the reverse migration of Americans like Henry James back toward the Old World.

The lesson of America's foreign relations and frequently abortive reform movements would suggest that the main impediment to maturity is an errant idealism which has too few ties with reality. Liberal reformer and conservative reformer, messianic internationalist and messianic isolationist would all do well to cultivate the kind of tragic sense of limitations possessed by Hawthorne, a confluence of the social progressive with a compassionate knowledge of human imperfection, including our own. This would require that we love and understand peoples (as individuals) who are different from ourselves in race, color, ethnic origin, economic and social class, occupation, and nationality. That is, we need badly to raise the threshold of our tolerance above the level of the local country club or parish house. Such a social philosophy would dispose us less to the spontaneous judgment, the unreasoning haste to force complex experience into simple moral categories. It would incorporate attitudes of unassuming self-confidence without self-righteous complacency, a greater esteem for intellectual eminence, more regard for the role of government in a democratic society, more concern and encouragement for the noneconomic aspects of individual fulfillment, a clearer understanding of what we are *for* and less emphasis on what we are *against*. Even then we will not have fulfilled the promise of the American Edenic dream, but we will be a more relaxed, less lonely people, with a greater sense of community.

The American Edenic dream, psychologically considered, expresses universal human impulses of self-assertion against restrictive environmental pressures in order to satisfy real or fancied needs which have been thwarted. Such self-assertion necessarily comes into conflict with authority. Historically, authority has most often been associated with social control and leadership in advanced stages of civilization. Therefore the revolt against authority has been accompanied historically by a repugnance for the refinements of civilization, expressed by the imagery of Hades, and by a preference for a simpler, freer life expressed by the state of nature, or image of Paradise. The Edenic dream is thus compounded of tendencies both assertive and regressive. The image of Paradise, taken by itself, would seem to be at once an image of desire and an image for the release of desire, an image for the realization and fulfillment of self and an image for the surrender of self. I have tried to resolve this paradox by suggesting that assertiveness grows out of the desire to achieve an ultimate state of blissful resignation, a theory which is remarkably similar to certain biological speculation about the tendency of organic life to revert to its origins.

The Edenic myth has been at different times a way of interpreting history, an effect of history, and a contributing factor to history. The event in modern history most responsible for removing the Edenic dream from its religious context and putting it in touch with earthly possibilities was the discovery of America. But as an interpretation of the significance of that discovery, it helped to map the revolutionary social and political changes which followed. The movement of the underprivileged peoples of western Europe to improve their lot was expressed in the imagery of the night journey and rebirth out of hell.

This "journey toward light" was also enacted in the westward trek to America and formed the basis for modern ideas of progress. Since Paradise and Hades were primarily moral categories, defining experience in terms of good and evil, the theme of a rebirth out of hell emphasized a moral regeneration. Moral regeneration became the collective mission of the American people, who identified their new country with a restoration to Eden. Associating material progress with a moral rise, they reconciled themselves to the change from an agricultural to an industrial nation without a serious wrench. The revolutionary implications of the Edenic dream seemingly realized, however, the Edenic image became a narcissistic symbol of conservative retrenchment. Beset by new worries and anxieties—the later, long-range effects of the world-wide industrial revolution—we Americans are not now altogether so sure that we have not been dispossessed from Eden. Perhaps we are bound on another journey, a journey quite as significant as that which began in Renaissance Europe. But perhaps, too, we are only, after all, taking the "long way round to Nirvana."

Index

268

THE QUEST FOR PARADISE

Empire, 90; as aristocrat, 105, 127, 129; and American distrust of government, 130, 179; identified with aristocracy, 160; identified with European industrialists, 162; identified with urban centers, 163; identified with U.S. industrialists, 166-167, 183, 184, 199; identified with southern slaveholders, 178; and invasion of U.S. by Europe, 190-191; and U.S. devil theory of Yalta, 248-249

Anti-intellectualism: and garden myth, 29-30, 58, 62-63, 64, 66, 67, 73, 74-75, 105, 131-132, 261-262

Appleton, Nathan: ambivalence toward manufacturing, 159; agrarian bias of, 163; Edenic sense of mission in, 168; opposes cultural dependency, 169; summarizes U.S. industrial story, 172; mentioned, 158, 168

—Labor, 159

Appleton, Samuel: agrarian bias of, 163; mentioned, 158

Appleton, William: contrasts U.S. and Europe, 161; Edenic sense of mission in, 168

Appleton family, 170

Aragon, Cardinal Ludovico de. See d'Aragon, Cardinal Ludovico

Archer, John, 81

Aretino, Pietro: nature as norm in, 61-62

Ariosto, Ludovico: and the sexual paradise, 15; ambivalence toward authority, 48; nature as norm in, 61; mentioned, 41

—Orlando Furioso, 43-44

Aristotle, 37

Ascham, Roger: ambivalence toward authority, 48

Assertion-submission impulses: and paradise quest, 15-16, 28,

265-266; and scientific knowledge, 20, 22-24; and imaginative reality, 24-25; and journey pattern of history, 34-35, 46-47, 56; and the Renaissance, 47-48; and the Reformation, 49-51, 75-77; and American Revolution, 98-103, 115; and cultural dependency, 100-101, 106-107, 138; the sublime versus the beautiful, 142; and classical revival in U.S., 156; and U.S. westward movement, 177; in U.S. foreign policy, 228, 230, 233-234, 241-242; and American language, 262-263

Audubon, John, 136

Augustine, Saint: on heaven as paradise, 8-9; on innocence of nature, 11; mentioned, 31, 36

—The City of God, 8-9

Augustus I, Emperor of Rome, 37

Authority, role of. See Assertion-submission impulses; Antichrist, or Satan

Baillie, Robert, 81

Bale, John, 79

Barlowe, Arthur, Captain, 83

Bartram, John and William, 135

Batchelder, Samuel, 170

Beach, Joseph Warren, 224

Becker, Carl, 123

Behaim, Martin: globe of, 37

Bellamy, Edward: polarity of past and future in, 185; as industrial reformer, 185-187; Edenic mission in, 186; nature as norm in, 186; rebirth theme in, 186; equates moral with material progress, 187; mentioned, 174, 196

—Looking Backward, 185-187

Bellamy, Joseph, 95

Bellingham, Richard, 82

Berkeley, George, Bishop, 54